D0231148

THE
Malt Whisky
FILE

The Essential Guide for
the Malt Whisky Connoisseur

JOHN LAMOND AND
ROBIN TUCEK

CANONGATE
Edinburgh · New York · Melbourne

This book is dedicated to

Karen and Kirsty
and
to the memory of
Jack and Marjorie Tucek

Original title *The Malt File* published 1989
Second edition published 1993
First edition of this work published 1995
Revised and reprinted 1996
Reprinted 1997
Second edition 1997
Reprinted 1998 and 2000
Revised third edition 2001
Revised and updated fourth edition published simultaneously in
Great Britain, the United States and Canada 2007
by Canongate Books Limited
14 High Street
Edinburgh EH1 1TE
Scotland

1

British Library Cataloguing-in-Publication Data
A catalogue record for this book is available from the British Library
ISBN 978 1 84767 005 2
Printed in Spain by mccgraphics

Contents

Tasting notes by
John Lamond

Background and history by
Robin Tucek

Introduction

Scotch whisky was a part of my upbringing. My grandmother owned the old Lochearnhead Hotel, which was located at the head of the loch where the A84 meets the A85, and my mother was born in the hotel. My maternal grandfather was a bank manager who "enjoyed his dram", as we say in Scotland. During the 1920s, he was the banker for several distilleries during his time in Dufftown. A time during which you could say he was in his own particular heaven.

Whisky was an ever-present in our family home. It was a given that whenever there was a celebration/visitor/mourning/cause for solace, the whisky came out. As such, it was natural that I should also be a whisky drinker when I reached the age of 18.

I grew up in Perth, where there were a number of whisky companies: Dewar's, Bell's, Matthew Gloag of Famous Grouse fame, Peter Thomson's, whose brand was Beneagles, J & T Currie's and R.B. Smith's Moorland. We were a Dewar's family, however. It was normal to have a brand loyalty and that often depended upon where in the city one lived.

In a curious instance of synergy, I started work with Dewar's in 1974, which served to give my family access to supplies of Dewar's White Label at better prices. Regrettably, there was a limit on staff purchases; we were only allowed 4 bottles of spirits per month, which meant that I could not get all our requirements at staff prices. My family did a LOT of entertaining!

Single Malt Whisky, however, was a high days and holidays drink and in the '60s and early '70s was a largely misunderstood spirit. It was for this reason that my first distillery visit was a complete revelation.

Dewar's was a very innovative company which saw that its future lay in the efficiency and ability of its staff. This meant a programme of staff training. As part of this training Dewar's arranged for ALL staff to visit Aberfeldy distillery around 1976. For some reason I was unable to visit on my scheduled date so I went in my own time, by myself. My host was the then manager, Ricky Robertson. After the tour he poured me a dram in his office, telling me to add water. In the naivety of my youth I drank my whisky neat. My inexperience was clearly demonstrated after my first mouthful of cask-strength spirit. Since then, I have added water! As a result of this fiery baptism, I became evangelical about malt whisky. The 30 years since have been a learning process for me. Scotch whisky is a fascinating subject and there remain many elements of production which are not fully understood. As an old-fashioned romantic, I hope that they will remain tantalisingly vague.

The raison d'être of this book, however, is malt whisky and not just Scotch malt whisky, even though my own preferences on the subject are well-known. As I write, in early 2007, malt whisky continues its expansion, with distilleries opening in England, Wales, Brittany and California since the last edition was published. On the downside, New Zealand and Japan have seen closures. The growth in the number of the world's malt distilleries has been driven by you, the consumer, aided and abetted by innovative and imaginative distillers who have, in many cases, been prepared to fly in the face of advice and open a distillery. To date, they look as if their instincts have been correct and that the market has been receptive to their product.

The Malt Whisky File is a celebration of the people involved in the production of this wonderful spirit. At the back of the book is a new section, "Ones to Watch", giving details of newly opened distilleries whose spirits are not yet mature enough to be presented to market. We have also created a section on pp21–24 about "Parent Companies" to give some background following the many changes of ownership which have occurred within the industry over the past few years.

JOHN LAMOND

As I write today, it hardly seems possible that I began the first pages in this book more than 22 years ago. At the time I was running a small public relations company from my then home in Kent. The company specialised in wines and spirits PR and one of the accounts it looked after included Tamnavulin malt whisky. By that time I had developed a keen interest in malt whisky, mostly centred around the history and heritage of Scotland's liquid gold.

I don't know whether whisky is in my blood in the same way as it obviously is in John's, but, if it is, it comes from my mother's side of the family. I was born in Farnborough, Kent, to wonderful and caring parents, an English mother and a Czech father, hence my surname, of which I am very proud. My mother, however, was of mixed Scots and Irish descent. Her father was a Shaw, the Shaws being originally a sept of the Mackintosh clan, of which they were the first chiefs. In all probability my grandfather Shaw was descended from one of the many Shaws in the "Young Pretender" Bonnie Prince Charlie's famous army of the Jacobite Rebellion of 1745. As my family history identifies the Shaws as coming from Derby before settling in Isleworth, West London, we figure our ancestor was one of the soldiers who stayed behind after Charlie's army reached no further south than Derby on its march on London.

Since history tells us nearly all of Charlie's army, including probably most of the Shaws, was slaughtered in the rout at Culloden in 1746, I believe my ancestor made a wise decision. As well as the Scotch, I also have more than a drop of the Irish running through my blood! My maternal grandmother was a McConnell, whose family originally came from Ireland to live in Highbury, North London around 1850. So perhaps my love of Scotland's and Ireland's precious drams is in my genes if not literally in my blood.

I first met John as a result of his winning a competition I had organised on behalf of Tamnavulin. The idea was to find an expert whisky nose from among the Scottish licensed trade. John entered the competition, run in 1987, and duly won to claim the title "Master of Malt". As part of winning this competition John correctly identified 6 out of 8 different blind samples of single malt whisky! Recognising John's whisky "nose" to be among the best there is, I asked him to write the tasting notes for the book I had by then been compiling for a couple of years. This was published in 1989 as *The Malt File*. The rest, as they say, is history.

Since that exciting day, John has gone on to become internationally recognised as one of the most respected independent whisky "noses", simultaneously working in the wine trade in Scotland. I have gone on to found a whisky company, Blackadder International. Our careers may have taken different paths but we continue to share the same passion for fine malt whisky!

Like all whisky lovers, we both have our own views and opinions and different favourites. However, we agree that malt whiskies should never be scored or rated, no matter how objective that scoring and rating is. We prefer to let you select and rate your own favourite drams, just as we select our own personal favourites ourselves. John's tasting notes are there to guide you. I hope, like me, you will find them both informative and helpful.

ROBIN TUCEK

Now turn the page, preferably with a glass in your hand, sit back and learn something new.

Slainté!

John Lamond	Robin Tucek
Master of Malt	Stockholm
Tullibody, Scotland	Sweden
April 2007	April 2007

A Guide to the Regions

There has been quite a bit of discussion in recent years as to whether or not regionalisation exists in the flavour of Scotch whisky, or whether the taste of each distillery's spirit is a result of nurture rather than nature. The overall consensus seems to be in favour of the distiller having the greater control over the ultimate outcome. Despite this, and some learned statistical viewpoints, we remain of the opinion that, while distilling practice can blur the outlines, nature has the overwhelming influence.

The French have a word "terroir" which, in wine-making, translates almost as "a sense of place". The definition of terroir takes in soil structure, micro-climate, indigenous wild yeasts, aromas in the air, ambience and hundreds of years of local culture, all topped with a certain indefinable *je ne sais quoi* peculiar to a particular spot. Terroir is something of which New World winemakers are also becoming aware. It is something which we believe defines the individuality of each distillery.

Of course, you can change the strain of barley you use; certainly, the yeast strains are cultured centrally – often outside Scotland even – and the same strains are used by very many distillers; of course, the shape of the stills also has a bearing on the ultimate character of the spirit; of course, distilling practices are going to change with the introduction of a new manager/dictates from the accountants at head office, but you CANNOT produce Talisker at Macallan. Likewise, you CANNOT recreate Linkwood at Glen Moray or even Glen Grant at Caperdonich. Each has their own unique combination of elements and influences which create the core characteristics of the spirit.

The cask has a very large influence on the maturing spirit. Other influences, less so, but 30% or so of a whisky's flavour characteristics come from sources other than the cask. Thus, around 25% of the flavour is down to terroir, or at least its Scottish equivalent.

Obviously, the water supply has an influence, although learned opinion has it that this amounts to only 2% of the total.

Many years ago, John had a colleague who swore that he could detect diesel in the aroma of Dalwhinnie – originating from the proximity of the distillery to the railway line! Even though this was probably in his fancy (did older Dalwhinnie feature coal from steam engines?) – this would have contributed to terroir.

To clarify things for you, the consumer, perhaps the whisky industry should delineate the regions in statute. Whether it is the simple Lowland, Highland, Speyside, Islay and Campbeltown currently annotated on the Scotch Whisky Association's website, or the categories detailed below which we first heard Wallace Milroy use in the 1980s, something positive could be set down. On the other hand, we have experienced many single cask bottlings from various distilleries that defy any attempts at regional classification.

The following is a sub-division of the traditional whisky regions, giving a more precise classification of the districts.

Islay Malts
Islay malts are generally the weightiest, most pungent and most heavily peated and are, therefore, the most easily identified. These malts take their dominant characteristics from the peat which is used to dry the barley, and their proximity to the sea. These elements give them what is often described as seaweedy and medicinal aromas and a distinct burnt peaty flavour.

Lowland Malts
Lowland malts are the driest of Scotland's offerings and, although often quite spirity, are lightly flavoured whiskies with a delicacy to their flavours.

Northern Highland Malts
Northern Highland malts are sweeter and have more body and character than their Lowland relations. They can have very distinctive and subtle characters, with a rich mellowness and fullness of flavour and, occasionally, a delicate fragrance. They are all influenced by the North Sea.

Speyside Malts
Speyside's malts are Scotland's sweetest. Although they do not have as much body as some Highland malts, their flavours are richer and more complex, showing fruity, leafy and honeyed notes and subtle delicacy of aroma which, once recognised, should be easy to identify.

Eastern Highland Malts
Eastern Highland malts come from the area between the North Sea coast and Speyside, stretching south into Angùs. Often quite full-bodied, they tend to be drier than Northern Highland malts with a fragrant, sweet, fruity flavour and a delicate peatiness.

Western Highlands
For some reason, we omitted the Western Highlands from the last edition. They have flavours akin to a baby Islay; with a more delicate Atlantic influence, they nonetheless have sweetness and quite a bit of weight.

Perthshire Malts
The Perthshire malts, although Highland by definition, stretch north from the area bordering the Lowland region. They tend to be medium-sweet,

clean-tasting whiskies which can be both light and fruity. Their identity may be best considered as falling somewhere between Highland and Speyside.

The Island Malts
The Island malts from Skye, Jura, Mull and Orkney are characterised by a peaty, smoky nose and flavour. Some could be said to resemble Islay malts, while others are more akin to Northern Highland malts. These have recently been joined by Arran.

Campbeltown
If it is possible to categorise Campbeltown malts nowadays (and Campbeltown's distillers are very defensive of their separate region), then we have to say that they fall between the Eastern and Northern Highlands in dryness, but show distinct smoky characteristics, Atlantic influence and a salty tang.

Irish Malt Whiskey
Irish malt whiskey (note the "e" in "whiskey") is much lighter, smoother and fresher than its Scottish cousin. This is, in part, due to the fact that it is mostly triple distilled, although there are a couple of Scotland's single malts which are also produced in this manner. Irish whiskey has traditionally used unpeated malt, although the Cooley distillery produces both peated and unpeated whiskey. Irish stills also tend to be larger than Scottish stills.

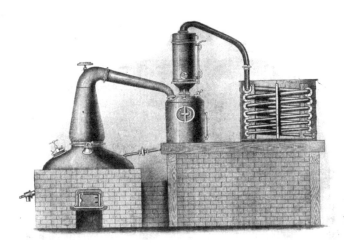

The Art of Nosing

It seems somewhat perverse that those who most appreciate the world's finest spirit should spend a great deal of their time NOT drinking it. They do not even go so far as serious-minded wine connoisseurs, who swill wine round their mouths before ejecting it. No, the master blender will use nothing other than his nose – and his experience – to assesses and evaluate a malt whisky. He noses rather than sips to preserve his ability to "taste" after the first sample. The reasoning behind this is simple: unlike wine, or other less alcoholic substances, a distilled spirit will anaesthetise the taste buds, the very mechanisms which need to be used time and again.

Aromatics

Our sense of aromatics (or "volatiles" as they are sometimes called) is derived from an organ known as the olfactory epithelium. This is located at the back of the nasal passage, and is directly linked to the brain. This helps to explain why we cannot taste so well when we have a cold.

Using the nose to detect aromatic ingredients provides a more immediate route to this area than via the back of the throat. The palate can detect only four taste elements: bitter, salt, sour and sweet. All other flavour characters are created when the palate warms the contents of your mouth and causes aromas to rise through your nasal passages to the olfactory epithelium. The palate merely confirms the aromas detected by the nose, although there will be slight differences and the strength of individual flavours will vary.

Our sense of smell is one of the most under-used of the human senses, being relegated in most cases by sight and taste to a subordinate role and only called into use for rather crude analysis of whether something smells good or bad. In fact, it is one of the most subtle of the senses, capable of detecting even faint changes in style or balance. It has a large "vocabulary" of its own. The tasting vocabulary used throughout this book has evolved over the years and, we hope, is easily understood by the reader.

The Master Blender

A Master Blender has an "educated" nose and can detect more than 150 separate flavours or characters in a whisky. Some of these will tell him that the product has been adversely affected in some way during maturation; others will indicate the type or style of wood in which it has matured. But although our senses are not as highly tuned as those of the blender, each whisky has a sufficient number of different characteristics to enable the whisky lover to distinguish one from another.

The Nosing

In general, the nosing of malt whiskies is carried out in a small, tulip-shaped or similar glass which, being bulbous at the base and reducing to a relatively narrow rim, releases the aromatics and concentrates them at the rim, where the nose can pick up these aromas. Glencairn Crystal has created the Glencairn Glass in consultation with Scotland's blenders. This is a good and readily available nosing glass. The sample is always diluted, or cut, with water: this releases the esters and aldehydes and thus makes the aroma more pronounced. The amount of water to be added depends on the alcoholic strength of the spirit which is being nosed. As a rough guide, malt whisky in the strength band 40% to 43% alcohol by volume (abv) should be cut with one third water, preferably a soft water – Scottish spring water – or clean tap water. Avoid waters with a high mineral content.

Higher Strength Whiskies

Higher strength whiskies should be cut with a greater quantity of water to reduce the sample to approximately the same strength – 25–30% abv. A high strength whisky of, for example, 60% abv, should be diluted with an equal volume of water for sampling. There is a very good reason for this: the olfactory senses are adversely affected by the high level of alcohol, even to the extent of causing pain, or burning them. Dilution removes the likelihood of this pain being inflicted. The quantity used for sampling should be fairly small to allow plenty of room for the aromatics to gather in the glass. There is enough spirit for an adequate assessment in a 25ml measure of whisky diluted with water.

You will find that different elements in the sample become dominant at different periods of the nosing. You may become confused by concentrating too hard. Very often, your first opinion will be the correct one. As you become more expert you will discover a greater range of aromas in the glass. Your palate is unique to you. You will pick up flavours differently from other people. For example, one person may detect a hint of rubber in a whisky, while that same characteristic will come over to another as liquorice. The difficulty with either tasting or nosing is in the descriptions used by individuals to describe sensation or flavour. Attempts have been made to categorise these flavours and several years ago John Lamond produced a "Malt Whisky Wheel" for Aberlour. This helped identify the principal flavour characteristics, and their taste relationships, using taste bands rather like spokes on a bicycle wheel. David Wishart extended the work on this theme in his book *Whisky Classified.*

While it is possible to create a common language to describe the aromas, the sense of smell is very subjective. Malt whisky is a gregarious spirit, so the next time you are with friends discussing flavour, let your nose lead your opinions. You will have as much fun trying to describe the aromas in your own words as you will from finally drinking the whiskies. This is one of the fascinations of single malts.

File Notes

John Lamond

There are three types of Scotch whisky: *malt* whisky, *grain* whisky and *blended* whisky. *Malt* whisky is produced only from 100% malted barley (in Ireland, they also add unmalted barley). *Grain* whisky is produced from a variety of cereals which may, but need not, include a proportion of malted barley. *Blended* whisky is a combination of *malt* whisky and *grain* whisky, mixed together before bottling. Recently there has been much discussion within the Scotch Whisky Association and at the time of going to press it is intended to set the following styles in statute.

Single Malt

Most of the whiskies covered in this book are *single malt* whiskies. The definition of Single Malt Scotch Whisky will become: "Scotch Whisky distilled at a single distillery (i) from water and malted barley without the addition of any other cereals, and; (ii) by batch distillation in pot stills". The actual distillery name need not be identified on the label; the whisky may come from different casks and be of various ages, but they must all originate from the same distillery. Not all distillers bottle their single malts under the name of the distillery, for example; the single malt from Macduff distillery is bottled as Glen Deveron by its owners. Likewise, different styles of whiskies can originate from within a particular distillery, e.g. Springbank and Hazelburn and Longrow or Loch Lomond and Inchmurrin and Rhosdhu.

Blended (Vatted) Malt

A Blended Malt Scotch Whisky "shall mean a blend of Single Malt Scotch Whiskies which have been distilled at more than one distillery". These whiskies have traditionally been called "vatted malts". However, we feel that this is an unnecessary and confusing change. From discussion with whisky club members, specialist whisky shops and many of the smaller independent whisky companies we have found it impossible to find anyone with a positive word to say about this idea. It is difficult to fathom why the great and the good in the whisky industry should want to put forward such a crazy idea, much less wish to persuade Parliament in London to legislate this into law. Our opinion is that this unnecessary change is certain to cause considerable confusion, not to mention sales problems for many fine vatted malt whisky brands which, in the public's eye, now seem certain to be considered only as blended Scotch in the traditional sense.

A dictionary definition of the word blended states: "to combine or mix so that the constituent parts are indistinguishable from one another". The idea of vatting, however, is to create a unique and individual flavour by combining the different malts together, usually re-casking them for a period to marry the flavours.

Many blenders believe such vatted malts give a fine, consistent product, each with a personality of its own. George Saintsbury, for example, in his *Notes on a Cellar-Book* dated 1920, believed that the finest whisky is a vatting of Clynelish, Longmorn and The Glenlivet. This whisky may well be given a distinctive name of its own, such as *Sheep Dip* or *Poit Dhubh*. Some "blended", we would say vatted, malts have been included in a section at the end of this book, as have some single malts bottled under the brand names of independent bottlers.

Grain Whisky
Grain whisky is to be similarly defined. Single Grain Scotch Whisky "shall mean Scotch Whisky distilled at a single distillery (i) from water and malted barley with or without whole grains of other malted or unmalted cereals, and; (ii) which does not comply with the definition of Single Malt Scotch Whisky". These other cereals include rye, wheat and maize. There is also to be a category for Blended Grain Scotch Whisky, which "shall mean a blend of Single Grain Scotch Whiskies which have been distilled at more than one distillery".

Blended Scotch Whisky
Blended Scotch Whisky "shall mean a blend of one or more Single Malt Scotch Whiskies with one or more Single Grain Scotch Whiskies". Blended Scotch Whisky falls outwith the scope of this book.

Scotch Whisky
All Scotch (and Irish) whisk(e)y is produced by first grinding the particular cereal to a coarse flour, known as grist, and then steeping this in hot water in a mash tun. The resultant sweet, sticky liquid, called wort, is then cooled to between 22°C and 24°C and run into a washback. Yeast is then added. When the yeast has been fermented out a strong ale, called wash, remains. This is between 8% and 10% alcohol by volume. The wash is then distilled

Scotland's Malt Distilleries

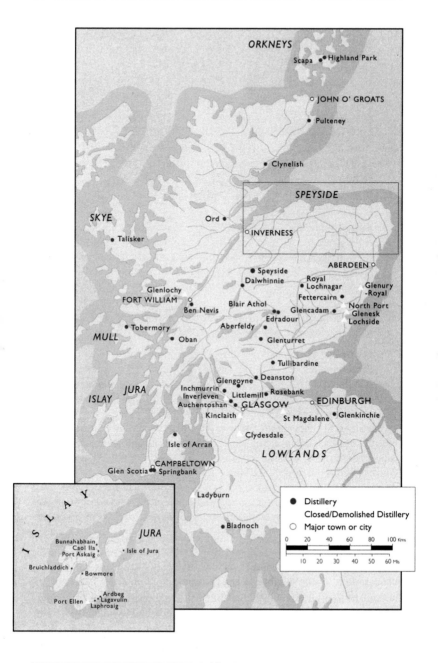

ORKNEYS
Scapa • Highland Park

○ JOHN O' GROATS

• Pulteney

• Clynelish

SPEYSIDE

SKYE
Ord •

○ INVERNESS

• Talisker

ABERDEEN ○

• Speyside
Dalwhinnie •   Royal
                     • Lochnagar   Glenury
Glenlochy   Fettercairn •   -Royal
FORT WILLIAM ○   Blair Athol   North Port
     Ben Nevis •   • Glencadam •   Glenesk
                    Edradour •   Lochside
• Tobermory   Aberfeldy •
MULL   • Oban   • Glenturret

JURA   • Tullibardine

                 • Deanston
         Glengoyne •
ISLAY   Inchmurrin •   • Rosebank
         Inverleven • Littlemill •
         Auchentoshan • • GLASGOW   ○ EDINBURGH
         Kinclaith   St Magdalene • Glenkinchie

              • Clydesdale

Isle of Arran   LOWLANDS

CAMPBELTOWN
Glen Scotia • • Springbank

Ladyburn

I S L A Y

JURA

Bunnahabhain
Caol Ila •
Port Askaig   • Isle of Jura

Bruichladdich •
          • Bowmore

Port Ellen • Ardbeg
       • • Lagavulin
     Laphroaig   • Bladnoch

• Distillery
Closed/Demolished Distillery
○ Major town or city

0   20   40   60   80   100 Kms
10   20   30   40   50   60 Mls

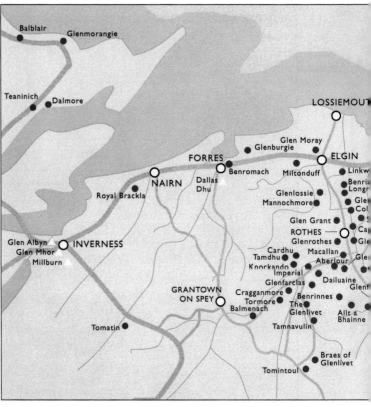

by heating it in copper stills, either in a continuous, or Coffey, still for grain whisky, or twice using a pair of pot stills for malt whisky. Three stills are used predominantly for Irish whiskey and the Scottish malts Auchentoshan, Benrinnes and the now closed Rosebank, these all being triple-distilled. Pot stills are usually onion-shaped, with tall, tapering swan necks falling over into what are known as lyne arms and condensers designed to help the alcohols condense, after which they are collected, cooled and put into casks.

A whisky, however it is produced, may only legally be described as Scotch Whisky if it has been matured in oak casks in Scotland for a minimum of three years. It must also have been bottled at a minimum strength of 40% alcohol by volume. There is no legal requirement for Scotch Whisky to be bottled in Scotland. We believe that there should be. The same legal restrictions also apply to Irish Whiskey in Ireland and to the new whiskies being distilled in Wales and England.

ʼhisky Distilleries

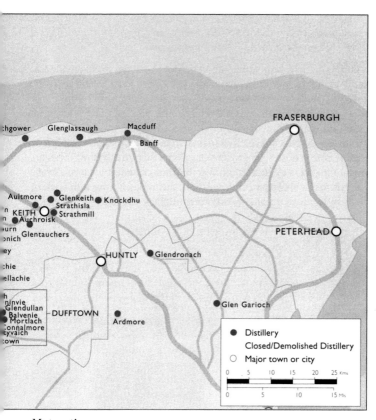

FRASERBURGH ○

hgower Glenglassaugh Macduff

Banff

PETERHEAD ○

Aultmore ● ● Glenkeith ● Knockdhu
Strathisla
ʼn KEITH ○ ● Strathmill
ʼn ● Auchroisk
ʼurn Glentauchers
ʼnich
ʼey
ʼhie HUNTLY ○ ● Glendronach
ʼellachie

h
ʼinvie
ʼGlendullan
●Balvenie DUFFTOWN
●Mortlach Ardmore ●
ʼonnalmore
ʼyvaich
ʼown

● Glen Garioch

	Distillery
●	Distillery
	Closed/Demolished Distillery
○	Major town or city

0   5   10   15   20   25 Kms

0   5   10   15 Mls

Maturation

Wood is now Scotch whisky's big fashion statement inasmuch as anything can be fashionable in an industry as conservative as that producing whisky. How has this come about?

To understand the reasons, you have to go back to 1912, when David Lloyd-George was Britain's prime minister. Lloyd-George was a teetotal Methodist and, therefore, anti-alcohol. A married man, he was, however, not so high-minded when it came to the subject of the fairer sex in general and other men's wives in particular. But then, nobody's perfect . . .

Up until this time, there was no minimum ageing requirement for whisky, with the result that whisky drunk in city bars was often very young indeed. At this time, if you bought a dram in a bar, it could have been as young as a day old. If you were lucky, it might have had some ageing, but the norm was to make it and sell it as quickly as possible. After all, ageing adds cost. Lloyd George thought that, by imposing a requirement to age the spirit before it could be called "Whisky", he would cut down on whisky drinking and, therefore, drunkenness, which was rife in the Britain at the turn of the 19th century. In 1912, the ageing requirement was set at two years; this was increased to three years in 1915. In the long term, ironically, Lloyd-George inadvertently improved the product, increased future sales and ensured the industry's continuity.

Initially, the distillers had great problems in sourcing sufficient casks. Everything available was pressed into service – wine barrels, rum barrels, liqueur casks, new wood. We have even heard of herring and butter casks being used! It would be obvious to assume that all types of wood: pine, beech, chestnut, oak, elm, etc. would have been pressed into service in the early days and with varying levels of success. The particular successes were *Quercus alba* (American white oak) and *Q. sessilis* and *Q. robur* (the European oaks). What you have to bear in mind is that Scotch whisky is a relatively delicate spirit. Its flavours can very easily be swamped by the influence of new oak. New casks, therefore, proved unsuitable for maturing whisky.

Some of you will be thinking: "Ardbeg or Talisker, delicate?!!" However, even such distinctive, powerful whiskies cannot assimilate the flavours of a new oak cask over a period of as little as 10 years without being dominated by the wood flavours. As American whiskies and the world's brandies are more robust spirits, the characters of these are much more resilient than those of Scotch whisky and can therefore survive the use of new wood.

In the longer term, the containers which proved to be the most suitable were ex-Bourbon and ex-Sherry casks. In the beginning, these had been fortuitous choices. The unions which were responsible for the coopers who made Bourbon's casks were powerful when the laws for Bourbon production were laid down in statute. They insisted that a new cask be used for each filling. In doing this, they safeguarded the jobs of the American coopers. Thus, when the cask was emptied after two or more years, it was useless. The Scottish distillers offered to take them off the Americans' hands and they got them cheaply. Likewise, historically, all Sherry was imported into Britain and Ireland in bulk in casks and was bottled in Bristol or Dublin. Once the casks had been emptied they, too, were useless so the whisky distillers made offers for the long-term supply of these casks – and they got them cheaply.

One could say that this is a typical, Scottish tight-fisted trait, but the fact is that Bourbon and Sherry both remove the harsh, young tannins from the oak, leaving a storage vessel which is not going to swamp the flavours of a whisky, but will give some of its character to the spirit it now contains, while permitting the harsher, lighter alcohols within that spirit to evaporate through its pores. Wood maturation involves the spirit being sucked into the pores of the oak and, in doing so, extracting flavour and colour from the wood. The alcohol levels are also important. Bourbon, at

68% vol., strips more of the harsher tannins than Sherry does. Thus, because of the lower alcohol levels of Sherry than Bourbon, the ageing potential of a Scotch whisky in a first-fill Sherry cask is shorter than that of the same whisky in a first-fill Bourbon cask.

Oak is a natural product. Primarily, it adds colour to the whisky and acts as an oxidation vehicle, no matter how old the wood; the oak itself absorbs sulphur and certain feinty, or impure, elements. In this way, wood can give a whisky as much as around 60% of its flavour. Within the cask lurk flavour compounds: vanillins (which give sweet, buttery characters), tannins (which give hard, bitter and chewy overtones), lactones (which give coconut and some creamy characters) and furfurals, which appear when the cask has been toasted.

If two casks are filled on the same day, lie in the same warehouse next to each other for the same number of years, one would expect the same result. In the section for Glengoyne, there are notes for casks 103 and 104 from February, 1985. You will see from the tasting notes that the result is different whiskies. The core flavours are the same and they are both obviously Glengoyne, but the "frill flavours" around the core vary.

Bearing in mind the above, the quality of the oak used, and its provenance, is of crucial importance to the continuity of flavour and quality of a whisky. Previously, the distillers' understanding of wood was whether it leaked or not, but in recent years much has changed. Wood management systems are now in place within most distillers' operations. These tell them:

a)   the origin of a cask
b)   how often the cask has been used
c)   what it contained during its life
d)   its size
e)   its location

The traditional method of pepping up the character of an old cask is to replace some of the more worn-out staves. This tended to extend the life of a cask by perhaps five years, but such a method was only used for casks which were necessary during the blending process. The industry has been experimenting with microwaving the staves and then treating them to high doses of infra-red light. At this stage, no-one is prepared to commit themselves to the success of this method of wood treatment. Traditionalists condemn it outright, however, believing it emphasises the harsher flavours of the spirit.

Coopers have traditionally air-dried their staves. Many cooperages in America, in particular, but also in Europe are now kiln-drying them. The process is faster (and therefore cheaper), but it increases the astringent wood flavours and gives the whisky an aggressive sharpness. However, Maker's Mark and Labrot & Graham use only air-dried timber and this is also widely, but not exclusively, used at Wild Turkey. Those who use kiln-dried admit that the move is driven by accountants and the major cooperages and state that they would rather use air-dried oak, but . . .

Glenmorangie has bought a forest in the Ozark Mountains in Missouri to ensure the continuity of supply of oak of the quality and character which it requires. This forest is north-facing, which means that the trees grow more slowly and develop tighter pores. Evaporation within the cask is slower and the dominance of lactones in the flavour is less. Not surprisingly, Glenmorangie insists its wood is air-dried. Macallan also insists on using air-dried wood. This time it is Spanish oak sourced in Galicia, which is also used by much of Macallan's parent company, the Edrington Group. Macallan insists that the wine (Sherry), which the casks must first hold, is fermented in the cask and then aged in it for two years. Wine fermentation within a cask is a tumultuous reaction which removes harsh wood tannins during the process. Fermentation, therefore, coats the cask and cleans it up before whisky maturation.

Another difference between Sherry and Bourbon wood is that Bourbon casks are charred, while Sherry casks are merely toasted. Charring leaches impurities out of the wood, while releasing lignins and vanillins. It also caramelises the cellulose, of which the oak is constructed. This gives the caramel, coffee, honey and vanilla notes to the whisky.

Cask size is also important. In a larger cask, there is a smaller percentage of the spirit in contact with the wood, so maturation is slower. Small casks mature relatively rapidly.

Cask sizes in total liquid content are approximately:

Quarter	127–159 litres
Barrel	173–191 litres
Hogshead	250–305 litres
Butt	500 litres

The traditional method of storage in old warehouses is known as "dunnage". This is in low, dark warehouses with slate roofs, thick stone walls and earthen floors. The earthen floors retain the humidity within the walls, while the thick walls maintain a cool, even temperature. A temperature swing of 2° C from winter to summer is fairly ideal. The casks are stored two or, at most, three high and have to be manhandled.

Experimentation began in the 1960s with large warehouses across the central belt of Scotland, these being built in locations such as Leven, Menstrie and Newbridge. These warehouses store casks in racks up to 13 high in thin-walled warehouses with (formerly) asbestos or steel roofs and concrete floors. Room is left between the racks for easy forklift access. The top level of casks can get very hot during the summer, with the sun beating down on the thin roof a metre or so above. As there is no insulation the temperature drops in winter. So a 50° C temperature swing from summer to winter is not unusual. The casks at the top mature much faster than the casks at the bottom, but, in so doing, they develop harsher, coarser flavours than they would have if kept in a dunnage warehouse. To alleviate this problem casks have to be moved to different positions within the warehouse on a regular basis. This increased handling adds to the maturation cost of a cask.

Most whiskies are reduced from their cask strength prior to bottling. The standard strength for the European markets is 40% abv, while the general export strength is 43% abv. However, some whiskies, such as non-cask-strength Springbank, are bottled at the "perfect strength" of 46% abv. Talisker is bottled at 45.8% abv and, more recently, Highland Park 25 and 30 years old are at 48.1% abv. A few selected casks may be bottled at higher strengths. Cask-strength whisky is whisky that has been bottled straight from the cask without the addition of water.

The respect of age
Much is made of the age of a whisky, and considerable prices are often paid for whiskies of more senior years. The age of a whisky, if stated on a bottle, must be that of the youngest whisky in that particular bottling. If all of the whisky used except for one centilitre is 21 years old and that one centilitre is 11 years old, then the whisky must carry an age statement to the effect that it is no more than 11 years old, although it could be described as being of a younger age, e.g. 10 years old. The date of distillation of a particular cask, as well as the date of bottling, may be given on a label, but the age of the whisky itself, unless given in days, may be given only as not more than the number of complete calendar years that the whisky has remained in cask in Scotland. For example, if a whisky was distilled in May, 1990 and bottled in April, 2003, then the whisky is 12 years old, although it could be sold as an 11- or 10-year-old, or less, or even not be given an age statement.

Whisky is usually about 70% abv when distilled, slightly higher in the case of triple-distilled whisky and Bruichladdich's quadruple-distilled X4 – Perilous Whisky, at 90% abv is just below the legal maximum of 94.8% abv. The remainder of the volume of a whisky is water from steam condensed with the distillation. New spirit is a clear, colourless liquid with limited characteristics and the actual volume of alcohol will vary slightly from batch to batch. With the exception of some distillations by a few distillers it is now industry practice to reduce all new spirit, known as new make, to 63.5% abv before filling into casks.

The longer a whisky remains in its cask, the more flavour it will acquire and the less spirit will remain. A 21-year-old whisky, for example, will usually have more complex flavours than a 12-year-old, although the degree of change is greatly dependant on the quality and type of cask used for filling. It will certainly be more expensive. Some whiskies are known to mature more quickly than others. Lowland whiskies are generally the quickest maturing, while others age particularly well, as is the case with many of the Speyside malts. However, although greater age usually means a more expensive whisky it does not necessarily mean a better one. Some will not care much for a very woody, tannic 25-year-old, preferring a soft, honeyed 18-year-old, while others may prefer a sherried 12-year-old. As with most things in life, it is all a matter of personal taste.

Filtration and the addition of colour
Most malt whiskies, especially those of the top-selling brands, are bottled from the "marriage" of several different casks. These big cask outturns are then chill-filtered and coloured with the addition of varying amounts of caramel before being bottled. Even whiskies that are not chill-filtered are normally bright-filtered. Chill-filtration – when the spirit is chilled to around 0°C prior to bottling – is done for cosmetic reasons, as it removes any possibility of cloudiness in a whisky. This clouding occurs naturally when a whisky is bottled at well below cask strength, such as at 40% or 43% abv. Unfortunately, chill-filtration also removes many of the natural fats, oils and flavours in the whisky, which in turn can also mean the removal of much of its individual character, as the esters, or flavour congeners, in the spirit tend to gather around these fats. The more a whisky is chilled when filtering, therefore, the greater the proportion of fats and esters removed. Chill-filtering a single cask of whisky removes around 5% of its total volume; bright-filtering around 3%.

Spirit caramel, which is often used to colour whisky, has its own flavour. This influences the final flavours of a whisky, even if only to a minimal extent when not heavily used. It is a fact that the majority of blended whiskies and many malt whiskies are treated with an addition of spirit caramel before being bottled.

The reason for doing this, it is argued, is to standardise the colour of a popular brand of whisky. The best-selling blends and malts are bottled in batches, often from as many as 100 casks at a time. Because the bottler cannot possibly standardise the colour of 100 different casks, even if these casks are used to the same "formula" of age and style at each bottling, he holds a set of colour references for each particular whisky. Once all of the casks have been vatted together a sample is then taken and compared with the library sample for that whisky. Spirit caramel is then added in the proportion required to bring the bottling to the required standard colour for that particular whisky. As it is not possible to lessen the colour of a bottling when it is too dark, it stands to reason that the standard level of colour for a particular whisky will be set to be at a darker shade than any potential vatting of casks for that whisky is likely to produce.

Unless they are being sold in countries such as Denmark or Germany, where the addition of caramel colouring must be declared by law, you will not be told that these whiskies have been altered in this way. You may be told other things, but never this information. Indeed, the whisky may even come in a coloured bottle so that you cannot see the actual colour of the whisky you are buying.

Many believe that such disclosure should be made part of the law relating to the bottling of Scotch and Irish whisky. This information is arguably more important and relevant to many consumers than the change of description of vatted malt whisky into blended malt whisky.

The following companies have interests in more than one distillery. Distilleries not mentioned in this section are either now closed or are single ownership distilleries and, as such, are covered under their entry within the tasting notes which follow.

Bacardi

Bacardi became a player in the whisky industry when, in 1993, they bought Martini & Rossi, which owned Macduff distillery through Willam Lawson subsidiary. They bought Dewar's in 1998 in the fall-out over the merger between Guinness and Grand Metropolitan. With Dewar's they also got Aberfeldy, Aultmore, Craigellachie and Royal Brackla distilleries.
John Dewar & Sons Ltd, 1700 London Road, Glasgow, G32 8XR

CL WorldBrands

CL WorldBrands Ltd, the Trinidadian-owned drinks group that also owns Angostura rum and bitters and Hine Cognac, has been the owner of Burn Stewart Distillers since 2002. Originally a small, family-owned whisky broker, Burn Stewart was taken over by Bill Thornton in 1988. Deanston was bought in 1990 and Tobermory (which also produces Ledaig) in 1993. The company acquired Black Bottle and Bunnahabhain from the Edrington Group in 2003.
Burn Stewart Distillers Ltd, 8 Milton Road, College Milton North,
East Kilbride, G74 5BU

Diageo

The first dominant company within the industry was The Distillers Company Limited (DCL), established on 24th April, 1877 by the amalgamation of the companies which owned six lowland grain whisky distilleries – Cambus, Cameronbridge, Carsebridge, Glenochil, Kirkliston and Port Dundas. The amalgamation was "to secure the benefits of combined experience and the advantage (which manufacturing and trading on a large scale alone can command) of reduced expenses and increased profits".

DCL built its first malt whisky distillery, Knockdhu, between 1893 and 1894. The company's growth made the quantum leap to market dominance following the collapse of the Pattison blending and bottling company in 1898. This growth was down to the foresight and business acumen of William Ross, Secretary of the company at that time. He saw the potential growth in demand for Scotch whisky and bought up distilling companies which had gone into liquidation following the Pattison collapse. The company gradually became an amalgam of semi-autonomous companies ruled by their own boards of directors. Each of these boards had, ultimately, to answer to the parent company board.

Following the takeover of DCL by Guinness in 1986 and the subsequent merger with Grand Metropolitan to form Diageo in 1997, this form of company structure changed, with many of the smaller companies owned by the parent company disappearing completely.

Diageo owns the following malt whisky distilleries that are still either operating or potentially operational as at April 2007: Auchroisk, Aultmore, Benrinnes, Blair Athol, Bushmills, Caol Ila, Cardhu, Clynelish, Cragganmore, Dailuaine, Dalwhinnie, Dufftown, Glendullan, Glen Elgin, Glenkinchie, Glenlossie, Glen Spey, Inchgower, Knockando, Lagavulin, Linkwood, Mannochmore, Mortlach, Oban, Ord, Pittyvaich, Royal Lochnagar, Strathmill, Talisker and Teaninich.
Diageo plc, 8 Henrietta Place, London, W1G 0NB

Edrington Group
The Edrington Group has grown out of the Robertson Trust, a charitable trust set up by the granddaughters of William Robertson, one of the founders of Glasgow whisky brokers and wine and spirit merchants, Robertson & Baxter. It transferred control of Robertson & Baxter to Edrington Holdings, which was managed by the Robertson Trust. In 1996, the companies were restructured to form the Edrington Group (still under the management of the Robertson Trust). In 1999, the group acquired Highland Distillers Ltd and its brands and distilleries – Macallan, Highland Park, Tamdhu, Glenrothes, Glenturret, Bunnahabhain and Glengoyne. Bunnahabhain was subsequently sold to Burn Stewart, and Glengoyne to Ian Macleod.
The Edrington Group, 2500 Great Western Road, Glasgow, G15 6RW

Inver House
Inver House was established in 1964 as a wholly-owned subsidiary of the American Publicker Industries of Philadelphia. It initially had a grain distillery which included in the complex a Lowland malt distillery, Glen Flagler, which was closed in 1985. During Publicker's ownership, the company bought (1973) and sold (1983) Bladnoch distillery. Publicker sold the business to its UK directors in 1988. Under their direction, the company acquired Knockdhu, Speyburn, Old Pulteney, Balblair and Balmenach. In 2001 the company was bought by Pacific Spirits (U.K.), a subsidiary of British Virgin Islands-based Great Oriole Group, itself owned by Thai businessman, Charoen Sirivadhanabhakdi.
Inver House Distillers Ltd, Airdrie, ML6 8PL

J & A Mitchell

An independent family-owned company. It is the owner of Springbank Distillery, which also produces the Longrow and Hazelburn malts. A subsidiary company, Mitchell's Glengyle Ltd, owns and runs the new Glengyle distillery, which produced its first spirit in 2004. Both companies are run under the guidance of Hedley Wright, a descendant of the Mitchell family, the original owners of both Springbank and the previous Glengyle distillery, which closed in 1925.

J. & A. Mitchell & Co Ltd, Springbank Distillery, Campbeltown, Argyll, PA28 6ET

Loch Lomond

The Loch Lomond Distillery Company owns two currently operating distilleries. One is the malt and grain whisky producing complex known as Loch Lomond in Alexandria; the other is Glen Scotia distillery in Campbeltown. The company was also for a while the owner of Littlemill distillery, which closed in 1992.

The Loch Lomond Distillery Company Ltd, Lomond Industrial Estate, Alexandria, G83 0TL

Moët Hennessy

LVMH Moët Hennessy Louis Vuitton SA, usually shortened to LVMH, is a French holding company. As well as being the world's largest luxury goods conglomerate, it is the parent of around 60 sub-companies that each manage a small number of prestigious brands. These include Moët Hennessy which, since 2004, has owned the Glenmorangie Company, whose distilleries are Ardbeg, Glenmorangie and Glen Moray.

The Glenmorangie Company, 18 Westerton Road, Broxburn, West Lothian, EH52 5AQ
www.glenmorangieplc.com

Pernod-Ricard

Pernod-Ricard's first foray into the whisky world was with their takeover of House of Campbell in 1974. This gave them Edradour and Aberlour distilleries (Edradour has since been sold to Signatory). They bought Glenallachie from Invergordon in 1989 and have since taken control of Allt a'Bhainne, Braeval, Caperdonich, Glen Keith, Glenlivet, Longmorn and Strathisla when Seagram was sold off and Glenburgie, Glendronach, Glentauchers, Imperial, Miltonduff, Scapa and Tormore when Allied Domecq was split up. Their UK distilling arm is now known as Chivas Brothers.

Chivas Bros Ltd, Chivas House, 72 Chancellors Road, London, W6 9RS

Suntory

Suntory was started by Torii Shinjiro, a wine and spirit merchant who opened his first store, Torii Shoten in Osaka, Japan, in 1899. Having studied whisky making in Scotland Torii Shinjiro opened Yamazaki Distillery, Japan's first whisky distillery, in December 1924. The company was originally named Kotobukiya, but changed its name to "Suntory" in 1963. In 1973, Suntory built another distillery in Hakushu at the foot of Mt Kaikomagatake in the southern Japanese Alps. Since 1994 the company has also owned Morrison Bowmore Distillers Ltd, operators of Auchentoshan, Bowmore and Glen Garioch distilleries.

Suntory Ltd, Head Office, Dojimahama 2-1-40, Kita-ku, Osaka,
Osaka 530–8203, Japan
www.suntory.com
Morrison Bowmore Distillers Ltd, Springburn Bond, Carlisle Street,
Glasgow, G21 1EQ

Whyte & Mackay

The company was established in 1881 when James Whyte and Charles Mackay bought a well-established Glasgow wine and spirit merchant's business. Dalmore became a part of the business, renamed Dalmore, Whyte & Mackay, in 1960. This was taken over by Scottish & Universal Investment Trusts in 1972. SUITS already owned Fettercairn and Tomintoul-Glenlivet was added in 1973. Following the takeover of Invergordon Distillers in 1993, Tamnavulin, Tullibardine (since sold during 2003) and Isle of Jura came into the group.

Whyte & Mackay Ltd, Dalmore House, 310 St Vincent Street,
Glasgow G2 5RG

William Grant & Sons

Another independent family-owned company. The proprietor of Glenfiddich Distillery, and also of Balvenie and Kininvie distilleries, all three being at Dufftown. It also owns the Girvan grain distillery, once also the home of the Ladyburn malt stills.

William Grant & Sons Distillers Ltd, Independence House, 84 Lower
Mortlake Road, Richmond, Surrey, TW9 2HS
www.williamgrant.com

INDEPENDENCE OF SPIRIT

As well as the whiskies bottled by the major brand-owning companies, there are today a great many whiskies available from independent, often family-owned companies, and some of the smaller distillery-owning companies. These companies usually bottle a variety of different ages of different whiskies, comprising mostly of single malt whiskies. Often their bottlings come from single or small batches of casks, with each cask, or batch, having its own, not to be repeated, distinctive flavours and characteristics. Many of these whiskies are today bottled at their natural cask strength, or at the very least at the sometimes called "perfect" strength of 46% abv. Most independent companies today consider it adulteration to add caramel colouring to the spirit before bottling, as they do not want to alter, enhance or control the natural flavour of the spirit. Nor do most of these companies chill-filter their whiskies, with one company, Blackadder, even going so far as to bottle a range of whiskies without any filtration at all.

The following are some of the main independent bottlers. They are listed alphabetically. We make no recommendations as to which you should seek out but would wish to note that the companies which follow have probably contributed much more to the growth of interest in malt whisky than could have been expected from their collective size of voice.

Adelphi
Established in 1993 by the great-grandson of the former owner of Loch Katrine Adelphi distillery, Glasgow, which ceased production in 1906, the company specialises in non chill-filtered, uncoloured single cask malt whiskies. Originally based in Edinburgh, the company was bought by new owners in late 2004 and is now based at the picturesque Glenborrodale Castle situated on the Ardnamurchan peninsula to the west of Fort William.
Adelphi Distillery Limited, Glenborrodale Castle, Ardnamurchan,
Argyll, PH36 4JP.
www.adelphidistillery.com

Angus Dundee
Angus Dundee is an independent company with over 50 years' experience in the production, bottling and distribution of fine Scotch whiskies and other spirits. The company now owns two malt distilleries: Tomintoul and Glencadam.
Angus Dundee Distillers Plc, 20/21 Cato Street, London, W1H 5JQ
www.angusdundee.co.uk

Berry Bros
The London St James's Royal Warrant-holding wine and spirit merchants. The business is the owner of the Cutty Sark brand of blended whisky and is also responsible for the worldwide marketing of Glenrothes single malt. For more than 100 years Berry Bros has also bottled malt whiskies under the "Berrys' Own Selection" label.
Berry Bros & Rudd, 3 St James's Street, London SW1A 1EG
www.bbr.com

Blackadder International
Blackadder International bottles only non chill-filtered, uncoloured single malt whiskies under the Blackadder and Blackadder Raw Cask labels. Other Blackadder-owned brands are: Aberdeen Distillers, Blairfindy, Clydesdale Original, Old Man of Hoy, Peat Reek and Smoking Islay. The company is owned by Robin Tucek, co-author of this book.

Blackadder International Ltd, Fairview House, Little London, Heathfield, East Sussex TN21 0BA
www.blackadder.com

Robin Tucek

William Cadenhead

Established as licensed grocers in Aberdeen in 1842, but now based in Campbeltown, William Cadenhead is Scotland's oldest-established firm of independent bottlers. The business is now owned by J. & A. Mitchell of Springbank fame. Cadenhead was for many years a pioneer in bottling whiskies that are uncoloured and non chill-filtered. The company has for several years run a malt whisky shop in Edinburgh's Royal Mile and, in 1995, a second, franchised, Cadenhead shop opened in Covent Garden, London. It now also has franchised stores in Odense, Denmark; Amsterdam, The Netherlands and Cologne, Germany.
Wm Cadenhead, 83 Longrow, Campbeltown, Argyll, PA28 6EX
www.wmcadenhead.com

Compass Box

This specialist, award winning and highly innovative whisky company was founded in 2000 by American John Glaser. John began his whisky career with United Distillers. He is a whisky purist, and does not believe in colouring, chill-filtering or putting age statements on his whiskies. He believes that age statements are misleading and that whiskies should be bottled at the age he feels that they are ready and not because they have reached a certain age. The company bottles a range of types of Scotch whisky: malt grain and blends. The company bottles under a colourful and imaginative names, including Asyla, Eleuthera, Flaming Heart, Hedonism, Oak Cross and The Peat Monster.

Compass Box Delicious Whisky Ltd, 9 Power Road, London W4 5PY
www.compassboxwhisky.com

Dewar Rattray

Founded by Andrew Dewar and William Rattray in 1868, A. Dewar Rattray began trading as an importer of French wines, Italian spirits and olive oil. In 2004 the company returned to the family of one of its original owners when purchased by Tim Morrison, previously of Morrison Bowmore Distillers and fourth-generation descendent of Andrew Dewar. The company bottles a range of single cask malt whiskies under the Dewar Rattray label and a malt called Stronachie.

A. Dewar Rattray Ltd, Whitefaulds, Culzean Road, Maybole,
Ayrshire KA19 8AH
www.dewarrattray.com

Douglas Laing

Established in 1948, this Glasgow-based family business is today run by brothers Fred and Stewart Laing, sons of the company's founder Douglas Laing. Although the company has only focused on single cask malt whisky bottlings since the late 1990s it is already one of the most respected names in this field. The company has an extensive portfolio of fine aged casks of single malt whiskies. These are bottled in a number of different ranges, the most important being Old Malt Cask, Platinum Selection, Premier Barrel, Douglas McGibbon's Provenance and Glen Denny.

Douglas Laing & Co. Ltd, Douglas House, 18 Lynedoch Crescent,
Glasgow, G3 6EQ
www.douglaslaing.com

Duncan Taylor

Today situated in Huntly, Aberdeenshire, the company was originally founded in Glasgow where the company originally operated as a broker and Scotch whisky merchant. Now run by Euan Shand, it produces a number of different ranges of whiskies, including those of the Duncan Taylor, Whisky Galore and Rarest of the Rare labels.

Duncan Taylor & Co. Ltd, 4 Upperkirkgate, Huntly, Aberdeenshire, AB54 8JU
www.dtcscotch.com

Gordon & MacPhail

Established as licensed grocers in Elgin, Moray in 1895, Gordon & MacPhail is Scotland's leading independent bottler. It was shipping single malt whiskies around the world when many of today's best-selling single malt whiskies were known only locally. The company is now also a distiller, having owned Benromach distillery since 1993. It is an independently minded and spirited family company and its owners are justly proud of what they have achieved in bringing single malt whisky to the world's attention. Gordon & MacPhail is a trading name of Speymalt Whisky Distributors Limited.

Gordon & MacPhail, 58–60 South Street, Elgin, Moray, IV30 1JY
www.gordonandmacphail.com

Hart Brothers

This Glasgow-based company offers a selection of single malt whiskies bottled from casks selected by Donald and Alistair Hart.

Hart Brothers, P.O. Box 5562, Glasgow, G77 9AP
www.hartbrothers.co.uk

Lombard

A family-owned company established on the Isle of Man in the 1960s. Its owners have a long history of connections with the wine and spirit trade as well as brewing. The company owns the Pebble Beach brand of Speyside malt whisky, and also bottles the "Jewels of Scotland" range.

Lombard Brands Ltd, Bourne House, College Street, Ramsey,
Isle of Man, IM8 1JW
www.lombardscotchwhisky.com

James MacArthur

James MacArthur was established in Edinburgh in 1982 with the aim of selecting whiskies from Scottish distilleries which were not very well known or had ceased production.

James MacArthur & Co. Ltd, 20 Knights Templar Way, High Wycombe,
Bucks HP11 1PY
www.james-macarthur.co.uk

Murray McDavid

The team which led the buy-out of Bruichladdich ran Murray McDavid before they became distillers. Their whisky selections are now made by Bruichladdich distiller Jim McEwan.

Murray McDavid Limited, Islay, Argyll, PA49 7UN
www.murray-mcdavid.com

Mackillop's Choice

The Mackillop's Choice is a range of whiskies selected by Master of Wine Lorne Mackillop, heir to the chief of the Mackillop clan.

Iain Mackillop & Co Ltd, 20–21 Cato Street, London W1H 5JQ
www.mackillopschoice.com

Ian Macleod

This now Broxburn-based company grew out of the originally Edinburgh-based whisky broker, Peter J. Russell & Co. It produces a number of single cask bottlings under the Chieftain's, Dun Bheagan and Macleod's labels. The company recently bought Glengoyne distillery.

Ian Macleod Distillers Ltd, Russell House, Dunnet Way,
Broxburn, EH52 5BU
www.ianmacleod.com

John Milroy

John, also known as Jack, Milroy was the original and former owner of Milroy's whisky shop in London's Soho. Today he bottles his own range of malt whiskies under his John Milroy label. His brother Wallace is the author of the *Malt Whisky Almanac*, one of the first whisky guides available.

Dram House, 9 Bittern Road, Saxmundham, Suffolk IP17 1WT
www.johnmilroywhisky.com

The Scotch Malt Whisky Society

This Edinburgh-based society bottles cask-strength whiskies for its members. Each cask is bottled under a numerical code, so as not to identify the source distillery on the label. The Scotch Malt Whisky Society is today owned by the Glenmorangie company, which is itself owned by the French company LVMH.

The Scotch Malt Whisky Society, The Vaults, 7 Giles Street,
Edinburgh, EH6 6BZ
Tel: +44 (0) 131 554 3451   www.smws.com

Scott's Selection

This is the name given to the distillery selection that was first made by Robert Scott, former distiller at Speyside Distillery, from the casks held by the owners of that company.

Speyside Distillers Co Ltd, Duchess Road, Rutherglen, Glasgow G73 1AU

Signatory

The Signatory Vintage Malt Whisky Company, to give the company its full name, was established by Andrew Symington in Leith in 1988. Signatory bottles an extensive selection of single malt whiskies and is today one of Scotland's premier independent bottling companies. The company bought Edradour distillery in July, 2002.

Signatory Vintage Scotch Whisky Company, Edradour Distillery,
Pitlochry, PH16 5JP

The Vintage Malt Whisky Company

The Vintage Malt Whisky Co. was founded in 1992 by Brian Crook, the former Export Director of one of Scotland's major distillers. The company bottles a range of single malt whiskies under the Cooper's Choice brand and also the brands Finlaggan, Tantallan and Glen Almond. The company is connected to the Highlands and Islands Scottish Whisky Company Ltd, which in turn owns the brands the Ileach, The Pibroch and Black Cuillin.

The Vintage Malt Whisky Company, 2 Stewart Street, Milngavie,
Glasgow, G62 6BW
www.vintagemaltwhisky.com

HOW TO USE THE GUIDE

Judging and understanding the differences

Each of our tasting notes contains its own numerical rating system. This system, developed by John Lamond and Robin Tucek, is designed to give you an approximate idea of Sweetness, Peatiness and Price for each whisky. It is intended as a helpful guide only and is not meant to be used as a qualitative rating system for malt whiskies. In our opinion, malt whisky is too much of a personal preference to justify any attempts to give rating scores to individual whiskies. After all, one man's Macallan is another woman's Laphroaig. Some will choose Bowmore and others Balvenie. Many whisky writers are big Islay fans, but we know from speaking with you, the consumers, that most of you prefer something softer and sweeter. We would not wish to position any malt before any other – all are to be respected and enjoyed for their relative qualities, all are made to similar quality levels and all are aged in oak casks. Only you can decide which whiskies are your favourites.

The Malt Whisky File Tasting Codes

The scale runs from 0 to 10, with 0 being the driest and least peated end of the scale. 10 is the sweetest and most pungent. The ratings are a statement of fact: a guide to help you find those malt whiskies which are most akin to your own taste. If, for example, you like a malt with a Sweetness factor of 7 and a Peatiness factor of 4, then other malts which have a similar rating could be of interest to your palate.

Having spoken with readers over the years, we realised our previous third rating, Availability, was, in some markets, not relevant. Accordingly, we have created another rating, Price. However, instead of a number, we have used symbols. Our ratings are based on British pricing and whiskies may be available in other countries at (slightly) different prices. Prices are in British pounds sterling:

*	low price	£15 – £29
**	reasonable	£30 – £59
***	mid-priced	£60 – £119
****	high-priced	£120 – £249
*****	prepare for a shock!	£250 +

Following the success of the independent companies in marketing single cask and cask strength whiskies, several of the major brand owners have now followed suit, making some very interesting whiskies available. These whiskies are bottled with little or minimum filtration and it is increasingly frowned upon to add caramel colouring to them. Such limited edition bottlings are an important and growing market, especially to the specialist whisky retailers, who never seem to get enough stock! With each single cask being an individual product, they cannot possibly have the same consistency of style, taste or colour as the more widely available malt whisky brands, each of which is bottled after blending together a number of carefully selected casks from the brand owner's warehouses of maturing whiskies. Even if the bottler is a small distiller, bottling runs of their brand may consist of fewer than a dozen casks. At this level, it is almost impossible to maintain consistency of colour or flavour. They will be close, but tasted against each other, the differences will be apparent.

The success of Single Malt Whisky today owes much to the efforts of the specialist bottler in making such whiskies available when, with one or two notable exceptions, the brand owners showed little interest in producing malt whisky for anything other than blending. In the past year, partly because of the growth in the Asian markets and partly because of the poor harvest and subsequent hike in price of malting barley, prices have risen and stocks have become less available than they were.

Shortage of supply because of market demands is not the only problem that the independent bottler faces today. It is a fact that some distillers now do all they can to try to restrict or stop independent companies obtaining and bottling casks of their malt whiskies, some to the extent of putting pressure on companies to prevent them doing what is perfectly legal within EC trade mark law through identifying on their labels the distillery that is the source of the cask of the whisky being bottled.

It is unfortunate that the larger distillers have taken this stance with the independents. Industry statistics show that the level of export sales of liquid in 2005 (277.904 million litres of alcohol) are fairly similar to that of 1978 (274.073 million litres of alcohol). With an increase of 1.3% over 27 years, and many of those years have shown a fall in liquid sales, there can be little rational thought behind their stance. The 2006 figures will be released by the time this book is published and there could be an increase in the 2006 figures, but we are not expecting any increase to be of a substantial nature.

When it comes to extending and expanding the market for whisky the bottom line must surely be that if malt whisky, and its blended sister, is to continue to grow and prosper, the whisky producers need to supply whiskies suited to all tastes and interests. It is our opinion that many distillers, not just the bigger ones, need to wake up to this fact and realise that the creation of a market that is based on a few centralised brand monopolies built around a limited number of key brands will eventually kill the goose that laid the golden whisky egg. The success of the whole must surely be dependent on the achievements of all of the constituent parts.

Vocabulary

We feel that, as any tasting note is necessarily a very personal and subjective matter, some of our descriptions may need explanation, in particular for readers outwith Scotland. "Tablet" is a delicious Scottish confection similar to a firm fudge, very sweet and sugary. We have created some words which pedants might object to – for this we apologise. Some of these are "toffeeyed", meaning having the character of toffee; "cerealy", having the aromas of the grain from which the malt is produced; "mashy", retaining the aromas of malt and sugars from the mash tun.

Labels

In some cases, the labels depicted above the tasting notes are not the vintage tasted. This is usually because of the bottler following on with the next vintage – which has not yet been tasted. When tasting the main distillery bottlings, the current vintage should be similar to the previous vintage when the whisky is bottled at a similar age. Space for labels is limited. However, we have attempted to include a representative selection from as many companies as possible.

Water

Although water from a kitchen tap is safe to drink in many parts of the world, it can be far from ideal as an accompaniment to fine malt whisky. In some areas, the water is naturally quite chalky or has a high mineral content. In others, for reasons we are told are to do with public health, various additives are put into public water supplies. In Britain, for example, varying amounts of chlorine are added to drinking water and this can affect the nose of a whisky.

In a perfect world, the water added to whisky would come from the distillery's own water supply, as you can experience in the garden behind Glen Grant. As an alternative, clear, pure, soft spring water with a low mineral content, such as one of the bottled Scottish waters, is eminently suitable. Do not use sparkling water.

Finally, don't be put off adding water. The belief that nothing but more malt whisky should be added to a glass of malt whisky is a misconception.

Taste the difference for yourself: one glass with neat whisky and one glass with one third water. Get used to the idea of adding water little by little according to your own taste. Be aware that your taste may also vary from day to day according to how you feel. It is your taste and opinions that matter when you sit down to enjoy a whisky!

Abbreviations used throughout this book

DCL   The Distillers Company Limited, later United Distillers & Vintners (UDV), now Diageo plc

D.o.b Distiller's own bottling

IDG   The Irish Distillers Group

IDV   International Distillers & Vintners Ltd, formerly a part of Grand Metropolitan Group

SMD   Scottish Malt Distillers. The malt distilling operational arm of DCL. Merged with Scottish Grain Distillers to form SMGD, Scottish Malt & Grain Distillers. Later United Malt & Grain Distillers (UMGD), now Diageo.

How to use this book

The pages are arranged in alphabetical order by distillery name. In cases where two, or more, distinct styles of whisky are produced at the same distillery, e.g. Springbank or Bruichladdich, the whiskies are found under the distillery building's entry. Where the whisky is from an independent bottling source, this has been noted in the tasting notes. Listed below are local nicknames, alternative or marketing brand names alongside the distillery from which each originates. Names marked with an asterisk are second malts distilled in a slightly different manner from the named distillery; *G are grain distilleries within which the malt stills are/were situated.

An Cnoc – Knockdhu	Hillside – Glen Esk
Drumguish – Speyside	Inverboyndie – Banff
Dumbarton *G – Inverleven	Ledaig – Tobermory
Girvan *G – Ladyburn	Moffat *G – Glen Flagler
Glencraig * – Glenburgie	Mosstowie * – Miltonduff
Glen Deveron – Macduff	Singleton – Auchroisk
Glen Ord/Glenordie – Ord	Strathclyde *G – Kinclaith

Visitors – [V] – indicates that the distillery welcomes visitors.

Key to geographical area of production:

Arran – [A]	Ireland – [IR]
Campbeltown – [C]	Speyside – [S]
Highland – [H]	Lowland – [L]
Islay – [I]	

Hints on Pronunciation

Unless you are an expert Gaelic speaker, you may have difficulty in pronouncing some of the names of the malts in this book or of the areas in which they are produced. The following list contains those names that may cause a problem, with their phonetic alternatives.

Aberlour	Aber-lower
Allt-a'Bhainne	Olt-a vane
Auchentoshan	Ochentoshen
Auchroisk	Othrusk
Balmenach	Bal-MAY-nach
Bruichladdich	Brew-ich-laddie
Bunnahabhain	Boon-a-havun
Caol Ila	Kaal-eela
Cardhu	Kar-doo
Clynelish	Klyn-leesh
Craigellachie	Krai-GELLachy
Dailuaine	Dall-YEWan
Dallas Dhu	Dallas Doo
Drumguish	Drum-oo-ish
Edradour	Edra-dower
Glen Garioch	Glen Gee-ree
Glenglassaugh	Glen Glass-och
Glen Mhor	Glen Voar
Glenmorangie	Glen-MORanjee
Glentauchers	Glen-tochers
Glenury-Royal	Glen-you-ree
Islay	Eye-la
Knockdhu	Nock-doo
Laphroaig	La-froyg
Ledaig	Led-chig
Old Pulteney	Pult-nay
Pittyvaich	Pit-ee-vay-ich
St Magdalene	Magdaleen
Strathisla	Strath-eye-la
Tamdhu	Tam-DOO
Tamnavulin	Tamna-VOO-lin
Teaninich	Tee-an-inich
Tomintoul	Tomin-towel
Tullibardine	Tully-bard-eye-n

and finally . . .

Slainté (Cheers!)	Schlan-jer

Aberfeldy

ABERFELDY, PERTHSHIRE [H] [V] EST. 1896
Website: www.aberfeldy.com

Built between 1896 and 1898 by Perth-based distillers, John Dewar & Sons Ltd. Run by SMD & UMD since 1930, Dewar's having joined DCL in 1925. The distillery building is very impressively Scots Presbyterian, with the still house and tun room having been rebuilt in 1972–3 using the original stonework. Four stills. The company was sold to Bacardi in 1998; Aberfeldy is the jewel in their portfolio. Award-winning visitor centre.

Location – Immediately to the east of the town of the same name; next to the former railway line and the main A827 road, overlooking the River Tay.

Notes – Previously about a dozen distilleries had been opened in the Aberfeldy neighbourhood by men who had been smugglers in earlier times. The distillery lies in a beautiful setting, with nearby woodland housing a rare colony of red squirrels. Tommy Dewar set off on a two-year world tour in 1892. He returned with 32 new agents in 26 different countries.

Water – The Pitilie Burn.

12 yrs, 40% abv

Sweetness – 5	Peatiness – 6	Price – *

Colour – Amber with old-gold highlights. *Nose* – Medium-bodied, medium-dry, gentle and creamy with a slight cherry fruitiness and a floral edge. *Palate* – Medium-dry, round, quite full-bodied and toffeeyed with a good, tangy cocoa peat character. *Finish* – Long, smooth and creamy with a touch of milk chocolate on the tail. *Notes* – D.o.b.

21 yrs, 40% *abv*

Sweetness – 5	Peatiness – 5	Price – ✳✳✳

Colour – Amber with old-gold highlights. *Nose* – Quite full, rich and honeyed with notes of green fruit and liquorice; water brings out a soft peat note and citrus zest, medium-sweet. *Palate* – Medium-bodied, medium-dry, rich and honeyed, quite fresh and smooth with a quite delicate peating. *Finish* – Long, clean and elegant with hints of orange and peach. *Notes* – D.o.b.

25 yrs, 40% *abv*

Sweetness – 5	Peatiness – 6	Price – ✳✳✳✳

Colour – Mid-amber with old-gold highlights. *Nose* – Round, mature, quite soft with rich, medium-sweet vanilla, notes of coffee, toffee, a definite touch of honey and an almost grapey character. *Palate* – Medium-dry, soft, quite full-bodied and elegant with sweet vanilla/toffee, a hint of banana and cocoa-flavoured peat. *Finish* – Very long, soft, complex and ethereal with notes of dark chocolate and espresso coffee. *Notes* – D.o.b.

1997, 46% *abv*

Sweetness – 5	Peatiness – 5	Price – ✳

Colour – Very pale straw with water-white highlights. *Nose* – Quite light with apple and a youthful mashy character; water brings out chocolate digestive biscuits, some citrus and smoke. *Palate* – Medium-dry with good richness, quite a solid peat note and softly chewy. *Finish* – Long, quite delicately smoky with a touch of spice and good richness. *Notes* – Berry's Own Selection from cask no. 2940.

1982, 43% *abv*

Sweetness – 6	Peatiness – 6	Price – ✳✳✳

Colour – Straw with pale yellow highlights. *Nose* – Medium-sweet, fresh, malty and quite delicately peated with a rich lemon-peel character. *Palate* – Smooth, round, medium-sweet and fruity with a good, soft peat character. *Finish* – Long, clean and fresh with a soft shortbread sweetness on the tail. *Notes* – Cooper's Choice bottling from the Vintage Malt Whisky Company.

Aberlour

ABERLOUR, BANFFSHIRE [S] [V] EST. 1826
Website: *www.aberlour.com*

Founded in 1826 by James Gordon and Peter Weir. Rebuilt in 1879 after an extensive fire. This is the date which appears on the label. Re-equipped with four stills in 1973. The Aberlour Glenlivet Distillery Company is a subsidiary of Chivas Brothers, itself a part of Pernod-Ricard.

Location – Aberlour is situated about a quarter of a mile below the Linn of Ruthrie, a 30-foot cascade on Ben Rinnes which falls into the pool which gives rise to the Lour Burn. The distillery is about 270 metres from the Lour's confluence with the River Spey.

Notes – Aberlour is a delightful village by the Lour at the foot of Ben Rinnes, from the 840-metre high summit of which ten counties (from Caithness in the north to Perthshire in the south) are visible. The early Christian missionary, St Dunstan (or Drostan, as he was known in Scotland), used the waters of the Lour for baptisms. The village itself was formerly known as "Charlestown of Aberlour", but renamed itself just "Aberlour" in honour of its most famous export.

Water – A spring on Ben Rinnes.

10 yrs, 40% abv

Sweetness – 7	Peatiness – 4	Price – *

Colour – Deep amber/golden. *Nose* – Full, rich, sweet and slightly toffee-like with apple and honey mingling. *Palate* – Quite full-bodied, smooth and medium-sweet with a well-balanced richness. *Finish* – Good, full and long, with delicate malty peat and smooth caramel toffee. *Notes* – D.o.b.

Sweetness – 7	Peatiness – 3	Price – ✳

Colour – Deep amber with old-gold highlights. *Nose* – Quite fresh, lanolin, oily character, ripe, almost walnut character with a touch of hedgerow greenness at the back, full-bodied and delicately peated. *Palate* – Medium-dry, full, fresh, walnuts, creamily smooth with a touch of spice and a hint of citrus. *Finish* – Long, clean and creamy with a gentle smokiness on the tail. *Notes* – D.o.b.

1990, 61.8% abv

Sweetness – 8	Peatiness – 4	Price – ✳✳

Colour – Very pale, watery straw with silver/lemon highlights. *Nose* – Light to medium-bodied, medium-dry, youthful, quite a floral, apple-blossom note and a perfumed malty character, quite soft and almost vinous. *Palate* – Soft, sweet, medium-bodied, a youthful floral note and quite rounded. *Finish* – Long and rich with notes of dark chocolate in the lingering peat. *Notes* – Clydesdale Original bottling.

1976, 43% abv

Sweetness – 8	Peatiness – 3	Price – ✳✳✳✳

Colour – Mid-amber with old-gold highlights. *Nose* – Full, round, medium-sweet, honeyed with a note of beeswax and aromas of toffee, coffee, cocoa and chocolate orange. *Palate* – Soft, ripe apple skins, good body, smooth, creamy, medium-sweet and delicately peated with touches of ginger and espresso. *Finish* – Long and elegant with ripe peaches and tangy coffee on the tail. *Notes* – D.o.b.

ABERLOUR SHERRY WOOD FINISH, 15 yrs, 40% abv

Sweetness – 7	Peatiness – 1	Price – ✳✳

Colour – Mid-amber with bronze highlights. *Nose* – Quite full-bodied, sweet, really rich, quite soft and honeyed with aromas of hazelnuts, ripe lemons and tangerines. *Palate* – Smooth, round, medium-sweet, creamy and delicately peated with notes of citrus, vanilla and chocolate. *Finish* – Very long, quite soft and elegant with a little belt of clean peat on the tail. *Notes* – D.o.b.

ABERLOUR ANTIQUE, No age statement, 43% abv

Sweetness – 8	Peatiness – 3	Price – ✳✳✳✳

Colour – Quite deep amber with bronze highlights. *Nose* – Full-bodied, medium-sweet with a slightly green apple perfumed hedgerow character, rich and softly oaky. *Palate* – Rich, sweet, quite full-bodied and with a touch of spice. *Finish* – Long, sweet and lingering. *Notes* – D.o.b.

Sweetness – 8	*Peatiness* – 3	*Price* – ✶✶

Colour – Quite deep amber with old-gold/bronze highlights. *Nose* – Quite full-bodied, almost stickily sweet, rich and honeyed with a slight green apple character. *Palate* – Sweet, soft and round, with good body, a slight green edge and a touch of spice. *Finish* – Long, slightly chewy, sweet and lingering. *Notes* – D.o.b.

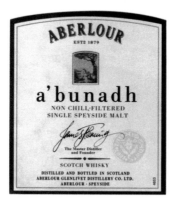

ABERLOUR A'BUNADH, No age statement, 59.6% *abv*

Sweetness – 7	*Peatiness* – 4	*Price* – ✶✶✶

Colour – Mid-amber with old-gold highlights. *Nose* – Quite big-bodied, mature, sweet and darkly nutty with a touch of a ripe maltiness and cooking apples. *Palate* – Rich, medium-sweet citrus and apples with a dark nuttiness and good cocoa-flavoured peat integration. *Finish* – Long, quite smoky, warm and spicy with a dollop of dark chocolate. *Notes* – D.o.b.

1990, 46% *abv*

Sweetness – 8	*Peatiness* – 3	*Price* – ✶✶

Colour – Straw with pale yellow highlights. *Nose* – Medium-bodied, sweet and rich with green apples, creamy toffee and some menthol; water makes it fresher, with a slightly vinous, Muscadet character. *Palate* – Medium-sweet, youthful, vinous, clean and quite smooth with good body. *Finish* – Stickily sweet with sugar-coated fruit, long and youthful with a soft and luxurious tail. *Notes* – Berry's Own Selection bottling from cask no. 16989.

Allt-a-Bhainne

NEAR DUFFTOWN, BANFFSHIRE [S] EST. 1975

A modern building of contemporary architecture, built in 1975 by Chivas Brothers, a subsidiary, at that time, of the Seagram Company of Canada. As a reminder of distilling's roots, four small pagoda roofs are set on the main roof. Sold to Pernod-Ricard in 2001.

Location –Sited on the southern slopes of Ben Rinnes, to the north of the B9009, some eight miles south-west of Dufftown.

Notes – Allt a'Bhainne is the Gaelic for "Burn of Milk".

Water – A spring on Ben Rinnes.

14 yrs, 46% abv

Sweetness – 3	Peatiness – 4	Price – **

Colour – Straw with pale yellow highlights. *Nose* – Quite youthful cereal and mashy characters and medium-bodied; with water it is less mashy and more vegetal with some kiwi fruit and peach. *Palate* – Medium-dry and mashy with a cereal note and lightly chewy tannins. *Finish* – Long, quite vegetal, too young. *Notes* – Duncan Taylor bottling.

1992, 46% abv

Sweetness – 8	Peatiness – 3	Price – *

Colour – Straw with pale yellow highlights. *Nose* – Sweet, rich and medium-bodied with a hint of apple and citrus; with water it is softer and has sweet oak and ripe orange notes with a touch of perfume. *Palate* – Sweet with good body and notes of bubble gum, cherries and American Cream Soda with a touch of spice. *Finish* – Clean, fresh, long and sweet with a perfumed tail. *Notes* – Whisky Castle Cask Collection bottling from cask no. 00960242 distilled 20 May 1992.

Ardbeg

NEAR PORT ELLEN, ISLAY, ARGYLL [I] [V] EST. 1794
Website: *www.ardbeg.com*

The original distillery was run by notorious smugglers, before excise men eventually overran the place, destroying the buildings. John McDougall established the present distillery in 1815. Owned from 1976 by Hiram Walker and latterly operated by Allied Domecq, Ardbeg was closed between 1981 and 1989 and again in 1996. It was bought, in 1997, by the Glenmorangie Distillery Co. Ltd.

Location –A very romantic, lonely site at the water's edge on the south coast of Islay.

Notes – *Ardbeg* has always been sought after by malt whisky aficionados. Following the Glenmorangie purchase, a visitor centre was opened and this has now become *the* place to eat for the ladies who lunch in Port Ellen.

Water – Supply from Lochs Arinambeast and Uigidale.

10 yrs, 46% abv

Sweetness – 2	Peatiness – 10	Price – *

Colour – Amber with pale gold highlights. *Nose* – Big-bodied, dark and pungent, good, solid peat character and an underlay of rich lemon-zest citrus, dry, but with a hint of sweetness, round with a delicate note of iodine. *Palate* – Full-bodied, earthily, smokily peaty and rich with touches of coffee/chocolate and tarry ropes/creosote. *Finish* – Long, tangy and quite pungent, the citrus notes reprise, together with dark chocolate and a little seaweed. *Notes* – D.o.b.

15 yrs, 43% abv

Sweetness – 2	Peatiness – 10	Price – ∗∗∗

Colour –Amber with old-gold highlights and a hint of lemon. *Nose* – Big, dark and powerful, a chunky peatiness with iodine, crabmeat and crashing breakers, dry but rich, soft, sweet vanilla and a round, nutty character. *Palate* – Big-bodied, dark and very heavily peated, good richness with notes of chocolate, tarry ropes and quite chewy tannins. *Finish* – Long, very tangy and initially very rich with notes of honey, orange, espresso coffee and dark chocolate. *Notes* – D.o.b.

17 yrs, 40% abv

Sweetness – 2	Peatiness – 10	Price – ∗∗

Colour – Quite full amber with old-gold highlights and a touch of lemon. *Nose* – Quite gentle and delicate peat, fruity! – orange/citrus, good body, slightly off-dry. *Palate* – Big-bodied and powerful, good peat and richness with a wee touch of sweetness. *Finish* – Long, elegant, very rich and complex, with a touch of spice. *Notes* – D.o.b.

30 yrs, 40% abv

Sweetness – 1	Peatiness – 9	Price – ∗∗∗∗∗

Colour – Amber with gold highlights. *Nose* – Big, dry, pungent, dark and tarry; quite elegant, full-bodied, a relatively light sea character with hints of creosote and cocoa. *Palate* – Big, dry, pungent and tarry, not overwhelmingly peaty and gently chewy. *Finish* – Long with just a hint of richness, quite elegant and almost delicate. *Notes* – Allied Domecq bottling.

1995, 15 yrs, 50% abv

Sweetness – 1	Peatiness – 10	Price – ∗∗

Colour – Pale amber with pale yellow/lemon highlights. *Nose* – Quite big-bodied with notes of citrus, sea pungency and honey; water brings out tarry rope, shellfish, soft peat and smouldering cigars. *Palate* – Big, powerful, smoky Cohibas, a touch of creosote and an earthy spiciness. *Finish* – Long, smoking, tangy and gently chewy. *Notes* – Douglas Laing Old Malt Cask bottling from hogshead no. 3059.

1976, 21 yrs, 49.2% abv

Sweetness 1	Peatiness 10	Price ∗∗∗

Colour – Pale amber with pale gold highlights. *Nose* – Full-bodied, pungent, dark and earthy with a dry medicinal peatiness and a sweet vanilla touch. *Palate* – Dry, powerful, dark, smoky and gently chewy with an edge of richness. *Finish* – Long, dry and finishes relatively delicately after the initial explosion. *Notes* – Adelphi bottling from cask no. 453.

32 yrs, 49% abv

Sweetness – 1	Peatiness – 10	Price – ✳✳✳✳

Colour – Deep amber with bronze highlights. *Nose* – Big, pungent, powerful and sea-tainted, really quite medicinal with aromas of tarry ropes, creosote, citrus, chocolate. *Palate* – Dry with a slight touch of richness, a big sea/smoky peat character and gently chewy. *Finish* – Long, softly chewy, medicinal, elegant and powerful. *Notes* – Douglas Laing bottling.

1978, 43% abv

Sweetness – 1	Peatiness – 10	Price – ✳✳✳✳✳

Colour – Full amber with bronze highlights and a hint of ruby. *Nose* – Quite full peat, but not overpoweringly, a touch of sweetness – like granulated sugar, a dark, earthy peatiness. *Palate* – Big-bodied, but delicate, the flavour expands on the palate. *Finish* – Very long, amazingly complex with notes of spice, chocolate and green coffee. *Notes* – D.o.b.

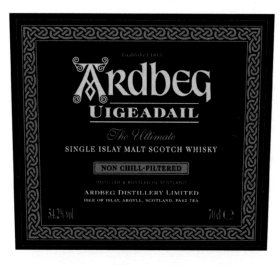

1976, 55.3% abv

Sweetness – 1	Peatiness – 10	Price – ✳✳✳✳✳

Colour –Deep amber with old-gold highlights. *Nose* – Big-bodied and medicinal with a rich sherried edge, showing citrus and sultanas, a big, slightly earthy peat character and notes of toasted oak, treacle, creosote and tarry ropes. *Palate* – Powerful and rich with quite a sweet edge, notes of chocolate and coffee and enormously peaty. *Finish* – Long, pungent and earthy with a perfumed edge and a whiff of cocoa. *Notes* – D.o.b. ex-cask no. 2392. Only available at the distillery and to members of the Ardbeg committee.

24 yrs, 50% *abv*

Sweetness – 1	Peatiness – 10	Price – ***

Colour – Pale amber with pale gold highlights. *Nose* – Big-bodied and sea-influenced with a touch of richness and a cereal note; water brings out a fresh touch of greenness and rounds out the aroma. *Palate* – Big-bodied, with notes of seaweed, burnt heather roots, a fishy tang and a creamy smoothness. *Finish* – Long, elegant and very pungent. *Notes* – Old Malt Cask bottling by Douglas Laing & Co.

ARDBEG UIGEADAIL, 54.4% *abv*

Sweetness – 2	Peatiness – 10	Price – **

Colour – Amber with old–gold highlights. *Nose* – Big-bodied, peaty, medicinal and tar-coated; water brings out cereal notes, warm peat and creosote. *Palate* – Big-bodied and rich, initially with ripe fruit, toffee and honey, followed by a big belt of smoky peat. *Finish* – Long, powerful, individual, eccentric and very smoky. *Note* – D.o.b.

ALMOST THERE, 1998, 54.1% *abv*

Sweetness – 3	Peatiness – 10	Price – **

Colour Straw with pale yellow highlights. *Nose* – Big-bodied and quite powerful with peat note aromas of smoked ham and tar; water softens and rounds it out, giving a melon fruitiness and a warm, earthy peat character. *Palate* – Off-dry, but with good richness, powerful with dark, cocoa-flavoured peat with a fresh green note and a touch of spice. *Finish* – Richness explodes initially! Very long, with good rich citrus, some milk chocolate underlaid by huge peat notes. Very complex. *Notes* – D.o.b.

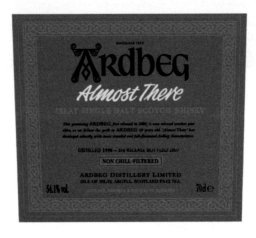

1990, 40% abv

Sweetness – 1	Peatiness – 10	Price – *

Colour – Amber with gold highlights. *Nose* – Big-bodied, dark and heavily peated, powerful, tarry rope and seaweed; water brings out the sea character, toasted cocoa and a slight edge of lemony citrus. *Palate* – Big-bodied, powerful, with creamy notes of cocoa and milk chocolate and creosote. *Finish* – Long, quite velvety, smooth intense, concentrated and explosive with just an edge of sweetness. *Notes* – Gordon & MacPhail Connoisseur's Choice bottling.

1974, 40% abv

Sweetness – 1	Peatiness – 10	Price – ***

Colour – Amber with gold highlights. *Nose* – Big-bodied, dark and pungent with a burnt peaty character and hints of ozone. *Palate* – Big, powerful and slightly salty with a burnt mahogany peatiness and quite firm tannins. *Finish* – Big, long, chewy and pungent with a nutty touch on the tail. *Notes* – Gordon & MacPhail bottling.

1967, 52% abv

Sweetness – 1	Peatiness – 10	Price – ***

Colour – Quite deep amber with bronze highlights. *Nose* – Big-bodied and pungent with a dark nuttiness, rich and full with a medicinal note – iodine/creosote/tarry rope. *Palate* – Big, powerful, and gently chewy with a burnt smokiness. *Finish* – Long, medicinal and smoky with a note of burnt Christmas cake richness on the tail. *Notes* – Signatory bottling.

ARDBEG 'LIMITED EDITION', 1975, 43% abv

Sweetness – 2	Peatiness – 10	Price – *****

Colour – Amber with old-gold highlights. *Nose* – Full-bodied, powerful sea character to the peat, a deep fruitiness. Almost apricot and really rich toffee/tablet vanilla. *Palate* – Dry, but really very rich, round, quite pungent, toffeeyed and gently chewy tannins. *Finish* – Long, elegant and complex, tangy and darkly peaty with good richness on the tail. *Note* – D.o.b. Distilled 1975, bottled 1999.

Ardmore

KENNETHMONT, ABERDEENSHIRE [H] EST. 1898

Built by William Teacher with two stills and doubled in size twice since – to four stills in 1955 and eight stills in 1974. The distillery was built as part of a major expansion programme for the company's popular blended whiskies. Now operated by Fortune Brands following the sale of Allied Domecq in 2005.

Location – Situated alongside the Aberdeen to Inverness railway line, below the 434-metre high Knockandy Hill. Close by is Leith Hall.

Notes – Fortune Brands use the make in blending Teacher's Highland Cream. The stills remain coal-fired and the steam engine, boiler front and other relics of the original distillery are preserved. One of the largest malt whisky distilleries in Scotland, Ardmore also houses extensive research laboratories.

Water – A spring on Knockandy Hill.

ARDMORE FOUNDED 1898 & HIGHLANDS
HIGHLAND SINGLE MALT
SCOTCH WHISKY | FULLY PEATED
TRADITIONAL CASK
MATURED FOR A FINAL PERIOD IN SMALL 19TH CENTURY STYLE 'QUARTER CASKS'
NON-CHILL FILTERED
DISTILLED AND BOTTLED IN SCOTLAND
OUR *TRADITIONAL METHODS* ENSURE A DISTINCTIVE TASTE THAT IS *FULL* AND *RICH*, WITH UNIQUE HIGHLAND *PEAT-SMOKE* NOTES
1ltr e | ARDMORE DISTILLERY, KENNETHMONT, ABERDEENSHIRE | 46% VOL

1977, 40% *abv*

Sweetness – 6	Peatiness – 6	Price – **

Colour – Pale amber with pale gold highlights. **Nose** – Quite full and smoky with a slight green touch, medium-dry with a touch of richness. **Palate** – Medium-bodied, quite smoky and medium-dry with good richness. **Finish** – Sweet with a good underpinning of smokiness, a touch of spice and quite chewy. **Notes** – Gordon & MacPhail bottling.

1989, 17 *yrs*, 55.8% *abv*

Sweetness – 6	Peatiness – 7	Price – **

Colour – Amber with old-gold highlights. **Nose** – Quite big and intense with hints of fresh greenness; water brings out green coffee, hints of hedgerows, apples and pears, shortbread and butterscotch. **Palate** – Rich, big-bodied, round, smooth and medium-sweet with quite a solid peat note. **Finish** – Long, tangy and quite ethereal with hints of Olde English Marmalade. **Notes** – Clydesdale Original bottling reference 0076/3060 distilled September 1989.

Auchentoshan

DALMUIR, DUMBARTONSHIRE [L] [V] EST. CIRCA 1800
Website: *www.auchentoshan.co.uk*

The name Auchentoshan derives from the Gaelic "achad oisnin", meaning "corner of the field". Building commenced in 1817, when the distillery was known as "Duntocher". It was renamed "Auchintoshan" in 1834 and the spelling changed to "Auchentoshan" in 1948. It is one of three distilleries owned by Morrison Bowmore Distillers, itself a part of Suntory of Japan. Although not the only distillery to experience war damage (see Banff), it had the misfortune to suffer heavily when the nearby Clydebank shipyards were the target of enemy bombing in 1941, an event which caused extensive damage and great loss of spirit.

Location – The distillery is situated close to the Erskine Bridge on the A82, between Duntocher and the River Clyde.

Notes – When Alfred Barnard visited in 1885, the name was spelt "Auchintoshan" and the distillery was silent as most of the staff were gathering in the harvest. Although situated geographically south of the Highland Line, the source of Auchentoshan's water is north of the line. Thus the distillery is a Lowland one, but its water supply is Highland. The make is triple distilled and unpeated. The first distillation takes an hour, the second five and the third nine hours. Currently marketed as "Glasgow's Malt Whisky".

Water – Near Cochna Loch in the Kilpatrick Hills.

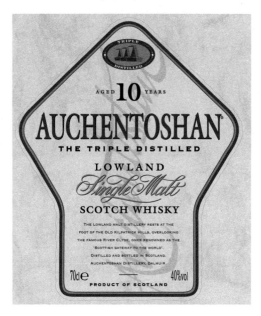

10 yrs, 40% abv

Sweetness – 4	Peatiness – 0	Price – *

Colour – Very pale straw with a slight green edge. **Nose** – Fresh, clean and floral. **Palate** – Light, soft, quite sweet and slightly fruity. **Finish** – Finishes quite well, although light. **Notes** – D.o.b.

21 yrs, 43% abv

Sweetness – 2	Peatiness – 0	Price – ***

Colour – Mid-amber with old-gold highlights. **Nose** – Soft, round, nutty and quite full-bodied with an almost buttery character. **Palate** – Dry, soft and smooth with a hint of richness, gentle tannins and medium-bodied. **Finish** – A hint of sweetness at first, nutty, quite delicate, long and complex. **Notes** – D.o.b.

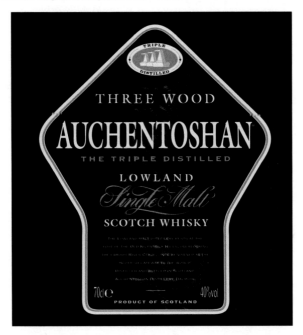

AUCHENTOSHAN THREE WOOD, No age statement, 43% abv

Sweetness – 2	Peatiness – 0	Price – **

Colour – Deep amber with ruby/bronze highlights. **Nose** – Quite full, round, warmly nutty with an almost over-ripe cheesy note (Camembert) and a cooked fruit (Madeira-like) character. **Palate** – Rich, but quite dry and intense with a gentle touch of nutty, oaky tannin and vanilla toffee. **Finish** – Long, with notes of dried fruit, toffee and nuts and a touch of spice. **Notes** – D.o.b. Matured in three different casks: Bourbon, Oloroso Sherry and Pedro Ximinez Sherry.

Auchroisk

MULBEN, BANFFSHIRE [S] EST. 1974

The Singleton of Auchroisk, to give the whisky its full name, is produced at the Auchroisk distillery. That name being rather a mouthful, the company's own bottlings are marked as "The Singleton". Independent bottlings are under the name "Auchroisk". The distillery is managed by Justerini & Brooks (Scotland) Ltd, a subsidiary of Diageo plc. Eight stills.

Location – On the north side of the A95 between Keith and Aberlour.

Notes – A new distillery producing its first make in 1974. Despite being a modern complex, the buildings are in the Scots vernacular style and the distillery received a Saltire Award (for outstanding architectural achievement in a traditional Scottish style). Sherry casks are used predominantly. Auchroisk is a showpiece distillery and has an old steam engine from Strathmill preserved in its entrance hall.

Water – Dorie's Well.

S P E Y S I D E
SINGLE MALT
SCOTCH WHISKY

In a striking *hilltop location, visible from ROTHES*, is sited the

AUCHROISK

distillery. The unusual name, *meaning "FORD of the RED STREAM" in Gaelic*, refers to the *MULBEN BURN from which the distillery draws its cooling water*. However, the *principal reason* for the *siting of the distillery is DORIES WELL* an abundant source *of soft, pure springwater.* Through the *smoke and nutty sweetness*, comes the *unmistakeable feel of DORIES silky water, followed by a dry*, well balanced *finish.*

A G E D **10** Y E A R S

43% vol   Distilled & Bottled in *SCOTLAND* AUCHROISK DISTILLERY, Mulben, Keith, Banffshire, *Scotland*   70 cl

---

THE SINGLETON OF AUCHROISK, 10 yrs, 40% *abv*

Sweetness – 7	Peatiness – 5	Price – ∗∗

Colour – Mid-amber with old-gold highlights. *Nose* – Quite full-bodied and medium-sweet with a dark peaty note, good nutty richness and a dark fruity character. *Palate* – Medium-bodied and quite sweet, round with a touch of greenness to the peatiness and a definite toffee character to the richness. *Finish* – Long and smooth with a vanilla tablet sweetness. *Notes* – D.o.b.

THE SINGLETON OF AUCHROISK, 1981, 43% *abv*

Sweetness – 7	*Peatiness* – 5	*Price* – **

Colour – Amber with gold highlights. *Nose* – Full-bodied, clean, medium-sweet and fresh with a slightly green, unripe peachy fruitiness and a delicately perfumed smokiness at the back. *Palate* – Medium-sweet, quite smoky, creamily smooth with an almost chocolatey flavour. *Finish* – Long and round with a hint of coffee. *Notes* – D.o.b.

THE SINGLETON OF AUCHROISK, 1983, 40% *abv*

Sweetness – 7	*Peatiness* – 3	*Price* – **

Colour – Full amber with old-gold highlights. *Nose* – Quite rich and medium-sweet with a dark nuttiness and reasonable weight. *Palate* – Medium-bodied, round, dark, nutty and medium-dry. *Finish* – Almost dry, slightly bitter and with a toffee-like tail. *Notes* – D.o.b.

THE SINGLETON OF AUCHROISK, 1976, 40% *abv*

Sweetness – 7	*Peatiness* – 4	*Price* – ***

Colour – Amber with gold highlights. *Nose* – Rich, quite full-bodied and minty with a peachy sweetness and good weight. *Palate* – Quite full-bodied and smooth with a sherried nuttiness, a vanilla oaky-oiliness and quite delicately peated. *Finish* – Quite long, nutty and dark with a smokiness on the tail. *Notes* – D.o.b.

1978, 12 *yrs*, 59.3% *abv*

Sweetness – 8	*Peatiness* – 3	*Price* – **

Colour – Pale straw with lemon/yellow highlights. *Nose* – Fresh, fruity – citrus and cherries, quite full-bodied with a touch of raisins at the back. *Palate* – Sweet, fruity, smooth and round with good oaky tannins and quite spirity. *Finish* – Smooth and spirity with a hint of cloves and quite long. *Notes* – Wm Cadenhead bottling as *Auchroisk*.

1989, Natural strength, 59.8% *abv*

Sweetness – 6	*Peatiness* – 3	*Price* – ***

Colour – Water-white with silver/white highlights. *Nose* – Very young, mashy and medium-sweet, floral with a slight fruity note and very light peat. *Palate* – Young, mashy, vegetal and medium-sweet. *Finish* – Long and spirity. *Notes* – Clydesdale Original bottling as *Auchroisk*.

Aultmore

KEITH, BANFFSHIRE [S] EST. 1895

Built by Alexander Edward of Sanquhar, Forres, with two stills. The first of the make was produced in early 1897. It became a part of DCL in 1925 and was managed by SMD from 1930. Rebuilt between 1970 and 1971 and doubled to four stills. Now operated by UMGD, a subsidiary of Diageo plc.

Location – An isolated building standing on the A96 Keith to Elgin road, close to the turning to Buckie.

Notes – Until 1969 a steam engine had been providing power, operating 24 hours a day, seven days a week since 1898. The old engine is still kept for show.

Water – The burn of Auchinderran.

12 yrs, 43% abv

Sweetness – 5	Peatiness – 4	Price – *

Colour – Pale straw with lemon highlights. *Nose* – Rich, round, medium-bodied, a cooked mash character, appley and spirity. *Palate* – Medium-bodied, lightly peated and medium-dry. *Finish* – Smooth, malty and quite long. *Notes* – D.o.b.

1990, 16 yrs, 50% abv

Sweetness – 7	Peatiness – 5	Price – **

Colour – Amber with gold highlights. *Nose* – Medium-bodied, rich and fruity – grapes and tangerines with quite delicate peat; water emphasises the grapiness and brings out a little warm, toasty character and honey. *Palate* – Quite big-bodied, gently chewy, medium-dry and rich, with orange and drying tannins. *Finish* – Long, with a touch of spice, a little honey and vanilla oak. *Notes* – Douglas Laing Old Malt Cask bottling from Sherry Butt no. 3333 distilled in May 1990.

Balblair

EDDERTON, ROSS-SHIRE [H]   EST. 1790
Website: *www.balblair.com*

The present distillery was built in 1872, when the then owner, Andrew Ross, decided to extend the business, the new buildings being higher up the slope of the hill. The older buildings were converted into a bonded warehouse. Two operational stills. These two large stills were added by Bertie Cumming in 1964 and the original, small still was only used occasionally. When Hiram Walker took over in 1970, they never used the wee still. Having fallen into disuse, it would need considerable repair work to bring it back into production. Sold to Inver House Distillers in 1996. The fermenting of ale on this site is said to have taken place as long ago as 1749.

Location – Less than a quarter of a mile from the Dornoch Firth, about six miles from Tain on the A9.

Notes – Distilling in the area predates Balblair by a considerable number of years, there being sources of water and peat in abundance. Indeed, the Edderton area has long been known as "the Parish of Peats" and once abounded with smuggling bothies.

Water – The Allt Dearg, a burn four miles from the distillery.

16 yrs, 43% abv

Sweetness – 6	Peatiness – 4	Price – *

Colour – Amber with gold highlights. *Nose* – Quite full-bodied, medium-sweet and fresh with a slight green fruit (peaches and apples) character. *Palate* – Quite soft and round with toffee and vanilla flavours, good body, quite a delicate peatiness and medium-dry. *Finish* – Long, quite dark and tangy with a hint of tarry rope. *Notes* – D.o.b.

BALBLAIR ELEMENTS, No age statement, 40% *abv*

Sweetness – 8	Peatiness – 3	Price – *

Colour – Amber with gold highlights. *Nose* – Quite full-bodied, rich, malty and medium-sweet with a slight fresh green peatiness, a floral hedgerow note and a light floral character. *Palate* – Sweet, rich, full-bodied, quite fresh and quite delicately peated with notes of toffee and vanilla, very smooth. *Finish* – Long, quite tangy, rich and malty. *Notes* – D.o.b.

1997, 43% *abv*

Sweetness – 6	Peatiness – 4	Price – *

Colour – Pale amber with gold highlights. *Nose* – Medium-bodied, malty with notes of treacle toffee, rich satsuma oranges and banana; water brings out a floral touch. *Palate* – Rich and medium-dry, quite full-bodied with a wee touch of spice, round and smooth with a charred peat note. *Finish* – Long and fresh with notes of medium-sweet toffee and white chocolate. *Notes* – D.o.b.

1989, 43% *abv*

Sweetness – 5	Peatiness – 4	Price – **

Colour – Amber with gold highlights. *Nose* – Light and quite delicate with slight lemon and sherbet notes; water brings out a more limey character and a toffee maltiness. *Palate* – Medium-bodied, quite fresh and round, gently chewy tannins and a touch of toffee. *Finish* – Long, clean, quite ethereal with dark, charred, tarry peat on the tail. *Notes* – D.o.b.

1979, 46% *abv*

Sweetness – 5	Peatiness – 4	Price – ***

Colour – Pale amber with gold highlights. *Nose* – Rich, round, soft citrus, honey and toffee; water brings out an old-fashioned sweet-shop aroma and good richness. *Palate* – Medium-dry with gently chewy tannins and good body, a floral touch and some tangy spice with an edge of juicy citrus. *Finish* – Long, quite dark and malty, quite unctuous and mouth-wateringly juicy. *Notes* – D.o.b.

Balmenach

BALMENACH, CROMDALE, MORAY [S] EST. 1824

The distillery was established in 1824 by James McGregor. At the time, it was at the centre of an area which was full of smugglers' bothies and illicit distilling was a way of life. Bought by SMD in 1930 and extended from four to six stills in 1962. A Saladin Box maltings was installed in 1964 and used until the mid-1980s. Over that period, it supplied most of SMD's Speyside malt requirements. Purchased by Inver House in December 1997.

Location – The distillery lies in a bowl in the hills off the A95 main road heading towards Bridge of Avon from Grantown-on-Spey. The distillery stands about a mile from the former Cromdale station on the Spey valley railway line.

Notes – A branch line was built to the distillery in the late 1880s and the steam engine which worked the line is preserved on the Strathspey railway at Aviemore. Local lore tells that farmer James McGregor was visited by an excise officer just after the 1823 Excise Act had been passed. He was shown around the farm and experienced typical hospitality with a quantity of fine whisky. The officer then pointed out an outbuilding and asked what it was used for. "That's just the peat shed," came the reply. The officer said nothing and continued to enjoy his whisky. After a few more drams, the officer made to leave. "If I were you, Mr McGregor," he said, "I'd take out a licence for that peat shed." McGregor took the hint and took out the necessary licence. In 1690, the Jacobites were defeated by William of Orange in a battle on the hills above the distillery.

Water – The Cromdale Burn.

SPEYSIDE
SINGLE MALT
SCOTCH WHISKY

Sometime in the early 19th, after *walking*
in the *CROMDALE* hills *with*
his 2 *BROTHERS*, *James McGregor* settled
and established

BALMENACH

distillery. *Spring water* from beneath those
same *HILLS* is still used to produce
this *RICH flavoured single MALT SCOTCH
WHISKY* of *exemplary* quality.

AGED **12** YEARS

43% vol   Distilled & Bottled in SCOTLAND.
BALMENACH DISTILLERY, Cromdale, Moray, Scotland.   70 cl

Sweetness – 7	Peatiness – 5	Price – ✲✲

Colour – Quite deep amber with bronze highlights. *Nose* – Quite full-bodied, heather floral characters, medium-sweet, rich and sherried with a light honeyed nuttiness. *Palate* – Full-bodied, sherried and nutty with a touch of oily vanilla. *Finish* – Long, nutty and medium-sweet with a touch of tannin. *Notes* – United Distillers bottling.

1981, 62.6% *abv*

Sweetness – 6	Peatiness – 5	Price – ✲✲

Colour – Very pale, watery straw with pale lemon highlights. *Nose* – Very mashy, youthful character, lightly spirity with a sweetness at the back. *Palate* – Medium-sweet, rich and unctuous with gentle tannins, a hint of austerity at the front of the palate and lightly peated. *Finish* – Quite short, but smooth with a light chewiness. *Notes* – Wm Cadenhead bottling.

1972, 40% *abv*

Sweetness – 6	Peatiness – 7	Price – ✲✲

Colour – Mid-amber with light bronze highlights. *Nose* – Medium-sweet, quite full-bodied, dark, rich, brazil nutty and smoky, oaky with a good unctuous richness. *Palate* – Medium-dry, nutty, of good body with a soft richness and smoky oak. *Finish* – Long and slightly chewy with a slight perfumed smokiness. *Notes* – Gordon & MacPhail bottling.

1971, 40% *abv*

Sweetness – 5	Peatiness – 7	Price – ✲✲

Colour – Amber/straw with yellow/gold highlights. *Nose* – Quite smoky and peaty, medium-bodied with a slight green nuttiness. *Palate* – Dryish, smoky, quite full and delicately peated with an edge of sweetness. *Finish* – Dry with oaky tannin and reasonable length. *Notes* – Gordon & MacPhail bottling.

1977, 18 *yrs*, 43% *abv*

Sweetness – 5	Peatiness – 7	Price – ✲✲

Colour – Very pale straw with pale yellow highlights. *Nose* – Medium-dry and quite full-bodied with a slightly earthy peat character and a slight burnt vegetal note. *Palate* – Medium-dry, smooth and creamy with good body and an earthy peatiness. *Finish* – Long and quite elegant with a slight edge of richness. *Notes* – Blackadder bottling distilled 18 November 1977.

Balvenie

DUFFTOWN, BANFFSHIRE [S] [V] EST. 1892
Website: *www.thebalvenie.com*

Built next to William Grant's Glenfiddich distillery in 1892. The stills came second-hand from Lagavulin and Glen Albyn. Three further stills were added to make eight in all (two in 1965 and one in 1971). Floor malting is still carried out at Balvenie, this supplying about 15% of the distillery's malt requirements. They also malt a small quantity for Glenfiddich. The peat used is hand-cut locally, and dried and seasoned before being used to fire the malt kiln. The stills at Balvenie are heated using the heat waste from Glenfiddich to produce steam heat to boil them.

Location – Situated just below Glenfiddich on the lower slopes of the Convals, the hills which dominate Dufftown.

Notes – The Balvenie is an excellent example of just how different single malts can be. Standing next door to its more famous sister, Glenfiddich draws its water from the same source and shares the same supply of malt – even the distiller is the same person – and yet the two whiskies are very different in character. In 1992, 100 years after Balvenie was built, the Grants opened another new distillery, Kininvie, next door.

Water – The Robbie Dhu (pronounced "doo") springs.

THE BALVENIE DOUBLEWOOD, 12 *yrs*, 40% *abv*

Sweetness – 7	Peatiness – 2	Price – ∗

Colour – Quite full amber with old-gold highlights and a hint of lemon. *Nose* – Quite full mashy/spirity and ripe with a slightly walnutty character and a fresh, almost Riesling-like diesel touch. *Palate* – Medium-sweet, slightly spicy, smooth and round with a dark nuttiness, a chocolatey/malty character and delicately peated. *Finish* – Fresh, warm, rich, quite tangy, long and with the walnut character of the nose. *Notes* – Partly aged in a Bourbon cask, its maturation is finished off in a Sherry cask, hence the name *DoubleWood*. D.o.b.

THE BALVENIE SINGLE BARREL, 1978, 15 *yrs*, 50.4% *abv*

Sweetness – 7	Peatiness – 3	Price – ∗∗

Colour – Bright, pale mid-amber with yellow-gold highlights. *Nose* – Quite full-bodied, ripe, rich and medium-sweet with an unctuous, oily, honeyed vanilla-oak character, delicately peated with hints of green apples. *Palate* – Medium-sweet, quite full-bodied, smooth and round with a backbone of oaky tannin, an oily-vanilla texture and a slight green edge to the peatiness. *Finish* – Very long and complex with hints of bitter chocolate, hazelnuts, toffee, honey and a nice green coffee tang. *Notes* – D.o.b. Bottle no. 134 from cask no. 199. This cask was filled on 17.1.1978 and bottled on 13.10.1991.

THE BALVENIE PORT WOOD, 21 *yrs*, 43% *abv*

Sweetness – 5	Peatiness – 4	Price – ∗∗∗

Colour – Mid-amber with bronze highlights and a slight ruby hue. *Nose* – Soft, round, quite full-bodied and sweet with a rich toffee and vanilla oak character, a touch of beeswax and a note of soft, ripe peach. *Palate* – Quite dry with chewy tannins, good body and richness and quite delicately peated. *Finish* – Long and gently chewy with a touch of beeswax. *Notes* – D.o.b., finished in a port pipe.

Banff

BANFF, BANFFSHIRE [H] EST. 1863

Built by James Simpson Junior to replace an earlier distillery of the same name built in 1824. Rebuilt after a fire in 1877. Owned by SMD from 1932. Two stills. Closed and dismantled in 1983.

Location – Half a mile west of Banff on the B9139.

Notes – One of the first distilleries located to take advantage of the railways. On Saturday, 16 August 1941, a single German plane machine-gunned and bombed the no. 12 warehouse. Exploding casks flew through the air and a local newspaper reported, ". . . thousands of gallons of whisky were lost, either burning or running to waste over the land . . . even farm animals became intoxicated". Cows were not milked because they could not be got to their feet. Banff was known locally as "Inverboyndie distillery".

Water – Springs on Fiskaildy Farm.

1976, 17 yrs, 60.5 % abv

Sweetness – 6	Peatiness – 6	Price – ***

Colour – Mid-amber with yellow/gold highlights. *Nose* – Fresh and clean with a soft green fruitiness, hints of perfume and a cedar note. *Palate* – Fresh, smooth, medium-dry and quite round with good body and gentle tannins. *Finish* – Of reasonable length, it has a light earthy smokiness with a green edge. *Notes* – Wm Cadenhead bottling.

34 yrs, 43% abv

Sweetness – 4	Peatiness – 6	Price – ***

Colour – Deep amber with bronze highlights. *Nose* – Medium-bodied, dark, nutty and meaty with notes of beeswax; water brings out a big, slightly burnt mahogany character and treacle toffee. *Palate* – Big-bodied, dark and very gently chewy, medium-dry and nutty (walnuts). *Finish* – Long with notes of beeswax and quite soft and gentle tannins. *Notes* – Douglas Laing Old Malt Cask bottling.

Ben Nevis

LOCHY BRIDGE, FORT WILLIAM [H] [V] EST. 1825
Website: *www.bennevisdistillery.com*

Founded by "Long John" Macdonald in 1825. Owned by various Macdonalds until taken over by Ben Nevis Distillery (Fort William) Ltd in 1955. A Coffey still installed at this time. Later sold to Long John (International) Ltd (a part of Whitbread) in 1981, when the Coffey still was removed. Four pot stills. Sold by Whitbread to the Japanese company, Nikka, early in 1989.

Location – Situated two miles north of Fort William on the A82.

Notes – A cask of *Ben Nevis* was presented to Queen Victoria on her visit to Fort William on 21 April 1848. The cask was not to be breached until the Prince of Wales reached his maturity 15 years later.

Water – Allt a' Mhuilinn (The Mill Burn), which flows from two small lochans, Coire Leis and Coire na' Ciste, situated over 915 metres up on Ben Nevis.

10 *yrs*, 46% *abv*

Sweetness – 5	Peatiness – 6	Price – *

Colour – Mid-amber with old-gold highlights. *Nose* – Fresh with a dark nuttiness, medium-dry with a leafy Demerara sugar character, rich and quite full-bodied, quite intense and showing fruit – orange and almost a grapiness. *Palate* – Quite full, soft, fresh and medium-sweet with a dark peat character, a touch of spice and sweet, oaky vanilla. *Finish* – Long, rich and smooth with a touch of toffee and chocolate. *Notes* – D.o.b.

21 yrs, 55.6% abv

Sweetness – 5	Peatiness – 6	Price – ✲✲✲

Colour – Quite deep amber with bronze highlights. *Nose* – Full-bodied, rich, oaky and medium-sweet with a firm peatiness. *Palate* – Full-bodied, dark and nutty with a rich peatiness, medium-sweet with quite gentle oaky tannins. *Finish* – Long, powerful and delicately smoky with a tangy touch of spice and just an edge of sweetness on the tail. *Notes* – D.o.b.

1972, 60.5% abv

Sweetness – 5	Peatiness – 6	Price – ✲✲✲✲

Colour – Pale amber with gold highlights. *Nose* – Quite full, earthy, medium-sweet, quite peaty for the region, with hints of hazelnuts. *Palate* – Medium-sweet, smoky and smooth with a little tannin and a green freshness. *Finish* – Long and gently smoky with a touch of spice. *Notes* – D.o.b. from cask no. 619.

1967, 26 yrs, 58% abv

Sweetness – 4	Peatiness – 5	Price – ✲✲✲

Colour – Mid-amber with old-gold highlights. *Nose* – Medium-sweet, quite rich and fresh with a touch of oily, oaky vanilla, a green character and medium-bodied. *Palate* – Medium-dry, quite full and rich with a slight oily smoothness. *Finish* – Long and gently smoky with good rich sweetness and a tail of bitter toffee. *Notes* – D.o.b.

1984, 61.2% abv

Sweetness – 4	Peatiness – 7	Price – ✲✲✲

Colour – Deep amber with bronze and ruby highlights. *Nose* – Quite big-bodied and round showing burnt toffee; water brings out a rich, creamy, treacle toffee character, a vegetal touch and quite a solid peat note. *Palate* – Medium-dry, big-bodied, smooth and elegant with quite a dark peat note and some chocolate. *Finish* – Long, darkly chocolate, very elegant and distinguished. *Notes* – Blackadder Raw Cask bottling from cask no. 258 filled on 21 November 1984.

1995, 10 yrs, 59.9% abv

Sweetness – 4	Peatiness – 6	Price – ✲✲

Colour – Amber with gold highlights. *Nose* – Big, dark, malty and nutty with cereal notes – sugar puffs; water emphasises the sugar puffs and a solid peat note. *Palate* – Big-bodied, and softly chewy with a dark peat note, malty, a note of brazil nuts. *Finish* – Long and quite chunky with a toasted breakfast cereal character. *Notes* – Clydesdale Original bottling from cask reference 0184/572 filled November 1995.

Benriach

LONGMORN, NR ELGIN, MORAY   [S]   EST. 1898
Website: *www.benriachdistillery.co.uk*

Established in 1898 as the whisky market moved suddenly into recession. It was then closed in 1900 and did not open again until 1965, when it was rebuilt by The Glenlivet Distillers Ltd. Owned by The Seagram Company of Canada from 1977, it was sold to Pernod-Ricard in 2001, who managed it under Chivas Brothers. In April 2004 three entrepreneurs, led by industry veteran Billy Walker, bought it. Four stills.

Location – Situated three miles south of Elgin to the east of the A941.

Notes – The floor maltings were closed in 1999, but remain in good working order and could be reactivated almost immediately. Previously only available through the independent bottlers, Seagram introduced their own bottling in 1994. The new owners have expanded that with a considerable number of single cask bottlings as well as some interesting finishes. They have styled their whisky with the definite article: "The BenRiach".

Water – The Burnside Springs.

12 yrs, 40% abv

Sweetness – 7	Peatiness – 2	Price – *

Colour – Amber with light gold highlights. *Nose* – Clean, quite rich, apple-flavoured; water brings out heather flowers, honey and vanilla and a slightly green edge to the delicate peat. *Palate* – Medium-sweet, velvety smooth, round, apple and peach characters with honey and a little spice. *Finish* – Long, elegant and spicy with a milk chocolate note. *Notes* – D.o.b.

CURIOSITAS 10 yrs, 40% abv

Sweetness – 6	Peatiness – 8	Price – *

Colour – Amber with pale gold highlights. *Nose* – Big-bodied, solid and quite pungent, notes of perfume and carbolic; water brings out a slightly rancid butter note, a slight creaminess and the peat becomes sooty. *Palate* – Darkly peaty, rich, medium-sweet and tangy with notes of apples and dried apricots. *Finish* – Long, very clean, quite ethereal and finishes dry. *Notes* – D.o.b. From 1983, Seagram produced a heavily peated style as well as the more traditional Speyside style. The new owners are maintaining this practice.

MADEIRA WOOD FINISH, 15 yrs, 46% abv

Sweetness – 7	Peatiness – 4	Price – **

Colour – Amber with gold highlights. *Nose* – Quite big-bodied and round, smooth and toffeeyed with clean peat at the back; water brings out notes of beeswax, pepper and citrus oil and a wee bit of spice. *Palate* – Rich and round with drying oak tannins in the middle of the palate surrounded by velvety smooth, malty citrus and peach notes. *Finish* – Long, ethereal and elegant with juicily mouth-watering citrus on the tail. *Notes* – D.o.b.

PEDRO XIMINEZ SHERRY WOOD FINISH, 15 yrs, 46% abv

Sweetness – 6	Peatiness – 4	Price – **

Colour – Mid-amber with honeyed old-gold highlights. *Nose* – Medium-bodied, soft, sweet and rich with lemon/tangerine characters; water brings out a nuttiness – walnuts, honey and a soft maltiness. *Palate* – Soft, medium-sweet, smooth and round with a touch of spice, notes of orange and toffee and delicately peated. *Finish* – Long, rich and complex with notes of honey and citrus. *Notes* – D.o.b.

16 yrs, 43% abv

Sweetness – 8	Peatiness – 5	Price – **

Colour – Amber with honeyed gold highlights. *Nose* – Quite big-bodied with a dark, heathery peat note and aromas of bog myrtle; water brings out a soft, floral, perfumed note and honey and apple. *Palate* – Decadently and almost overwhelmingly rich, quite big-bodied, sweet with citrus and honey, the peat is present, but subdued by the richness and notes of golden syrup, toffee and marmalade. *Finish* – Peat to the fore in the finish, delicately done though, quite ethereal and very long. *Notes* – D.o.b.

AUTHENTICUS 21 yrs, 46% abv

Sweetness – 6	*Peatiness* – 9	*Price* – ✳✳

Colour – Mid-amber with gold highlights. *Nose* – Powerful and dark with an earthy, charred, peat note; water emphasises the charred note, which is reminiscent of spent fireworks. *Palate* – Big, powerful and darkly peaty, with notes of breakfast cereal – puffed wheat and burnt paper, medium-sweet and rich with a red apple character. *Finish* – Long and impressive; peat without the sea supported by fine sweetness. *Notes* – D.o.b.

Barley receipts record book from Benriach showing entries from 1948

Benrinnes

ABERLOUR, BANFFSHIRE [S] EST. 1835

The original distillery was located at Whitehouse Farm, three quarters of a mile to the south-east, and was washed away in the great flood of 1829. The present building was founded in 1835 by William Smith & Co. as an extension of the farm steading. Acquired by Dewar's in 1922 and thereby became part of DCL in 1925. Run by SMD from 1930, the licensees were A. & A. Crawford Ltd. Major reconstruction took place between 1955 and 1956. Doubled from three to six stills in 1966. Now part of Diageo.

Location – Situated one and a half miles south of the A95 on a loop of an unclassified road which runs between the A95 at Daugh of Kinermony and the B9009 at Succoth in Glen Rinnes.

Notes – A form of triple distillation is practised.

Water – The Scurran and Rowantree Burns.

15 yrs, 43% abv

Sweetness – 8	Peatiness – 4	Price – ✵✵

Colour – Amber with old-gold highlights. *Nose* – Medium-bodied, biscuity-yeasty, fresh, vanilla and medium-sweet with a slight floral note. *Palate* – Medium-sweet, round, smooth, biscuity and honeyed. *Finish* – Nice, sweet, round, biscuity and honeyed. *Notes* – Diageo Flora & Fauna bottling.

1982, 14 yrs, 43% *abv*

Sweetness – 7	Peatiness – 5	Price – **

Colour – Pale amber with bright gold highlights. *Nose* – Quite full-bodied, medium-sweet and rich with a slight hint of green apples and a rubbery peatiness. *Palate* – Quite big-bodied, medium-dry and slightly smoky. *Finish* – Dry, long and gently chewy. *Notes* – Signatory bottling from cask nos. 95/1171/4 distilled 25 November 1982.

BLACKADDER

SINGLE SPEYSIDE MALT WHISKY
from

Benrinnes

distillery

16 years old

Distilled 19th March 1980
Cask no.1350 Bottled September 1996

Benrinnes distillery, which is named after a dominant mountain peak overlooking the Spey Valley, is notable for the use of a form of triple distillation in its production process. This bottling gives a medium-dry whisky with good body, an almost fragrant peatiness and a long, clean finish.

70cl   Blackadder International
Larkhall ML9 1DA   43%vol

Product of Scotland

1980, 16 yrs, 43% *abv*

Sweetness – 6	Peatiness – 6	Price – **

Colour – Pale straw with pale yellow highlights. *Nose* – Quite a mashy cereal note, soft and medium-dry with quite gentle peatiness. *Palate* – Medium-sweet with an almost fragrant peatiness, smooth, round and of good body. *Finish* – Long, fragrant and clean. *Notes* – Blackadder bottling from cask no. 1350 distilled 19 March 1980.

1968, 40% *abv*

Sweetness – 6	Peatiness – 6	Price – ***

Colour – Straw/gold with good bright highlights. *Nose* – Sweet, nutty and slightly fatty in an unctuous way. *Palate* – Medium-sweet, smoky, spicy and oaky. *Finish* – Good, smoky and dry, smooth and creamy. *Notes* – Gordon & MacPhail bottling.

Benromach

FORRES, MORAY [S] [V] EST. 1898
Website: *www.benromach.com*

Built by the Benromach Distillery Company. Bought by Associated Scottish Distilleries Ltd in 1937, who sold it to DCL in 1953. It was managed by SMD and the licensees were J. & W. Hardie. The still-house was rebuilt in 1966 and the mash-house was rebuilt and the tun-room modernised in 1974. Two stills. Bought by Gordon & MacPhail in 1992, who re-opened it in 1996.

Location – North of Forres on the north side of the railway line.

Notes – Benromach was designed by Elgin architect Charles Doig and has the high-pitched gables and narrow-mullioned windows in the Scots vernacular style of the 17th century. In 1925, the mash tun was wooden.

Water – Chapeltown springs near Forres.

BENROMACH TRADITIONAL, 40% *abv*		
Sweetness – 6	*Peatiness* – 4	*Price* – ✳

Colour – Pale amber with pale yellow highlights. *Nose* – Malty and medium-dry with a good cereal note, quite full-bodied with aromas of green pine needles; water brings out the peat which has a slight burnt mahogany note, cloves, a hint of richness and a slight citrus fruity note. *Palate* – Medium-sweet, with good body, round and malty with nice weight and a youthful cereal note. *Finish* – Long, slightly tangy with a wee touch of spice and cocoa/chocolate on the tail. *Notes* – D.o.b.

12 yrs, 40% *abv*		
Sweetness – 7	*Peatiness* – 4	*Price* – ✳✳

Colour – Amber with yellow highlights. *Nose* – Medium-bodied and medium-sweet with a rich, almost bubble-gum fruitiness and a touch of apple with good background peat. *Palate* – Medium-sweet, round and smooth with good, quite chunky peat flavours. *Finish* – Long, very gently smoky and quite complex. *Notes* – D.o.b.

15 *yrs*, 40% *abv*

Sweetness – 7	Peatiness – 5	Price – ✳✳✳

Colour – Amber with pale gold highlights. *Nose* – Full, malty, rich and medium-sweet with a slightly green vegetal note and darkish peat character, showing notes of heather honey and lemon curd. *Palate* – Medium-dry, rich and quite creamy with gently chewy oaky tannins and a good dark peat character. *Finish* – Long and softly chewy with creamy toffee on the tail. *Notes* – UDV bottling.

CENTENARY, 17 *yrs*, 43% *abv*

Sweetness – 7	Peatiness – 5	Price – ✳✳✳

Colour – Amber with pale gold highlights. *Nose* – Medium-sweet, round and slightly malty with notes of vanilla, cereals, cocoa and coffee. *Palate* – Medium-sweet, round and malty with a quite delicate, but also quite solid peatiness and a rich, fruity character. *Finish* – Long and clean, showing creamy vanilla and richly smoky. *Notes* – D.o.b.

PORTWOOD FINISH, 45% *abv*

Sweetness – 4	Peatiness – 4	Price – ✳✳

Colour – Amber with gold highlights. *Nose* – Full, round, soft, rich and raisiny with notes of bread and butter pudding; water brings out more fruit – plum pudding and a floral note. *Palate* – Medium-dry, round, quite intense with dried fruit – apricots and raisins, smooth and quite full-bodied. *Finish* – Long, quite ethereal and fruity with the whisky, cereal and vanilla kicking in at the tail. *Notes* – D.o.b.

1974, 40% *abv*

Sweetness – 7	Peatiness – 4	Price – ✳✳✳✳

Colour – Amber with gold highlights. *Nose* – Quite soft, medium-sweet and malty, quite delicately peated, showing characteristics of toffee, ripe, sweet apples and almost peaches. *Palate* – Quite big, soft, medium-sweet and honeyed with a quite delicate peatiness. *Finish* – Long, clean, rich and quite elegant with a toffee apple character. *Notes* – D.o.b.

Ben Wyvis

INVERGORDON, ROSS-SHIRE [H] EST. 1881

Built within the Invergordon grain distilling complex in 1965 by Invergordon Distillers Ltd, Ben Wyvis had two stills. These were closed down in 1977 and subsequently dismantled. The vast bulk of Ben Wyvis' output was included in blends and it has only very rarely appeared as a single malt.

Location – Within the Invergordon grain complex to the west of the town of the same name.

Notes – Invergordon is the deepest port in Britain. A regular port of call for cruise ships, the Cromarty Firth, on the shores of which the harbour is situated, is a storage area for deep sea oil rigs.

Water – Loch Glass.

1968, 51% *abv*

Sweetness – 7	Peatiness – 4	Price – *****

Colour – Amber with yellow highlights. **Nose** – Quite full-bodied, medium-sweet, slightly honeyed vanilla note with sweet, soft oak, beeswax and lemon oil. **Palate** – Quite soft, round, smooth and of good body, with gently chewy tannins and delicately peated **Finish** – Long, rich and elegant with lingering shortbread flavours. **Notes** – signatory bottling.

Bladnoch

BLADNOCH, WIGTOWNSHIRE [L] [V] EST. 1817
Website: *www.bladnoch.co.uk*

Founded in 1817 by John & Thomas McClelland. Sold by Dunvilles, the Irish Whiskey distillers, in 1936 for £3,500. This "representing a considerable loss for the premises and plant." Closed from 1938 to 1956. Owned by Inver House from 1973 to 1983 when sold to Arthur Bell & Sons. Licensed to UMGD in 1992 and closed in 1993. Bought by Raymond Armstrong as a visitor centre and finally recommenced distilling in November 2000.

Location – The southernmost distillery in Scotland, situated on the river of the same name, just a mile outside Scotland's Book Town, Wigtown.

Notes – Close to the distillery is Baldoon Farm, where stands the ruined castle to which Janet Dalrymple, the "Bride of Lammermoor", came to die after her marriage to David Dunbar of Baldoon. Bladnoch is home to the Whisky School, where, for three days, students get hands-on experience in making whisky.

Water – The River Bladnoch.

15 yrs, 55% abv

Sweetness – 4	Peatiness – 3	Price – ✳✳

Colour – Straw with pale gold highlights. *Nose* – Medium-bodied and rich with chocolate, tobacco and fruity notes of orange; water brings out tangerines and juicy satsumas, delicate peat and some blossom. *Palate* – Medium-dry, rich and quite full-bodied with citrus – satsumas and a delicate coffee/chocolate peat character. *Finish* – Long, smooth and elegant with citrus notes lingering. *Notes* – D.o.b.

10 yrs, 43% abv

Sweetness – 4	Peatiness – 4	Price – ✳✳

Colour – Straw/amber with yellow highlights and a green tinge. *Nose* – Fresh, quite full, fruity and floral, medium-dry with an attractive grape spirit-like aroma. *Palate* – Fresh with good weight, a sweet edge and a touch of spice. *Finish* – Fresh with nice sweetness and quite light. *Notes* – United Distillers bottling.

22 yrs, 50% abv

Sweetness – 8	Peatiness – 2	Price – ✳✳✳

Colour – Amber with yellow highlights. *Nose* – Medium-bodied, fresh, quite fat and rich, medium-sweet and lightly peated with notes of apple, orange, dried bananas and sweet, oaky vanilla. *Palate* – Sweet, rich, lightly peated, quite full-bodied with flavours of vanilla and banana. *Finish* – Long, rich, quite fresh and appealingly fruity. *Notes* – Douglas Laing & Co. Ltd bottling.

1992, 46% abv

Sweetness – 3	Peatiness – 4	Price – ✳✳

Colour – Pale straw with pale lemon highlights. *Nose* – Fresh, malty and fruity – red apple and peach; water brings out a touch of floral perfume, some buttery vanilla and delicate peat. *Palate* – Off-dry and fresh with a citrus note, good body and clean with a touch of spice, delicate peat and some perfume. *Finish* – Long, clean, fragrant and floral – lavender-scented. *Notes* – Berry's Own Selection bottling.

Blair Athol

PITLOCHRY, PERTHSHIRE [H] [V] EST. 1798

Although originally founded almost 30 years earlier, the present buildings were established in 1826, when they were revived by John Robertson. It passed into the hands of John Conacher and Company in 1827. It closed in 1932 and, although purchased by Arthur Bell & Sons the following year, it did not come into production again until 1949 after rebuilding. Extended from two to four stills in 1973. Now a part of Diageo plc.

Location – Not at Blair Atholl (note that the town is spelt differently), as its name suggests, the distillery is to be found on the southern approaches to Pitlochry, just off the main A9.

Notes – The Conacher family, who owned the distillery for a time in the 1800s, are said to be descended from the chivalrous young Conacher who so admired Catherine Glover, the Fair Maid of Perth. The distillery has a large, modern visitor centre and was rebuilt internally in the mid-1990s to make it more accessible for visitors. Blair Athol is well worth a visit.

Water – From a spring on the nearby 841-metre high Ben Vrackie.

12 yrs, 43% abv

Sweetness – 7	Peatiness – 6	Price – **

Colour – Pale, mid-amber with gold highlights. *Nose* – Quite full with touches of nuttiness and greenness, medium-sweet with a fresh smokiness. *Palate* – Medium-sweet and quite full-bodied, spicy and round with a definite smoky tang. *Finish* – Fresh, quite long and smoky with a sweetness on the tail. *Notes* – D.o.b.

1977, 54.7% abv

Sweetness – 6	Peatiness – 5	Price – ✳✳✳

Colour – Amber with old-gold highlights. *Nose* – Medium-sweet, quite rich and medium-bodied with beeswax and toffee notes; water softens and emphasises the wood. *Palate* – Medium-sweet, rich and honeyed with softly chewy tannins and dried fruit – raisins. *Finish* – Long, clean and smooth. *Notes* – Duncan Taylor bottling from cask no. 36852D.

1966, 23 yrs, 57.1% abv

Sweetness – 6	Peatiness – 5	Price – ✳✳✳

Colour – Mid-amber with yellow/gold highlights. *Nose* – Medium-sweet, quite good body and round with nice vanilla-oak and a citrus oil tang. *Palate* – Soft, smooth, medium-sweet with a dry oakiness, quite gentle tannins and good body. *Finish* – Long with a distinctive perfumed sweetness and a gentle smokiness. *Notes* – Wm Cadenhead bottling distilled October 1966.

27 yrs, 54.7% abv

Sweetness – 7	Peatiness – 5	Price – ✳✳✳

Colour – Mid-amber with old-gold highlights. *Nose* – Medium-sweet, with notes of butter, citrus, nuttiness – hazelnuts and chocolate; water pulls out the lemon, a fresh smoky character and a rich, almost Christmas cake character. *Palate* – Gently chewy, medium-sweet, nutty, ginger, honey and citrus. *Finish* – Chewy oaky tannins with ginger lasting, a sooty smoky tang and cocoa rising. *Notes* – D.o.b. from the Rare Malts range.

Bowmore

BOWMORE, ISLE OF ISLAY, ARGYLL [I] [V] EST. 1779
Website: *www.bowmore.co.uk*

In 1776, an Islay merchant, David Simpson, obtained permission from the local laird to build dwellings and "other buildings". The "other buildings" were soon converted into a distillery. Taken over by J.B. Sheriff & Co. for £20,000 in 1925. Bought by Stanley P. Morrison in 1963 for £117,000, the distillery is now owned by Morrison Bowmore Distillers, who were themselves purchased outright by Suntory of Japan in 1994. The company had been part-owned by Suntory for some years previously, having had a long-term trading relationship with the Japanese company.

Location – Bowmore stands, almost fortress-like, beside the harbour in the town of Bowmore.

Notes – The distillery uses a revolutionary waste heat recovery system to reduce energy costs. The distillery donated a warehouse to the town of Bowmore which has been converted to a swimming pool. The waste heat from the distillery is used to heat the swimming pool. The distillery was built early in the town's history, at the foot of Hill Street, and has proved important to its economic survival.

Water – Laggan River.

LEGEND, No age statement, 40% *abv*

Sweetness – 1	Peatiness – 8	Price – *

Colour – Light amber with gold highlights and a touch of green. *Nose* – Full, pungent, a touch perfumed and a phenol character with a little greenness. *Palate* – Dry with an edge of richness, perfumed and quite pungent. *Finish* – Long, gently smoky and perfumed. *Notes* – D.o.b.

1991, 15 yrs, 56.5% abv

Sweetness – 2	Peatiness – 8	Price – **

Colour – Mid-amber with old-gold highlights. *Nose* – Quite big-bodied, with a soft cocoa-flavoured peat character and a slight floral note; water brings out a breakfast cereal note, a touch of the sea and a slight edge of citrus. *Palate* – Almost dry with good richness, fruit – cherries and bubble gum, quite solid peat and a slight tar/creosote note. *Finish* – Long, dark chocolatey, smoky, quite creamy and complex with a touch of lime on the tail. *Notes* – Dewar, Rattray bottling ex-Sherry cask no. 2057 distilled 15 July 1991.

16 yrs, 53.8% abv

Sweetness – 2	Peatiness – 8	Price – **

Colour – Amber with old-gold highlights. *Nose* – Big-bodied and quite powerful with notes of dampened peat fire, tobacco and fruit; water brings out raisins, fennel and seaweed. *Palate* – Dry, perfumed, carbolic violets, softly chewy and a little creamy toffee. *Finish* – Long and perfumed with charred smoky characters and an edge of toffee. *Notes* – D.o.b.

17 yrs, 43% abv

Sweetness – 2	Peatiness – 8	Price – **

Colour – Quite full, deep amber with old-gold highlights. *Nose* – Rich, medium-bodied with a delicate pungency; water brings out heather and violets, tobacco, brazil nuts and chocolate. *Palate* – Round, quite full-bodied and rich with gently chewy tannins and a carbolic note. *Finish* – Soft, gently smoky, quite elegant and slightly salty with a final note of liquorice. *Notes* – D.o.b.

21 yrs, 43% abv

Sweetness – 2	Peatiness – 8	Price – ****

Colour – Mid-amber with old-gold highlights. *Nose* – Quite big-bodied, dark and smoky, rounded and quite dry with just a hint of ozone. *Palate* – Big, round, burnt heather roots, quite pungent with a delicate floral note at the back. *Finish* – Long with a hint of sweetness/ richness and finely smoky with a touch of bitter chocolate on the tail. *Notes* – D.o.b.

Sweetness – 3	Peatiness – 7	Price – ****

Colour – Quite deep amber with pale bronze highlights. *Nose* – Quite full-bodied, rich with a slightly green hedgerow freshness, the peat is less obvious; water brings out some sea characters – shellfish, a floral smokiness and crème brulée character. *Palate* – Full-bodied, fresh and round, medium-dry but rich with, a slightly perfumed dark peaty smokiness and a touch of gently chewy oaky tannins. *Finish* – Long, gently chewy, almost floral, quite delicately smoky with just a hint of seaweed and bitter chocolate – very complex. *Notes* – D.o.b.

1996, 10 yrs, 50% abv

Sweetness – 1	Peatiness – 8	Price – ***

Colour – Pale straw with gold highlights and a rosé hue. *Nose* – Quite big-bodied with a sea-influenced smokiness; water brings out a little cocoa and some citrus. *Palate* – Big and peaty, soft and dry, gently chewy. *Finish* – Long and clean with a fruity (cherries) touch. *Notes* – Douglas Laing Old Malt Cask bottling from a claret barrique filled in June 1996.

1989, 63.3% abv

Sweetness – 2	Peatiness – 8	Price – ***

Colour – Straw with yellow highlights. *Nose* – Quite light, almost closed with a good, dark peat character; with water it opens out fully – slightly medicinal, an edge of sweetness, a floral note and a creaminess to the peat. *Palate* – Big-bodied, dry and gently tannic with a charred peat note and hints of seaweed and creosote. *Finish* – Long, quite intense and darkly smoky. *Notes* – Blackadder bottling from cask no. 22531.

1987, 52.1% abv

Sweetness – 2	Peatiness – 8	Price – ***

Colour – Mid-amber with gold highlights. *Nose* – Medium-bodied, quite delicate with a sherried richness; water brings out toffee, honey and a touch of perfume. *Palate* – Dry with an edge of richness, a floral note and some smooth, unctuous oak. *Finish* – Big – the peat explodes on the finish with quite a violet-flavoured floral note. *Notes* – Duncan Taylor bottling from cask no. 18052.

BLACK BOWMORE, 1964, 50% *abv*

Sweetness – 2	*Peatiness* – 7	*Price* – ✻✻✻✻✻

Colour – Very deep, dark mahogany/teak with deep bronze highlights. *Nose* – Big-bodied, full, dark, nutty and rich, quite delicately peated, dry with slight notes of burnt mahogany. *Palate* – Big, powerful, full-bodied, quite tannic with dark nutty flavours, smooth, though chewy. *Finish* – Long, full-flavoured, quite chewy with a smoky/nutty character, a good perfumed peatiness and a rich salty tang on the tail. *Notes* – D.o.b. Known as *Black Bowmore*, this is from a very rare old sherry cask bottling. There were three issues of *Black Bowmore*, the first and the last being the most rare.

BOWMORE DARKEST, No age statement, 43% *abv*

Sweetness – 3	*Peatiness* – 8	*Price* – ✻✻

Colour – Deep amber with bronze highlights. *Nose* – Fresh, clean, big and perfumed, sherrily nutty; water brings out a floral touch and tideline seaweed with a wee hint of toffee at the back. *Palate* – Big-bodied and powerful, fragrant with treacle toffee seriously underpinned by cocoa-flavoured peat. *Finish* – Long, with liquorice and a perfumed note wrapped in heathery peat. *Notes* – D.o.b. 12 years in Bourbon casks and finished in Oloroso Sherry butts.

BOWMORE DAWN, No age statement, 51.5% *abv*

Sweetness – 3	*Peatiness* – 8	*Price* – ✻✻

Colour – Deep amber with bronze highlights. *Nose* – Big-bodied, dark, sooty peat notes with fruit and a floral touch; water brings out a vinous character, red fruits and citrus – tangerines, seaweed and heather. *Palate* – Full, dry and peat smoky, toffee and Demerara sugar with fruit – cherries and cloves, gently chewy and tarry. *Finish* – Long, with an earthy peat character and a touch of liquorice on the tail. *Notes* – D.o.b. Matured in bourbon barrels and finished in port pipes.

BOWMORE DUSK, No age statement, 50% *abv*

Sweetness – 3	*Peatiness* – 8	*Price* – ✻✻

Colour – Deep amber with bronze and ruby highlights. *Nose* – Unusual, the peat seems subservient to the wine cask. Medium-bodied, but powerful, hints of blackcurrant and cedar surrounded by quite delicate peat; water seems to broaden the fruit characters – cherries and orange with cocoa peat. *Palate* – Big and spicy, medium-dry with chocolate, orange and Demerara sugar, the peat hovers over the top of the palate. *Finish* – Very long and rich with fruit (blackcurrants and forest fruits) fighting to come through. *Notes* – D.o.b. Matured in bourbon barrels and finished in claret barriques.

Braeval

Originally called Braes of Glenlivet, Braeval was built between 1973 and 1974 by Chivas Brothers, at the time a subsidiary of the Seagram Co. Ltd of Canada. Now a part of Pernod-Ricard. Originally three stills with two more being added in 1975 and a sixth in 1978. Although a very modern distillery, it is nevertheless of a most attractive design, with a decorative, albeit non-functional, pagoda-style roof.

Location – High up above the remote hamlet of Chapeltown off the B9008. It is one of the most remote distilleries in Scotland. It, at some 350 metres above sea-level, is the highest distillery in Scotland.

Notes – The distillery's name was changed to Braeval to avoid confusion with its illustrious sister, The Glenlivet. Braeval is currently (April 2007) temporarily silent.

Water – The Pitilie Burn.

SHERRY CASK, 1996, 8 *yrs*, 46% *abv*

Sweetness – 7	Peatiness – 4	Price – **

Colour – Straw with pale gold highlights. *Nose* – Sweet, rich, butterscotch; water brings out beeswax and baked apples and cloves and a delicate peat note at the back. *Palate* – Quite full-bodied, smooth and unctuous oily oak, ripe apples, cherries and soft peat. *Finish* – Long, smooth, a little spice and some vanilla oak. *Notes* – Douglas Laing bottling from the Provenance range.

Brora

BRORA, SUTHERLAND [H] EST. 1819

Brora was known as Clynelish until 1969. Established by the Duke of Sutherland, who had cleared his tenant farmers off the land to make way for sheep. Having moved some of the inland farmers to the coastal strip, the distillery was established to create a market for the farmers' grain. Owned by SMD from 1930; now a part of Diageo plc.

Location – Just off the A9 at Brora.

Notes – After the modern distillery had been built in 1967–68, the old Clynelish opened in April 1969, housed in the former mash house, which had been rebuilt. It subsequently ceased distillation in May 1983. The old buildings are now used as warehouses and the visitor centre for the "new" Clynelish. Brora had two stills.

Water – The Clynemilton Burn.

1982, 20 yrs, 58.1% abv

Sweetness – 3	Peatiness – 8	Price – ✲✲✲

Colour – Amber with old-gold highlights. *Nose* – Big, delicately pungent and smooth with citrus and lilac notes; water pulls out the peat which has a delicate sea nature – aromas of the beach, the citrus is now definitely lemons and tangerines, along with honey and pear. *Palate* – Velvety smooth and unctuous, beeswax, citrus and spice underpinned by solid, dark peat. *Finish* – Long and ethereal, with liquorice and juniper floating over the peat. *Notes* – D.o.b. from the Rare Malts Collection.

30 yrs, 52.4% abv

Sweetness – 3	Peatiness – 8	Price – ✲✲✲✲

Colour – Deep amber with bronze highlights and an edge of ruby. *Nose* – Huge! Fantastically powerful, rich, heathery smoky and almost a pine character; water expands it even further: toffee, coffee, liquorice, Parma ham and tangerines overlaid with a touch of the beach. *Palate* – Big-bodied, medium-dry, peppery, spicy, warm, sweet oak and iodine. *Finish* – Very long and spicy, the embers of a fire on the beach and a medicinal note on the end. *Notes* – D.o.b. from the Rare Malts Collection.

Bruichladdich

BRUICHLADDICH, ISLAY, ARGYLL [I] [V] EST. 1881
Website: *www.bruichladdich.com*

Built by Robert, William & John Gourlay Harvey (of the Dundashill & Yoker Harveys). Became the Bruichladdich Distillery Company (Islay) Ltd in 1886. Doubled from two to four stills in 1975. Owned in recent years by Invergordon Distillers, who were taken over by JBB (Greater Europe) plc in late 1993. A lot of very old machinery and distillation techniques were employed in the distillery, making it an exciting distillery to visit. Mothballed abruptly at the end of January 1995, it was sold in December 2000 to the Bruichladdich Distillery Co. Ltd, a consortium of 25 shareholders. Production started again in May 2001.

Location – Sited on the western shore of Loch Indaal on the A847 to Port Charlotte and the picturesque village of Portnahaven.

Notes – The distillery's make has a lighter, more delicate character than the other Islay malts. It is thought that this is because it is sheltered from the prevailing winds – and weather – by the Rhinns of Islay, a range of hills which lie between Bruichladdich and the Atlantic. The current owners are very innovative in their bottlings and techniques, much of this being driven by the holes in their stocks caused by the distillery's mothballing over the years. Plans have been announced to build a distillery at Port Charlotte on the site of the former Lochindaal distillery. Watch this space.

Water – A reservoir in the local hills.

WAVES, 7 *yrs*, 46% *abv*

Sweetness – 2	Peatiness – 6	Price – *

Colour – Pale amber with pale gold highlights. *Nose* – Medium-bodied, fresh, a little touch of a medicinal character; water enhances the youthful character and pulls out perfume. *Palate* – Youthfully fresh, clean with a nice, soft peat touch, an edge of richness and medium-dry. *Finish* – Long and perfumed with a slight tang of tarry ropes and dried wrack. *Notes* – D.o.b. created from a mix of ex-Bourbon and ex-Madeira casks.

ROCKS, No age statement, 46% *abv*

Sweetness – 3	Peatiness – 6	Price – *

Colour – Amber with gold highlights and a pale ruby hue, almost onion-skin rosé. *Nose* – Medium-bodied, fruity! Very! Grapes and delicate peat; water brings out grapes and raspberries, Demerara sugar and very rich. *Palate* – Big-bodied and rich, creamy, delicate peat mingling with raspberries and toffee. *Finish* – Delicately smoky peat, long, quite ethereal and rich. *Notes* – D.o.b.

10 *yrs*, 46% *abv*

Sweetness – 3	Peatiness – 4	Price – **

Colour – Pale amber with pale lemon highlights. *Nose* – Fresh, clean, malty, toffee/tablet; water brings out fruit – pears and pear drops and hedgerow characters. *Palate* – Medium-dry, clean, fresh, quite rich and medium-bodied with notes of green stone fruit and delicate peat. *Finish* – Long, elegant and squeaky clean. *Notes* – D.o.b.

15 *yrs*, 46% *abv*

Sweetness – 3	Peatiness – 3	Price – **

Colour – Mid-amber with gold highlights. *Nose* – Medium-bodied, a touch of nuttiness – hazelnuts and peanuts; water brings out a malty, rich note of tablet and beeswax. *Palate* – Round, smooth, malty, medium-bodied and medium-dry with softly chewy tannins and gently peated with a peanut character on the end. *Finish* – Long, quite ethereal, delicately perfumed and elegant. *Notes* – D.o.b.

XVII, 17 *yrs*, 46% *abv*

Sweetness – 3	Peatiness – 3	Price – **

Colour – Amber with pale gold highlights. *Nose* – Medium-bodied and rich; water pulls out a slightly overcooked fruitcake and a fresh greenness. *Palate* – Medium-dry with a green peat note and chewy oaky tannins. *Finish* – Long, very clean, delicately and freshly peated. *Notes* – D.o.b.

ISLANDS THIRD EDITION, 20 *yrs*, 46% *abv*

Sweetness – 3	*Peatiness* – 4	*Price* – ✱✱✱

Colour – Amber with old-gold highlights. *Nose* – Round and quite good-bodied, slightly charred; water brings out fruitcake, beeswax and sultanas. *Palate* – Quite big-bodied, but delicate, an edge of sweetness, charred peat, gently chewy and fruit – plums? *Finish* – Gently chewy oak tannins and walnuts with medium-sweet vanilla. *Notes* – D.o.b.

1991, 46% *abv*

Sweetness – 2	*Peatiness* – 6	*Price* – ✱✱

Colour – Pale straw with pale lemon highlights. *Nose* – Quite light and delicate with a shellfish note; water brings out the aroma of fish and chips from the van at Bowmore, a creamy butteriness and some banana and kiwi fruit. *Palate* – Dry, medium-peated with a slight sea influence, of good body with a delicate medicinal note and smooth. *Finish* – Long, clean and quite ethereal with a wee touch of spice. *Notes* – Berry's Own Selection bottling from cask no. 2512.

1970, 53.8% *abv*

Sweetness – 3	*Peatiness* – 4	*Price* – ✱✱✱

Colour – Mid-amber with old-gold highlights. *Nose* – Light and delicate; water brings out a fresh, round and vinous character, a nutty (hazelnut and coconut) character, creamy and beeswax notes. *Palate* – Medium-bodied, rich and gently chewy with quite a soft peat character. *Finish* – Long, elegant and quite subtle with a little coconut and fruit. *Notes* – Blackadder Raw Cask bottling from cask no. 4840 distilled 16 November 1970.

1967, 44.7% *abv*

Sweetness – 4	*Peatiness* – 5	*Price* – ✱✱✱

Colour – Deep amber with blood-red highlights. *Nose* – Quite delicate, but rounded, warm and nutty with a slight hint of burnt mahogany and notes of toast, honey, beeswax and toffee. *Palate* – Soft, round, smooth and rich with very delicate chewy tannins and creamy toffee. *Finish* – Long, ethereal and complex, showing beeswax, honey and citrus on the tail. *Notes* – Signatory bottling.

Bunnahabhain

NEAR PORT ASKAIG, ISLAY, ARGYLL   [I] [V]   EST. 1880
Website: *www.bunnahabhain.com*

Became part of Highland Distilleries Ltd in 1887 when it was amalgamated with William Grant & Co. of Glenrothes. Extended from 2 to 4 stills in 1963. The distillery was bought by Burn Stewart Distillers in 2003.

Location – Situated towards the north-east tip of Islay on the bay from which it takes its name.

Notes – Bunnhabhain means "mouth of the river". Prior to the building of the distillery, which is the island's most northerly, the surrounding area was inhospitable and uninhabited. Now a small hamlet has built up around the distillery.

Water – Margadale Springs.

12 yrs, 40% abv

Sweetness – 3	Peatiness – 6	Price – *

Colour – Straw with golden highlights. *Nose* – Distinctive, flowery with a soft Sherry nuttiness and quite light sea-peat character. *Palate* – Smooth, soft and malty, a delicate pungency and easy-drinking. *Finish* – Long, smooth, round, long, malty/toffee/Sherry with soft vanilla. *Notes* – D.o.b.

1979, 17 yrs, 58.4% abv

Sweetness – 3	Peatiness – 5	Price – ✳✳

Colour – Full amber with old-gold highlights. *Nose* – Full, ripe and nutty with a fine, delicate peatiness, medium-dry with a slight hint of liquorice and trout fishing basket. *Palate* – Smooth, medium-dry and nutty with good body and a very gentle peatiness. *Finish* – Nuttily soft, lingeringly complex and round. *Notes* – Signatory bottling from butt no. 5110 distilled 18 April 1979

18 yrs, 43% abv

Sweetness – 3	Peatiness – 6	Price – ✳✳

Colour – Pale amber with old-gold highlights. *Nose* – A slight medicinal note with apples and some acetone; water emphasises the fruit and richness and brings out a buttery vanilla character. *Palate* – Off-dry, Sherry notes – brazil nuts, smooth, warm and a sensation of the sea, at the end there is smoked ham. *Finish* – Long, toasted oak and Sherry notes. *Notes* – D.o.b.

25 yrs, 43% abv

Sweetness – 3	Peatiness – 6	Price – ✳✳✳✳

Colour – Mid-amber with old-gold highlights. *Nose* – Quite full-bodied and round, with a sherried nuttiness; water converts the nuttiness to coconut, vanilla, butterscotch and a background hint of sea-tainted peat. *Palate* – Quite big-bodied, with an unctuous smoothness, digestive biscuits, toffee and a touch of spice. *Finish* – Long with gently chewy, oaky tannins and a belt of dark chocolate and cocoa. *Notes* – D.o.b.

1979, 60.2% abv

Sweetness – 3	Peatiness – 6	Price – ✳✳✳

Colour – Straw with yellow highlights. *Nose* – Quite full-bodied, gently peated, puffed oats, rich sherbet lemon; water opens a vinous note akin to Riesling's racy character, almost diesel. *Palate* – Dry, medium-bodied, gently medicinal with a hint of citrus, medium peat, creamy and malty with an almost hoppy note. *Finish* – Long, hoppy, clean and softly peated – with American Cream Soda on the tail. *Notes* – Blackadder bottling.

Bushmills

COUNTY ANTRIM, NORTHERN IRELAND   [IR] [V]   EST. 1608
Website: *www.bushmills.com*

Bushmills was granted a licence to distil in 1608, making it by far the earliest legal distillery of all. Operated by Irish Distillers which, in 1988, was the target of a hard-fought takeover battle between British giant Grand Metropolitan and French rival Pernod-Ricard. Pernod-Ricard won.

Location – Near the Giant's Causeway on the north coast of Ulster.

Notes – Bushmills is triple-distilled, although it is not alone in this regard. Forms of triple distillation are/were also practised at Auchentoshan, Rosebank and Benrinnes, not forgetting Hazelburn. Bushmills is available in duty-free markets at 43% abv. Irish whiskey is mostly unpeated, unlike most Scotch whisky. Pernod-Ricard own two distilleries: Bushmills and the Midleton complex near Cork. Between them, they have a considerable number of still shapes. Irish blends such as Jameson, Original Bushmills, Black Bush, Power's, Paddy and Tullamore Dew, all very different, are produced from whiskeys distilled at these two distilleries. In 1885/86, when Alfred Barnard visited Ireland, there were 21 distilleries in the republic and a further 7 in the north.

Water – Saint Columb's Rill.

Sweetness – 7	Peatiness – 0	Price – *

Colour – Amber with yellow-gold highlights. *Nose* – Fresh, clean, and grassy with a bubblegummy sweetness (medium-sweet) and a slight nettley character. *Palate* – Medium-sweet with quite good body and round with a nice vanilla wood note. *Finish* – Clean, long and fresh. *Notes* – D.o.b.

16 *yrs*, 40% *abv*

Sweetness – 5	Peatiness – 0	Price – **

Colour – Mid-amber with old-gold highlights and an edge of ruby. *Nose* – Full-bodied, fresh and slightly green with a gooseberry character, it has a rich, woody nuttiness and is medium-sweet with a nutty toffee character. *Palate* – Almost dry with good body, smooth, dark and nutty; round with a slight gooseberry ripeness and a touch of toffee. *Finish* – Long, with a good, nutty richness, a dark complexity and an almost mahogany-flavoured chewiness. *Notes* – D.o.b. Aged in a mixture of Bourbon barrels and Sherry butts, then finished off for six months in Port pipes.

DISTILLERY RESERVE, 12 *yrs*, 40% *abv*

Sweetness – 6	Peatiness – 0	Price – *

Colour – Mid-amber with old-gold highlights. *Nose* – Clean, rich and creamy with notes of toffee, almonds, rich vanilla, marzipan and a fresh, grapey fruitiness. *Palate* – Medium-sweet, rich, quite full-bodied, tangy, smooth, quite elegant and thoughtful. *Finish* – Long, round and rich with lingering sweet vanilla. *Notes* – D.o.b. Only available from the distillery.

Caol Ila

PORT ASKAIG, ISLAY, ARGYLL   [I] [V]   EST. 1846
Website: *www.malts.com/en-gb/Malts/summary/CaolIla*

Built by Hector Henderson on what, when you are standing at the distillery, seems a very isolated spot. The distillery was taken over in 1863 by Bulloch, Lade & Co., who extended and rebuilt it in 1879. It came under DCL's control in 1927 and management has been by SMD and UMGD from 1930. It was completely rebuilt, apart from the warehouses, between April 1972 and January 1974, when it was extended from two stills to six. Now a part of Diageo plc.

Location – Another distillery which is literally at the end of the road, in this case, the northern end of the A846.

Notes – Caol Ila's stillhouse has arguably the finest view in the Scotch whisky industry. It overlooks Caol Ila (the Gaelic name for the Sound of Islay) to the Paps of Jura. Hot water from the condensers is pumped through a sea water condenser, cooled and returned for use in the still-house condensers. Diageo seem to be putting more emphasis on Caol Ila and have bottled a number of expressions recently. Long overdue.

Water – Loch Nam Ban (Torrabolls Loch).

CAOL ILA™

AGED **12** YEARS

ISLAY SINGLE MALT WHISKY

Out of sight, in a remote cove near Port Askaig lies Caol Ila, hidden gem among Islay's distilleries since 1846. Not easy to find, Caol Ila's secret malt is nonetheless highly prized among *devotees* of the Islay style.

43% vol   *Caol Ila Distillery, Port Askaig, Isle of Islay.*   70 cl ℮

Caol Ila lies close to *Loch nam Ban*, source of its pure mash water. The sea provides water for cooling and once brought steamers to collect a whisky appreciated for its *balanced, fresh style* – lighter-bodied than many Islay malts, yet with all their typical peatiness.

---

12 yrs, 43% abv

Sweetness – 2	Peatiness – 9	Price – ✳

Colour – Straw with lemon highlights. *Nose* – Big-bodied, burnt heather roots and a little floral note; water brings out soft charred vanilla, almost crème brulée and an aroma of docken leaves. *Palate* – Big, powerful, banana-tinged and dry with a dark, charred peat flavour. *Finish* – Long, with notes of cocoa and chocolate, dying embers on the beach and crisp citrus on the very tail. *Notes* – D.o.b.

10 yrs, 43% abv

Sweetness – 2	Peatiness – 10	Price – *

Colour – Straw with yellow highlights. *Nose* – Big-bodied, dry, malty and rich with a powerful, earthy peat character. *Palate* – Full-bodied, quite soft (relatively), rich and gently chewy with a solid peat character. *Finish* – Long, smooth, earthy and rich. *Notes* – Hart Brothers bottling.

1993, 15 yrs, 56.5% abv

Sweetness – 2	Peatiness – 10	Price – **

Colour – Pale amber with pale lemon highlights. *Nose* – Big, dark, dry and peaty with smoky creosote; water brings out a cereal note, burnt heather roots and digestive biscuits. *Palate* – Powerful, rich, quite chewy tannins and big charred peat. *Finish* – Long, charred, the embers of a fire. *Notes* – Clydesdale Original bottling from cask no. 001/6980.

1991, 15 yrs, 58.8% abv

Sweetness – 2	Peatiness – 10	Price – **

Colour – Straw with lemon highlights. *Nose* – Big-bodied, dark charred heather roots with a slight antiseptic note; water brings out the richness and a slight note of melon. *Palate* – Big-bodied, round, smooth, charred and gently chewy with dark chocolate. *Finish* – Long, very rich, cocoa-flavoured and strongly smoky. *Notes* – Bladnoch Forum bottling from hogshead no. 3870 filled 11 March 1991.

18 yrs, 43% abv

Sweetness – 2	Peatiness – 10	Price – **

Colour – Amber with gold highlights. *Nose* – Big and powerful, classic burnt heather roots, but matched by oaky vanilla; water adds a touch of antiseptic and citrus/soft vanilla. *Palate* – Dry, big, rich, smooth and charred with an edge of sweetness and a hint of fruit. *Finish* – Tar and chocolate, dry smoke and melon. *Notes* – D.o.b.

Sweetness – 2	Peatiness – 10	Price – **

Colour – Amber with pale gold highlights. *Nose* – Big, smoky and burnt heather roots; water gives more of the same, but softer and rounder. *Palate* – Powerful, sea-influenced, and heathery peat flavoured with a floral touch and just an edge of sweetness. *Finish* – Very long, impressive with notes of tarry ropes, creosote and cocoa/chocolate. *Notes* – Douglas Laing Old Malt Cask bottling.

PROVENANCE, 1995, 10 *yrs*, 58% *abv*

Sweetness – 1	Peatiness – 9	Price – **

Colour – Mid-amber with old-gold highlights. *Nose* – Big and quite rich with notes of burnt heather roots and spent fireworks; water gives breakfast cereal, liquorice and cocoa characters. *Palate* – Big, powerful and smooth with the flavour of a smoky fire on the beach at Camusdarrach. *Finish* – Long, smoky and definitely salty with a suggestion of chocolate. *Notes* – Douglas McGibbon Spring Distillation bottling from 6 hogsheads.

1991, 46% *abv*

Sweetness – 3	Peatiness – 10	Price – **

Colour – Straw with pale yellow highlights. *Nose* – Big and smoky with burnt heather roots and a slight earthy note; water brings out a hint of Demerara sugar and crème brulée and Oddfellow sweets. *Palate* – Big and powerful with a sweet rim, very earthily smoky with a fresh green note to the peat. *Finish* – Very long, rich and unusually sweet with notes of burnt crème caramel and butterscotch on the tail. *Notes* – John Milroy Selection bottling.

1989, 46% *abv*

Sweetness – 2	Peatiness – 9	Price – ***

Colour – Straw with yellow/lemon highlights. *Nose* – Full and big-bodied, fresh and heavily earth-peated with a green edge and a hint of menthol. *Palate* – Big-bodied, pungent, intense and powerful with an earthy peatiness and a slight sea character. *Finish* – Long, intensely smoky, rich with an edge of sweetness and a touch of salt. *Notes* – Murray McDavid bottling.

Caperdonich

ROTHES, MORAY   [S]   EST. 1897

Following the industry slump at the end of the 19th century, Caperdonich was closed in 1902 and did not produce again until 1965 following rebuilding. Extended from two to four stills in 1967 under Seagram's ownership. Sold to Pernod-Ricard in 2001 and now operated by Chivas Brothers.

Location – Situated at the north end of the small town of Rothes, across the road from its sister distillery, Glen Grant.

Notes – The distillery was built to supplement the output of Glen Grant and was long known as Glen Grant no. 2. The whisky, using the same water, is lighter and fruitier than Glen Grant. The two distilleries were originally joined by a pipe which carried spirit from Caperdonich to Glen Grant across the town's main street. Rothes supports five distilleries, with Caperdonich the last to be built. Glen Grant, established in 1840, was the first.

Water – The Caperdonich Well, adjacent to the Glen Grant burn.

1968, 54.7% *abv*

Sweetness – 7	Peatiness – 3	Price – ∗

Colour – Amber with honeyed gold highlights. *Nose* – Warm, medium-bodied and rich with toffee and honey notes; water brings out delicate honey and lemon, tangerines and a little tobacco. *Palate* – Medium-sweet, toffeeyed and gently chewy with soft, delicate peat. *Finish* – Long, rich, medium-sweet and toffeeyed, almost sticky. *Notes* – Duncan Taylor bottling.

Cardhu

KNOCKANDO, MORAY   [S] [V]   EST. 1824
Website: *www.malts.com/en-gb/Malts/summary/Cardhu*

Built on Cardow farm, the distillery also being known by that name until fairly recently. The original licensee was John Cumming, who had previously gained a string of convictions as a whisky smuggler. Acquired by John Walker & Son in 1893, it became part of DCL in 1925 and was managed by SMD/UGMD from 1930. Rebuilt in 1960 and extended from 4 to 6 stills. Now part of Diageo plc.

Location – Situated high up above the River Spey on its north bank, on the B9012 between Knockando and Craigellachie.

Notes – A "flagship" of UDV, the malt has long played an important role in the success of Johnnie Walker's Red and Black Label brands. Cardhu has been responsible for a redefinition of the terms relating to Scotch whisky (see File Notes p11). In 2003, Diageo introduced Cardhu as a blended malt, making the argument that world demand for the brand meant that the distillery could not produce sufficient spirit. There was public outcry, Diageo backed down under a hail of criticism from within the industry and a committee was established to enshrine the various categories in statute.

Water – Springs on the Mannoch Hill or the Lyne burn.

12 yrs, 40% abv

Sweetness 8	Peatiness – 7	Price – *

Colour – Pale mid-amber with a definite green tinge. *Nose* – Quite full-bodied, rich, medium-sweet and smoky with a green-apple character. *Palate* – Round and mellow, sweet with a delicate peatiness. *Finish* – Long, peaty and sweet. *Notes* – D.o.b.

Clynelish

BRORA, SUTHERLAND   [H] [V]   EST. 1967
Website: *www.malts.com/en-gb/Malts/summary/Clynelish*

The original Clynelish distillery was the old, now closed, Brora distillery next door. It was founded by the Marquess of Stafford, later the first Duke of Sutherland. It was intended as a ready market for barley produced by crofters who had been evicted from inland farms to make way for sheep and moved down onto the coastal plain. Established as a brewery in 1817, it was turned into a distillery two years later. Operated by UMGD and now part of Diageo plc. Six stills.

Location – Just off the A9 north of Brora on the north side of the extensive plain which forms the mouth of Strathbrora.

Notes – Brora was known as Clynelish until 1969. After the modern distillery had been built in 1967–68, the old Clynelish opened in April 1975, housed in the rebuilt mash-house. It subsequently ceased distillation in May 1983. There is no little confusion as Brora is often called "Clynelish". The whisky from the old distillery was only bottled as Clynelish prior to 1967. Between 1967 and 1983, production from the old distillery was stencilled as "Brora" on casks.

Water – The Clynemilton Burn.

14 yrs, 43% abv

Sweetness – 4	Peatiness – 6	Price – *

Colour – Mid-amber with pale old-gold highlights. *Nose* – Quite big-bodied, medium-dry, a citrus fruitiness and floral note with Demerara sugar, soft sweet oak; water brings out the richness, a soft maltiness, orange and chocolate/cocoa notes. *Palate* – Medium-dry with a soft sweetness, quite solid, dark oaty peat note, creamy vanilla and a hint of ripe hazelnuts – very complex. *Finish* – Long and elegant with a touch of bitter whole-nut chocolate and seaweed at the back. *Notes* – D.o.b.

1992, 46% abv

Sweetness – 4	Peatiness – 6	Price – **

Colour – Straw with yellow highlights. *Nose* – Quite light and fresh with a green vegetal note, some apples and a hint of Demerara sugar; water pulls out boiled garden peas, mint, a slight floral touch and some cherries. *Palate* – Big-bodied, medium dry and rich with a good dark peat note and some cocoa. *Finish* – Long, impressive and quite chunky, but with good richness. *Notes* – John Milroy Selection bottling from cask no. 7167.

1983, 50% abv

Sweetness – 4	Peatiness – 6	Price – ***

Colour – Pale amber with pale gold highlights. *Nose* – Medium-bodied and rich with citrus/orange notes, quite soft peat in the background and a hint of chocolate; water softens it and brings out breakfast cereal, apple and honey. *Palate* – Medium-dry, of good body with toffee, coffee and chocolate and quite a solid peat note. *Finish* – Long, flavoursome and rich with notes of toffee, tobacco and honey on the tail. *Notes* – Douglas Laing Old Malt Cask bottling from hogshead no. 1354 distilled April 1983.

1983, 43% *abv*

Sweetness – 4	Peatiness – 7	Price – ✻✻

Colour – Pale straw with pale lemon highlights. *Nose* – Slightly closed, rich, medium-dry with a hint of mint, good creamy peat integration and notes of Demerara sugar and toffee. *Palate* – Medium-dry, rich, round, smooth and quite creamy with a good dollop of peat and quite solid body. *Finish* – Long, intense, rich, fresh and quite delicately, almost earthily smoky on the tail. *Notes* – The Vintage Malt Whisky Co. Ltd bottling.

1976, 59% *abv*

Sweetness – 3	Peatiness – 6	Price – ✻✻✻

Colour – Deep amber with bronze highlights. *Nose* – Slightly closed, a dark nuttiness with beeswax and honey; water brings out oak flavours, sweet, concentrated dark fruit purée with quite solid peat at the back. *Palate* – Big-bodied, nutty – brazil nuts – chewy tannins, medium-dry and quite delicately peated. *Finish* – Long, chewy, darkly smoky and perfumed, almonds come in at the end. *Notes* – Blackadder Raw Cask bottling from cask no. 6501 filled 5 August 1976.

1965, 28 yrs, 50.7% *abv*

Sweetness – 3	Peatiness – 6	Price – ✻✻✻

Colour – Mid-amber with yellow/gold highlights. *Nose* – Quite full-bodied, fresh, round and medium-sweet with an unctuous sweet-oak character. *Palate* – Dry, but with a nice edge of sweetness, rich, round, good, dry, oaky tannins, nutty and softly unctuous. *Finish* – Long, elegant and gently smoky with just a touch of sweetness at the front. *Notes* – Signatory bottling.

Coleburn

LONGMORN, ELGIN, MORAY [S] EST. 1897

Built by John Robertson & Sons. Became part of DCL in 1925 and managed by SMD/UGMD from 1930. Two stills.

Location – Situated to the east of the A491, four miles south of Elgin. It is "faced on the one side by a plantation of Scotch firs and birches and swept by the cool mountain breezes of Brown Muir" according to Robertson's original announcement in 1896.

Notes – The distillery was built from warm-coloured Moray sandstone and roofed with blue Welsh slates. A problem which faced Charles Doig, the architect, was the provision of a lavatory to the excise office – it took 18 months to resolve! The excise officer's house took even longer to be completed. Closed in 1985 and unlikely to reopen. The maltings, disused from 1968, had two kilns, one with a normal pagoda roof and the other with a flat roof. This second kiln was used for drying barley at a controlled temperature; the process was slow, but gave good results.

Water – A spring in the Glen of Rothes.

1979, 59.4% *abv*

Sweetness – 5	*Peatiness* – 6	*Price* – ♥♥♥

Colour – Mid-amber with old-gold highlights. *Nose* – Medium-bodied with quite solid peat, a flowery touch; water brings out an almond character, apple and citrus. *Palate* – Malty and medium-sweet, chewy, oaky tannins, drying out. *Finish* – Smooth, quite creamy, then chewy tannins. *Notes* – D.o.b. Rare Malts.

Convalmore

DUFFTOWN, BANFFSHIRE [S] EST. 1894

Founded 2 June 1893 by the Convalmore-Glenlivet Distillery Co. Ltd. Purchased from the liquidator in March 1905 for £6000 plus stock at 2s 6d (12.5p) per gallon by W. P. Lowrie & Co. Ltd which was controlled by James Buchanan & Co. Ltd from 1906. Fire broke out on 29 October 1909 and the malt barn, mash-house and tun-room were destroyed. After the distillery was rebuilt, it was used for experimentation into the continuous distillation of malt. W. P. Lowrie joined DCL in 1925 and production was carried out by SMD/UMGD from 1930. Doubled from two to four stills in 1964, it was closed in 1985 and the site was sold to Wm. Grant & Sons in 1990.

Location – Just north of Dufftown on the A941.

Notes – The distillery accommodated a signals detachment of the 51st (Highland) Division from 1940 to 1942 and then gunners of the 52nd (Lowland) Division until 1944.

Water – Springs in the Conval Hills.

1977, 28 yrs, 57.9% abv

Sweetness – 7	Peatiness – 5	Price – ✱✱✱

Colour – Amber with gold highlights. *Nose* – Rich, sweet and clean, citrus and medium-bodied; water lifts lemon and American Cream Soda and a floral note. *Palate* – Smooth, medium-sweet, fennel, juicy apples and quite good body. *Finish* – Spicy with a little liquorice, some mint and some light peat. *Notes* – UD bottling in the Rare Malts range.

Cooley

RIVERSTOWN, DUNDALK, CO. LOUTH   [IR]   EST. 1987
Website: *www.cooleywhiskey.com*

The Cooley Distillery plc was established in 1987 when the company took over the site of the former state-owned potato alcohol plant in the Cooley peninsula on Ireland's east coast. Coffey and pot stills were installed and the first spirit was distilled in 1989.

Location – At Riverstown, Dundalk, not far from the border of the Irish Republic and Northern Ireland.

Notes – The Cooley distillery produces two different styles of Irish malt whiskey; a traditional unpeated malt and the peated malt which the company markets under its Connemara brand.

Water – A spring on Slieve Na gCloc in the Cooley Mountains.

CONNEMARA, No age statement, 40% *abv*

Sweetness – 5	Peatiness – 6	Price – ✳

Colour – Mid-amber with old-gold highlights. *Nose* – Quite full-bodied, fresh and medium-dry with a round fruitiness and a good measure of slightly green peatiness. *Palate* – Medium-sweet, with good body, a nice weight of peat and a round, dark nuttiness. *Finish* – Long and clean with a good background smokiness. *Notes* – Peated Irish single malt from Cooley.

THE TYRCONNELL, No age statement, 40% *abv*

Sweetness – 7	Peatiness – 0	Price – ✳

Colour – Straw with yellow highlights. *Nose* – Fresh and clean with a touch of liquorice, a good, ripe richness, medium-sweet and quite round with a slight unctuous character. *Palate* – Medium-sweet, fresh, round and smooth with quite good body. *Finish* – Long and clean with honey and an almost barley-sugar sweetness and a slight citrus note. *Notes* – Unpeated Irish single malt from Cooley.

LOCKE'S, 8 yrs, 40% *abv*

Sweetness – 6	Peatiness – 0	Price – ✳

Colour – Straw with yellow highlights. *Nose* – Quite full-bodied, fresh and clean with a slight menthol character and a rich maltiness; water brings out a malty leather character, rich apples and peaches and a soft green touch. *Palate* – Round, appley, soft, rich and medium-sweet with notes of Macintosh Red apples. *Finish* – Long, clean, soft and quite gentle with lingering apple skins. *Notes* – Single malt from Cooley.

COOLEY PEATED, 1992, 60% *abv*

Sweetness – 4	Peatiness – 8	Price – ✳✳

Colour – Straw with pale yellow highlights. *Nose* – Big-bodied with a medicinal peat character; water brings out a slight richness, the damp embers of tree prunings and juniper, very clean and refreshing. *Palate* – Dry, quite rich, gently chewy with flavours of wet wood, round and slightly spicy. *Finish* – Long and flavoursome with a touch of spice. *Notes* – Peated sample from Cooley.

Ireland – land of magic and mystery

Cragganmore

BALLINDALLOCH, BANFFSHIRE [S] [V]* EST. 1869
Website: www.malts.com/en-gb/Malts/summary/Cragganmore

Built by John Smith, the lessee of Glenfarclas from 1865 to 1869, manager of Macallan in the early 1850s, Glenlivet from 1858 and Clydesdale in the early 1860s. The distillery never closed for even a fortnight in any year up until the summer of 1901, when reconstruction began. Extended from two to four stills in 1964. Now part of Diageo plc.

Location – Cragganmore occupies a site north of the A95 between Grantown-on-Spey and Ballindalloch, close to the River Spey. It was the first Speyside distillery to be sited to take advantage of railway transport, the former railway line (now the Speyside Way footpath) passing its doors.

Notes – Originally available only at the distillery or through independent bottlers, the make is now widely available as one of UDV's Classic Malts portfolio. An interesting feature is that the spirit stills have flat-topped, T-shaped lyne pipes instead of the usual swan necks. The stills have cooling worms rather than condensers.

Water – The Craggan Burn, a spring on the Craggan More hill.

DISTILLER'S EDITION, 1984, 40% *abv*

Sweetness – 6	Peatiness – 7	Price – **

Colour – Mid-amber with old-gold highlights. *Nose* – Full, medium-sweet and honeyed and nutty with a quite solid peatiness, quite dark, rich, oaky vanilla and notes of Demerara sugar and mandarin oranges. *Palate* – Medium-dry, quite big-bodied, rich and creamy with a nutty oakiness and a quite solid peat note. *Finish* – Long, quite fruity and spicy with a dark peaty note. *Notes* – D.o.b. Fnished in a Port pipe.

12 yrs, 40% abv

Sweetness – 6	Peatiness – 7	Price – ❋

Colour – Amber with pale gold highlights. *Nose* – Clean with quite good body, medium-dry, smokily peaty, slightly creamy with a light green touch. *Palate* – Quite full-bodied, round with a touch of spice, smoky and creamy. *Finish* – Quite long, clean and fresh. *Notes* – D.o.b.

17 yrs, 56% abv

Sweetness – 6	Peatiness – 7	Price – ❋❋

Colour – Amber with gold highlights. *Nose* – Big, solid, marzipan, apple and crème brulée; water brings out a green, herbal note with sweet oaky vanilla and the peat has a touch of cinnamon and cloves. *Palate* – Quite big-bodied, chunky and creamily smooth with a spicy apple character, maybe baked toffee apples. *Finish* – Long, quite darkly peaty with a fruity note and gently chewy with coconut and cocoa evident. *Notes* – D.o.b.

1978, 40% abv

Sweetness – 7	Peatiness – 7	Price – ❋❋

Colour – Amber with good yellow highlights. *Nose* – Quite full-bodied and medium-sweet with a quite chunky peatiness, a touch of citrus and an almost jammy note. *Palate* – Rich and medium-sweet with quite solid peat and of good weight. *Finish* – Long and sweet with a note of cocoa to the peat. *Notes* – Gordon & MacPhail bottling.

Craigellachie

CRAIGELLACHIE, BANFFSHIRE [S] EST. 1891

Built by the Craigellachie Distillery Co. Ltd, a partnership formed by a group of blenders and whisky merchants. Rebuilt in 1964–5 and doubled to four stills. Sold to Bacardi during 1998.

Location – The distillery stands on the spur of a hill overlooking the village of the same name, the precipitous Rock of Craigellachie, the River Spey and James Telford's elegant single-span bridge of 1815.

Notes – Sir Peter Mackie, founder of White Horse blended whisky, was one of its original owners. The workers in 1923 lived in tied cottages and tended their gardens as lovingly as they tended the spirit. The owners of the best-kept gardens received prizes annually from the White Horse board.

Water – A spring on Conval Hill.

14 yrs, 40% abv

Sweetness – 8	Peatiness – 4	Price – *

Colour – Straw with lemon/gold highlights. *Nose* – Fresh and cerealy with good body and a touch of greenness, a waxy, candle aroma; water brings out sherbet, lemon and gooseberries. *Palate* – Fresh, round, smooth and sweet with a dark chocolate note, some sooty peat and cereal reprising. *Finish* – Long and sweet with a hint of cinnamon spice and the smoke underpinning the tail. *Notes* – D.o.b.

15 yrs, 46% abv

Sweetness – 7	Peatiness – 6	Price – *

Colour – Very pale, almost crystal clear, watery coloured. *Nose* – Pungent, peaty, burnt heather with a slight orange/citrus tang to the edge. *Palate* – Heavy, pungent, peaty, but with an edge of sweetness. *Finish* – Good, spicy and long – reminiscent of Islay. *Notes* – Wm Cadenhead bottling.

Dailuaine

CARRON, BY ABERLOUR, BANFFSHIRE [S] EST. 1852

Founded by William Mackenzie, a farmer at Carron and Rinnachat, the business was amalgamated with Talisker on Skye and nearby Imperial to form Dailuaine-Talisker Distilleries Ltd. Became part of DCL in 1925 and run by SMD/UMGD from 1930. Rebuilt after a fire in 1917 and again in 1959–60, when it was increased from four stills to six. Now part of Diageo. The old floor maltings were converted to a Saladin box system, the use of which was discontinued in 1983.

Location – Situated in a natural hollow by the Carron Burn with river meadows all around it on an unclassified road between the A95 and B9102 at Archiestown. It is to the south of the River Spey.

Notes – The name 'Dailuaine' comes from the Gaelic 'dail uaine', meaning 'green valley', an apt description of its location. Although electricity reached the Carron area in 1938, it was not introduced to Dailuaine until 1950. For some years from the late 1880s, the distillery operated a rail link to the Spey Valley line at Carron Station, a few hundred yards away. The steam locomotive which once worked the line is preserved on the Strathspey Railway, which runs from Aviemore to Boat of Garten. The Spey Valley line itself fell to the Beeching axe in 1967, but much of it is given over to walkers as The Speyside Way. Like its near neighbour, Dailuaine is one of the principal malts used in the Johnnie Walker blends.

Water – The Bailliemullich Burn.

SPEYSIDE
SINGLE MALT *SCOTCH WHISKY*

DAILUAINE

is the GAELIC for "the green vale". The *distillery*, established
in 1852, lies in a hollow by the *CARRON BURN* in *BANFFSHIRE*. This
single Malt Scotch Whisky has a *full bodied fruity* nose and a *smoky* finish.
For more than a *hundred years* all *distillery supplies* were despatched by
rail. The *steam locomotive* "DAILUAINE NO.1" was in use
from 1939 ~ 1967 and is *preserved* on the *STRATHSPEY RAILWAY*.

A G E D **16** Y E A R S

43% vol   Distilled & Bottled in SCOTLAND. DAILUAINE DISTILLERY, Carron, Aberlour, Banffshire, Scotland.   70 cl

16 yrs, 43% abv

Sweetness – 5	Peatiness – 7	Price – ✷✷

Colour – Deep, full amber with bronze highlights. *Nose* – Quite full and sherried, a nutty, rubbery and damp oak character, medium-dry, slightly spirity. *Palate* – Full-bodied, nutty, rubbery, medium-dry with a touch of tannin and a hint of richness. *Finish* – Long, dark and quite smooth with a touch of peat. *Notes* – D.o.b.

1996, 46% *abv*

Sweetness – 4	Peatiness – 7	Price – *

Colour – Pale straw with pale lemon highlights. *Nose* – Quite big-bodied with dark peat and mixed spice; water brings out a green, fresh touch with bananas, fennel and limes. *Palate* – Medium-dry, smooth and creamy with buttery vanilla, an edge of richness, a touch of spice with quite solid peat. *Finish* – Long, quite ethereal and spicy with rich liquorice and smoky. *Notes* – John Milroy Selection bottling.

1986, 20 *yrs*, 53.3% *abv*

Sweetness – 6	Peatiness – 6	Price – **

Colour – Straw with yellow highlights. *Nose* – Big, rich with aromas of toffee, coffee and chocolate; water brings out honey and a touch of apple. *Palate* – Medium-sweet, rich and gently chewy with good body and quite a solid peat note. *Finish* – Very long and honeyed with apple and mixed spice notes. *Notes* – Clydesdale Original bottling from cask ref. 0220/4566 filled in December 1986.

1985, 46% *abv*

Sweetness – 5	Peatiness – 6	Price – **

Colour – Amber with gold highlights. *Nose* – Fresh and malty with a fresh, slightly green peat note , a bit of liquorice and some candle wax; water brings out Christmas cake icing, marzipan, tobacco and honey. *Palate* – Medium-sweet, rich and malty with good body and smooth with layers of peat in the background. *Finish* – Long and quite peaty with a touch of spice, finishing almost dry. *Notes* – Berry's Own Selection bottling from cask no. 1064.

1975, 40% *abv*

Sweetness – 5	Peatiness – 6	Price – ***

Colour – Amber with pale gold highlights. *Nose* – Quite soft, medium-bodied and medium-sweet, a citrus note with quite earthy peat; water brings out toffee and lemon with some forest fruits and light chocolate. *Palate* – Delicately peated, rich and medium-sweet, some gently chewy tannins and a little spice. *Finish* – Long and delicately smoky with a floral touch and quite clean. *Notes* – Gordon & MacPhail bottling.

1974, 46% *abv*

Sweetness – 4	Peatiness – 6	Price – ***

Colour – Pale amber with golden brown highlights. *Nose* – Quite light with good richness and honeyed apple; water brings out hints of citrus, vanilla oak and comb honey. *Palate* – Medium-bodied, rich and medium-sweet with gently chewy tannins and a fresh, leafy green note. *Finish* – Long and clean with a note of tea, a touch of spice and a hint of citrus. *Notes* – Berry's Own Selection bottling from cask nos. 111/2.

Dallas Dhu

FORRES, MORAY [S] [V] EST. 1899
Website: *www.historic-scotland.gov.uk/properties_sites_
detail.htm?propertyID=PL_085*

Originally to be called "Dallasmore" in 1898, the plans for the new distillery, designed by local Elgin architect, Charles Doig, caused much correspondence in the local paper, the *Forres Gazette*. This included some verse from a local councillor. The fillings were eventually advertised as Dallas Dhu in November 1899, when it came on stream. Dallas Dhu was built by Glasgow blenders, Wright & Greig Ltd, the proprietors of Roderick Dhu, a whisky brand which was popular in the 19th century. The still house was burned down on 9 April 1939 and it did not reopen until 1947. It closed in 1983 and the licence was cancelled in 1992.

Location – Built in a hollow to the east of an unclassified road which forks south off the A940 on the southern outskirts of Forres.

Notes – The distillery buildings were handed over by SMD to the Historic Buildings and Monuments department of the Scottish Executive which now runs them as a model example of a distillery on the tourist trail. It is still possible to obtain special bottlings from old casks, although supplies of the whisky are dwindling. Dallas Dhu is a perfectly preserved example of what a small Highland distillery would have been like at the turn of the century. Had its water supply been more plentiful, it is most likely that the distillery would have been one of those chosen for expansion in more recent years. As it is, its single pair of old stills has been preserved, as have all the old plant and machinery and the fine old distillery buildings.

Water – The Altyre Burn (known locally as the Scourie Burn).

1978, 18 yrs, 43% abv

Sweetness – 4	Peatiness – 6	Price – **

Colour – Amber with yellow highlights. *Nose* – Quite full-bodied, slightly spirity and medium-dry with a dark, burnt-stick peaty character. *Palate* – Smooth, slightly chewy and medium-dry with good body. *Finish* – Long, smoky and gently chewy. *Notes* – A Cooper's Choice bottling from the Vintage Malt Whisky Co.

1974, 18 yrs, 60.8% abv

Sweetness – 4	Peatiness – 3	Price – **

Colour – Mid-amber with gold highlights. *Nose* – Medium-bodied, nutty and malty, medium-dry with an edge of richness and a touch of lanolin. *Palate* – Medium-dry, gently peaty, oaky tannins and a woody character. *Finish* – Quite dry, almost astringently tannic and spirity. *Notes* – Signatory bottling.

24 yrs, 60.6% abv

Sweetness – 4	Peatiness – 4	Price – ***

Colour – Pale amber with pale gold/lemon highlights. *Nose* – Medium-dry, slightly peppery with oaky vanilla. *Palate* – Oaky, quite full, round and medium-dry. *Finish* – Chewy, spirity and gently oaky. *Notes* – United Distillers bottling.

1978, 59.7% abv

Sweetness – 4	Peatiness – 6	Price – ***

Colour – Amber with pale gold highlights. *Nose* – Mature, slightly musty oak, medium-dry; water brings out ripe apple and peach. *Palate* – Quite big-bodied, round and gently chewy with sweet vanilla oak and a quite solid peat character. *Finish* – Long, medium-sweet, round and very smooth with a little touch of greenness on the end. *Notes* – Signatory bottling.

1974, 40% abv

Sweetness – 6	Peatiness – 4	Price – **

Colour – Straw/amber with yellow/gold highlights. *Nose* – Quite full, gently peated, oaky vanilla and a slight greenness. *Palate* – Round, smooth, medium-sweet with a touch of nuttiness. *Finish* – Almost dry, oaky. *Notes* – Gordon & MacPhail bottling.

Dalmore

ALNESS, ROSS-SHIRE [H] EST. 1839
Website: *www.thedalmore.com*

Alexander Matheson was a partner in the Hong Kong firm Jardine Matheson & Co., traders in everything from tea to opium and, of course, whisky. In 1839, the very year of the first Opium Wars between China and Britain, Matheson purchased Ardross Farm on the shore of the Cromarty Firth and opened a distillery. Whisky production at Dalmore was taken over by the Mackenzie family, who were to buy the distillery and land as a result of the 1886 Crofters Act. Much of the whisky went to supply long-standing customers and friends, James Whyte and Charles Mackay, who owned the popular blend of Whyte & Mackay. The two businesses eventually merged in 1960. After a few years of ownership by JBB (Greater Europe) plc, Whyte & Mackay was the subject of a management buy-out in October 2001. In May 2007, as I wrote this, the company was finally bought by Bangalore-based Vijay Mallya's United Breweries Group.

Location – Situated just off the A9, the distillery is in a beautiful position overlooking the Cromarty Firth to the Black Isle and the Cairngorms beyond.

Notes – The distillery was well sited by its founders in the middle of a fine barley-growing district. Its handsome offices are panelled with carved oak taken from a nearby shooting lodge. During the First World War it was used by the US Navy as a base for manufacturing deep-sea mines and was burned down as a result of a fire. Production resumed again in 1922. Doubled from four to eight stills in 1966. The top half of each spirit still is surrounded by a tulip-shaped copper cooling jacket which contains a series of tubes through which cold water flows. This serves as a condenser and allows only the finest alcohols to evaporate through the lyne arm. The top half of one of these stills dates from 1874.

Water – The River Alness, which flows from Loch Morie.

12 yrs, 40% abv

Sweetness – 6	Peatiness – 6	Price – ✳

Colour – Full, deep amber with good gold highlights. *Nose* – Fresh, clean, slightly sweet and delicately oaked with a grapey/mandarin orange fruitiness and a floral note. *Palate* – Very good body, with a solid masculine note, a touch of sweetness and an elegantly-knit peat character. *Finish* – Smooth, almost dry, lightly malty and very distinguished. *Notes* – D.o.b.

CIGAR MALT, 43% abv

Sweetness – 6	Peatiness – 5	Price – ✳✳

Colour – Deep amber with bronze highlights. *Nose* – Big-bodied, intense, enormously rich with notes of chocolate and orange; water releases dried fruits, cocoa, toffee and blackcurrants and plums with an almost understated oak note. *Palate* – Huge! Wonderful! Rich, fat, tangerines and lemons, marmalade and delicate chocolate peat, mouth-wateringly juicy! *Finish* – Very long, concentrated and complex, toasty oak, very rich chocolate/cocoa and malt. *Notes* – D.o.b.

21 yrs, 43% abv

Sweetness – 6	Peatiness – 5	Price – ✳✳✳

Colour – Mid-amber with gold highlights. *Nose* – Fresh, soft oak character, medium-dry, quite full-bodied and yet delicate with a slight citrus note. *Palate* – Full-bodied, medium-sweet and rich with a slight oaky unctuousness, a floral note and zesty tangerines. *Finish* – Long, elegant, a hint of chocolate and citrus with a final smokiness. *Notes* – D.o.b. Bourbon-cask aged.

STILLMAN'S DRAM, 30 yrs, 45% abv

Sweetness – 6	Peatiness – 5	Price – ✳✳✳

Colour – Quite full amber with old-gold highlights. *Nose* – Big-bodied, elegant, rich, dark and medium-dry with a slight malic note. *Palate* – Medium-dry, with an oaky-oily untuousness, quite big-bodied and silkily smooth. *Finish* – Very long, elegant and rich with complex notes of chocolate and Cooper's Olde English marmalade. *Notes* – D.o.b.

CABERNET SAUVIGNON FINISH, 1973, 45% *abv*

Sweetness – 5	Peatiness – 4	Price – ✱✱✱

Colour – Deep amber with ruby highlights. *Nose* – Big and intense with notes of cassis, cedar, tobacco and creamy toffee; water brings out a slight medicinal note, mint and nutty (almond) marzipan. *Palate* – Big-bodied, with a tobacco and a fresh green note, gently chewy tannins, medium-dry with a touch of spice and crème caramel. *Finish* – Long, powerful, complex and muscular, finishing with rich notes of caramel and chocolate. *Notes* – D.o.b. Finished in Chateau Haut-Marbuzet casks.

40 *yrs*, 40% *abv*

Sweetness – 6	Peatiness – 5	Price – ✱✱✱✱✱

Colour – Deep amber with bronze and pale ruby highlights. *Nose* – Big and dark, showing muscovado sugar, tar and honey; water brings out a medicinal note, richness, delicate peat and thick Olde English marmalade and tangerines. *Palate* – Big, round and velvety smooth with some tingling spice, rich, medium-sweet, very gently chewy and a toffee note. *Finish* – Long, elegant and ethereal with a soft peat note. *Notes* – D.o.b.

1939, 52 *yrs*, 51.5% *abv*

Sweetness – 6	Peatiness – 3	Price – ✱✱✱✱✱

Colour – Full, rich amber. *Nose* – Enormous! Soft, gentle and smooth with a dark nuttiness, a slight delicate smokiness, very complex and with a liquorice character at the back. *Palate* – Very full, still quite a fresh green flavour, reminiscent of hedgerows. *Finish* – Long, powerful and very distinguished. *Notes* – A cask sample by Whyte & Mackay for a tasting at Christie's in Glasgow.

Dalwhinnie

DALWHINNIE, INVERNESS-SHIRE [H] [V] EST. 1897
Website: *www.malts.com/en-gb/Malts/summary/Dalwhinnie*

Originally called Strathspey distillery, the company went into voluntary liquidation the year after it opened. Its name was changed circa 1900 when it was purchased from the liquidator by the Dalwhinnie Distillery Co. The distillery was then sold at auction for £1,250 in 1905 to Cook & Bernheimer of New York and Baltimore who, in turn, sold it to Macdonald Greenlees of Edinburgh in 1919. Macdonald Greenlees joined DCL in 1926 and SMD/UMGD took over its management in 1930. Badly damaged by fire in 1934, it reopened in 1938. The distillery is now owned by Diageo plc. Two stills.

Location – The distillery is sited next to the main railway line at the junction of the A9 (Inverness to the north, Perth to the south) and the A899 (Road to the Isles) to Fort William.

Notes – "Dalwhinnie" derives from the Gaelic word meaning "meeting place". At 326 metres above sea level, Dalwhinnie is Scotland's second highest and the highest in production as I write in the spring of 2007. The distillery was located to take advantage of plentiful supplies of local peat, the railway line and the abundant supply of pure Highland water. The distillery is Station 0582 of the Meteorological Office and it is the manager's duty to take daily readings of maximum and minimum temperatures, the number of hours of sunshine, wind speed, rainfall and snow depth. In 1937, snowdrifts were over 6 metres deep and people had to scramble out of their houses through first floor windows.

Water – Lochan an Doire-Uaine.

Sweetness – 7	Peatiness – 5	Price – ∗

Colour – Straw with honeyed golden highlights. *Nose* – Quite aromatic, delicately peated and medium-sweet; water brings out the peat with a heathery touch and honey and toffee. *Palate* – Round and sweet, with honey and citrus, rich vanilla and malt. *Finish* – Long, of excellent length, sweet richness and smoke and peat. *Notes* – D.o.b.

DISTILLER'S EDITION, 1990, 15 yrs, 43% abv

Sweetness – 6	Peatiness – 5	Price – ∗∗

Colour – Amber with old-gold highlights. *Nose* – Quite big-bodied, Sherry-rubber medium-bodied and honeyed; with water, the rubber becomes fainter and the honey more beeswax, liquorice comes through, as does peat. *Palate* – Sweet, quite big-bodied with toffee flavours, honey and lemon, a slight green-edged peat, vanilla oak and a nuttiness. *Finish* – Sweet, long and honeyed with peat and smoky oak dominant on the tail, very complex. *Notes* – D.o.b.

1966, 27 yrs, 45.5% abv

Sweetness – 5	Peatiness – 4	Price – ∗∗

Colour – Pale amber with pale gold highlights. *Nose* – Quite full-bodied, medium-sweet and oaky with an aroma of wet cement, a slight burnt-wood character and a touch of mint. *Palate* – Quite good body, fairly dominant wood, slightly chewy and medium-dry. *Finish* – Of reasonable length, with a burnt-wood tang and a chewy tail. *Notes* – Wm Cadenhead bottling.

Deanston

DOUNE, PERTHSHIRE [H] EST. 1965
Website: *www.burnstewartdistillers.com/deanstondistillery*

Founded by the Deanston Distillery Co. Ltd and sold to Invergordon Distillers in 1972. Silent from 1982 until sold to Burn Stewart Distillers in 1990. Four stills.

Location – Situated on the south bank of the River Teith within two miles of the centre of Doune village.

Notes – Burn Stewart have decided to use only unpeated barley in the production of Deanston, the company believing there to be sufficient peat for their purposes in the waters of the Teith. Part of the buildings originally housed a textile mill. This was established in 1748 and was designed by Richard Arkwright of Spinning Jenny fame. Like the distillery, the mill also required good water supplies. The River Teith, as well as supplying all the process water, drives generators which provide all the distillery's electrical power needs – and also export power to the National Grid. The distillery complex includes cathedral-like historic warehouses, many underground in which are housed 45,000 casks of maturing whisky. The film *Monty Python and the Holy Grail* was shot at nearby Doune Castle.

Water – The River Teith.

DEANSTON

Single Highland Malt
Scotch Whisky

A fine mellow Single Highland MALT, with a fragrant fruity flavour and a lingering pleasant aftertaste

40% vol   DEANSTON DISTILLERY DOUNE PERTHSHIRE   **1 Litre**

78039

Sweetness – 6	Peatiness – 3	Price – ＊

Colour – Pale amber with pale gold highlights. *Nose* – Clean with a cereal note and a delicate floral peat character; water pulls out vanilla, honey, lemon caramel and cappuccino. *Palate* – Medium-sweet, rich, round with a wee touch of spice, some creamy toffee and a smooth underlay of quite softly smoky peat. *Finish* – Long, quite citrus tangy, rich, creamy and with a gentle peat note on the end. *Notes* – D.o.b.

17 yrs, 40% abv

Sweetness – 7	Peatiness – 3	Price – ＊＊

Colour – Amber with yellow highlights. *Nose* – Quite full, fresh and sweet with a slight green edge, medium-peated with quite unctuous creamy oak and notes of banana and coconut. *Palate* – Medium-sweet, quite full-bodied with a nice caress of peat and a toffeeyed richness. *Finish* – Long, sweet, showing citrus and coconut. *Notes* – D.o.b.

21 yrs, 40% abv

Sweetness – 4	Peatiness – 6	Price – ＊＊＊

Colour – Full amber with old-gold highlights. *Nose* – Light and quite delicate, medium-sweet with notes of honey, chocolate and vanilla, toffee and a hint of tobacco. *Palate* – Medium-dry, of good body, slightly chewy, smooth and rich with flavours of cocoa and toffee. *Finish* – Long, elegant and softly chewy with a smoky toffee character. *Notes* – D.o.b.

25 yrs, 40% abv

Sweetness – 4	Peatiness – 6	Price – ＊＊＊

Colour – Quite deep amber with bronze highlights. *Nose* – Soft, round, quite light and delicate, a light hazelnut character and sweet vanilla. *Palate* – Medium-dry, smooth, quite creamy with a firm but delicate peaty note at the back and very gently chewy. *Finish* – Long, creamily smooth with notes of coffee and toffee. *Notes* – D.o.b.

1977, 55.8% abv

Sweetness – 4	Peatiness – 3	Price – ＊＊＊

Colour – Straw/very pale amber with lemon/yellow highlights. *Nose* – Fresh and medium-sweet, round with a slight cereal note, lightly peated. *Palate* – Medium-dry and round with a gentle smokiness and light oaky tannins. *Finish* – Fresh, quite zingy, lightly smoky and with a hint of coffee. *Notes* – Wm Cadenhead bottling.

Dufftown

Converted from a former meal mill in 1896 by the Dufftown-Glenlivet Distillery Co. and acquired in 1897 by P. MacKenzie & Co., also owners of Blair Athol distillery. Purchased by Perth blenders Arthur Bell & Sons in 1933. The two original stills were extended to four in 1974 and six in 1979. Owned by Guinness from 1985 and licensed to UMGD from 1992. Now a part of Diageo plc.

Location – Situated in the Dullan Glen on the outskirts of Dufftown near the 6th-century Mortlach Parish Church.

Notes – From Dufftown, which has always been a source of good whisky. It is said that Rome was built on seven hills, but Dufftown was built on seven stills. Dufftown was the sixth distillery to be established in Dufftown, but the fourth in the 1890s. The original water mill at Dufftown is still in working order. Dufftown plays an important role as one of the principal constituents in the *Bell's* blend

Water – Jock's Well in the Conval Hills.

THE **SINGLETON**
Single Malt Scotch Whisky
ESTD 1896 *of Dufftown*
MATURED FOR **12** TWELVE YEARS

15 *yrs*, 43% *abv*

Sweetness – 8	Peatiness – 3	Price – **

Colour – Pale amber with lemon/gold highlights. *Nose* – Medium-bodied, medium-sweet, quite rich and fruity with a slight floral note. *Palate* – Medium-sweet and fresh, quite rich and delicately peated with a nice sweetness. *Finish* – Clean and gently smoky with the good sweetness lasting. *Notes* – D.o.b.

Edradour

PITLOCHRY, PERTHSHIRE [H] [V] EST. 1825
Website: *www.edradour.co.uk*

Founded on land rented from the Duke of Atholl, Edradour appears little changed by the passing of time. The distillery has gone through several interesting changes of ownership, the most notable being becoming a subsidiary of William Whitely & Co. Whitely's were primarily blenders and their most famous blends were *King's Ransom* (Round the World Whisky) and *House of Lords*. Acquired by Pernod-Ricard in 1982 and they released *Edradour* as a single malt in 1986. Bought in the summer of 2002 by independent bottler, Signatory Vintage Malt Whisky Co. Ltd, who are to move their bottling operation from Edinburgh to Perthshire. Since acquiring the distillery Signatory have broadened the range of Edradour products and also started distilling a heavily peated malt which will be known as *Ballechin*.

Location – Situated on the A924, just outside the village of Moulin, at the foot of a steep hill; a collection of old farmstead-like buildings past which tumbles a fast-flowing burn. An idyllic setting.

Notes – Scotland's smallest distillery whose actual output is only enough spirit to fill 12 casks per week. The last remaining of the once numerous Perthshire farm distilleries, it is run by just three people. The output of single malt is a mere 95,000 litres of alcohol a year; only very small quantities of *Edradour* are now used in blends. Previously also bottled as *Glenforres*. An excellent visitor centre with a well-stocked tasting bar.

Water – A spring on Moulin Moor, some 4 miles above the distillery.

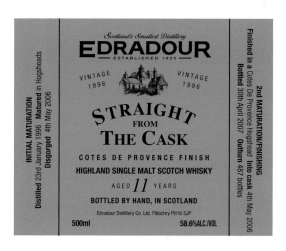

10 *yrs*, 40% *abv*

Sweetness – 8	Peatiness – 2	Price – ✳

Colour – Pale amber with pale gold highlights. *Nose* – Medium-bodied, medium-sweet, fruity and rich with soft perfume and honey; water brings out sweet vanilla, some apple and orange. *Palate* – Medium-sweet, of good body, rich, round, very smooth with notes of honey and rum. *Finish* – Long, clean and quite ethereal with the sweetness lingering long. *Notes* – D.o.b.

CÔTES DE PROVENCE FINISH, No age statement, 58.6% *abv*

Sweetness – 7	Peatiness – 2	Price – ✳✳

Colour – Honeyed mid-tawny with pale gold highlights and a ruby hue. *Nose* – Medium-bodied, with notes of coffee – creamy latte, brioche and custard; with water there is more of general French patisserie and some spent fireworks aromas. *Palate* – Medium-sweet, round and smooth with a charred oak note, some fireworks and chocolate. *Finish* – Very complex, long, clean, medium-dry and gently chewy with notes of cocoa, tobacco and marmalade, the sweetness comes back on the tail. *Notes* – D.o.b. Finished in ex-Château Roubine casks.

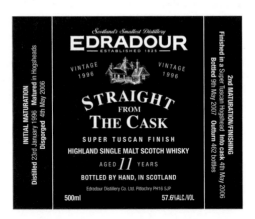

SUPERTUSCAN FINISH, No age statement, 58% *abv*

Sweetness – 8	Peatiness – 2	Price – ✳✳

Colour – Dusky rosé with pale ruby highlights. *Nose* – Medium-bodied, grappa-like with a note of chocolate-dipped cherries; water brings out olives, a slightly unctuous character and a forest fruits note. *Palate* – Medium-sweet and very complex with notes of vanilla custard and dark fruit with spice tingling across the tongue and some chocolate. *Finish* – Very long with delicate fruit – strawberries and a little floral touch. *Notes* – D.o.b. Finished in ex-Ornellaia casks.

Fettercairn

FETTERCAIRN, LAURENCEKIRK, KINCARDINESHIRE [H] [V] EST. 1824

The Fettercairn distillery originally stood two miles further up the mountain in the heart of a smuggling district, but this was abandoned in 1824 when the present building, converted from a former cornmill, was opened. It was extensively destroyed by a fire in 1888 when "much excellent whisky was lost in the flames or in the nearby burn". The distillery remained silent for the next two years before renovation in 1890. Silent between 1926 and 1939, when it was acquired by a subsidiary of National Distillers of America. Extended from two to four stills in 1966. Now owned by Whyte & Mackay.

Location – Situated just off the B974, close to the River Esk on the outskirts of Fettercairn, the distillery rests at the foot of the Cairngorm mountains.

Notes – According to Rev. Robert Foote, the village minister in 1892, the village was home to 50 weavers, 10 millers, 7 shopkeepers, 5 flaxdressers and 1 surgeon. He made no mention of distillers, but there were many who practised their illicit trade on the slopes of the nearby Cairngorms. John Gladstone bought the Fasque estate in 1829 and, consequently, became the landlord of James Stewart, the distiller at Fettercairn. John Gladstone was the father of William Ewart Gladstone, one of Britain's most illustrious prime ministers and probably the best friend the whisky industry ever had amongst their number. He introduced several reforms crucial to the industry, the most important of which was in 1853, when he abolished the crippling Malt Tax. Another was to permit the selling of bottled whisky to the public. Extensive warehouses contain some 25,000 casks of maturing whisky.

Water – Springs in the nearby Cairngorm Mountains.

Sweetness – 4	Peatiness – 4	Price – *

Colour – Straw with good gold highlights. *Nose* – Quite full, dryish with notes of oaky vanilla and malt. *Palate* – Dry, spicy, of medium weight, creamy and smooth. *Finish* – Dry, long and softly chewy. *Notes* – D.o.b.

1980, 43% abv

Sweetness – 3	Peatiness – 6	Price – **

Colour – Quite deep amber with ruby-bronze highlights. *Nose* – Quite big and nutty with a dark, deep, burnt character, a hint of rubber and quite gently peated. *Palate* – Good body, round and well-peated with a slight burnt character, medium-dry with oaky tannins. *Finish* – Long and smoky with a touch of richness and spicy with an almost salty tail. *Notes* – Signatory bottling.

STILLMAN'S DRAM, 30 yrs, 45% abv

Sweetness – 3	Peatiness – 5	Price – ***

Colour – Deep amber with bronze highlights. *Nose* – Medium-bodied, medium-dry with notes of citrus, heather and rubbery Oloroso; water brings out some liquorice and some honey/vanilla with quite soft peating. *Palate* – Medium-bodied, drying and with a waxy citrus note followed by a burnt cough-linctus character. *Finish* – Long, dryish, but with a rich edge and quite a bit of smoke. *Notes* – D.o.b.

1824, 12 yrs, 40% abv

Sweetness – 4	Peatiness – 4	Price – *

Colour – Pale amber with gold highlights. *Nose* – Lights, clean and fresh; with water some caramel is apparent with a little spicy oak, a note of children's sweets and some quite pungent, rubbery peat. *Palate* – A nutty dryness, some perfume, medium-dry, of quite-good body and with some creamy toffee. *Finish* – Quite elegant and well-balanced and quite delicately peated with some spice popping up. *Notes* – D.o.b.

Glen Albyn

Founded by James Sutherland, the then Provost of Inverness, on the ruins of the Muirtown brewery which had catered for the thirst of the men who built the Caledonian Canal. Rebuilt 1884 after being used as a flour mill during a period of disuse. Acquired in 1972 by DCL from Mackinlay & Birnie Ltd, a company owned by 14 members of the Mackinlay family of the Leith distillers and 11 members of the local Birnie family, John Birnie having been the manager and distiller in 1892. Managed by SMD until its demolition in 1988; distilling had ceased in 1983. When operational, it had two stills.

Location – Situated on the east side of the A9 to the north of Inverness. It faced Glen Mhor across the Great North Road where it crosses the Caledonian Canal.

Notes – The distillery was closed between 1917 and 1919 and used as a US Naval Base for the manufacture of mines. For a long time, supplies were delivered by sea. Demolished, along with Glen Mhor, to make way for a supermarket development. Prior to 1745, Inverness had been the chief malting town in Scotland.

Water – Loch Ness.

1977, 30 yrs, 50% abv

Sweetness – 4	*Peatiness – 5*	*Price – ✱✱✱*

Colour – Amber with gold highlights. *Nose* – Medium-dry, cerealy – with an aroma of the mash tun – and wood shavings; water brings out a character of citrus; it is, though, light and delicate. *Palate* – Medium-bodied, gently chewy, medium-dry with a touch of maltiness and woody. *Finish* – Long, quite wine-like, slightly ethereal. *Notes* – Douglas Laing Old Malt Cask bottling.

CONNOISSEURS CHOICE

SINGLE HIGHLAND
MALT SCOTCH WHISKY
GLEN ALBYN
DISTILLERY

DISTILLED **1972** DISTILLED

70cl   **GORDON & MACPHAIL**   40%vol

1972, 40% *abv*

Sweetness – 7	Peatiness – 5	Price – ✱✱✱

Colour – Amber with yellow highlights and a green tinge. *Nose* – Quite good body, medium-sweet, ripe and fruity, a slight buttery toffee character with a nice, dark smokiness. *Palate* – Medium-sweet, rich and cerealy with an almost hop-like flavour, good body and delicately peated. *Finish* – Clean, quite rich and of good length. *Notes* Gordon & MacPhail bottling.

1965, 40% *abv*

Sweetness – 7	Peatiness – 4	Price – ✱✱✱

Colour – Full amber with gold highlights. *Nose* – Medium-sweet, rich, lanolin and peppery characters with an almost raisiny fruitiness. *Palate* – Rich, oaky, of medium weight and quite smooth. *Finish* – Peppery, oaky and dry. *Notes* – Gordon & MacPhail bottling.

1963, 40% *abv*

Sweetness – 7	Peatiness – 4	Price – ✱✱✱✱

Colour – Peaty gold with greenish tinges. *Nose* – Quite sweet, creamy and fruity with hints of almonds. *Palate* – Sweet, nutty and creamy. *Finish* – Fine, long and delicately sweet. *Notes* – Gordon & MacPhail bottling.

Glenallachie

RUTHRIE, ABERLOUR, BANFFSHIRE [S] EST. 1968

Built in 1967–68 by Mackinlay McPherson Ltd, a subsidiary company of Scottish & Newcastle Breweries Ltd. Sold to Invergordon Distillers in 1985 along with its then sister distillery, Isle of Jura. Closed in 1987 and reopened again in 1989 after being purchased by Campbell Distillers, a subsidiary of the French company Pernod-Ricard. Now a part of Chivas Brothers. Four stills.

Location – The distillery nestles at the foot of Ben Rinnes, a short way from the A95.

Notes – One of three distilleries designed by William Delme-Evans, the other two being Isle of Jura and Tullibardine. A distillery, 100% of whose output is intended for blending and is only very rarely found as a single.

Water – Springs on Ben Rinnes.

12 yrs, 40% abv

Sweetness – 7	Peatiness – 4	Price – ✱✱✱✱

Colour – Pale, soft golden. *Nose* – Full and delightfully leafy. *Palate* – Full-bodied, lightly peated, slightly sweet. *Finish* – Elegant and smooth. *Notes* – Invergordon bottling.

1985, 11 yrs, 43% abv

Sweetness – 7	Peatiness – 3	Price – ✱

Colour – Very pale straw with pale lemon highlights. *Nose* – Medium-bodied, quite fresh with a slightly youthful mashy character. *Palate* – Medium-sweet, quite smooth and lightly peated with a touch of spice. *Finish* – Lingeringly sweet with hints of smoke and vanilla tablet on the tail. *Notes* – Signatory bottling from cask nos. 4072–4.

Glenburgie

ALVES, NR FORRES, MORAY [S]   EST. 1829

Founded on this site as Kilnflat by William Paul, the grandfather of Dr Listen Paul, a celebrated London surgeon of the latter part of the 19th century. Silent from 1927 to 1935. Managed by Hiram Walker from 1930 and purchased outright by them in 1936. Now a part of Chivas Brothers. Six stills.

Location – Sited in a valley to the south of the A95, some five miles to the east of Forres.

Notes – The distillery did once have two short-necked Lomond stills which produced a heavier malt known as Glencraig. These Lomond stills were removed in 1981. Aeneas Macdonald in his classic book, *Whisky*, lists Glenburgie as one of his 12 great malts. Despite this accolade, neither Hiram Walker/Allied nor Chivas have bottled Glenburgie; the task of keeping its make out there on the public's tastebuds seems to be exclusively down to Gordon & MacPhail.

Water – Local springs.

CONNOISSEURS CHOICE

Connoisseurs Choice, a range of single malts from various districts of Scotland.

The distilleries situated in the area of the valley of the River Spey produce some of the finest malt whiskies.

SINGLE SPEYSIDE
MALT SCOTCH WHISKY
DISTILLED AT
GLENBURGIE
DISTILLERY
PROPRIETORS: Jas. & Geo. Stodart Ltd
DISTILLED **1968** DISTILLED
SPECIALLY SELECTED, PRODUCED AND BOTTLED BY
75cl   GORDON & MACPHAIL   40%vol
ELGIN - SCOTLAND
PRODUCT OF SCOTLAND

1948, 40% *abv*

Sweetness – 5	Peatiness – 6	Price – ****

Colour   Deep amber with bronze highlights. **Nose** – Very big, dark and powerful, with characters of linseed and soft oak with a slightly green touch, medium-dry with a slight "burnt" character and a pleasant spiritiness. **Palate** – Big, rich and smoky with a not too dominant oakiness, the "burnt" character again and quite big tannins. **Finish** – Long, quite elegant, slightly chewy and gently smoky. **Notes** – Gordon & MacPhail Centenary Reserve bottling.

1960, 40% *abv*

Sweetness – 7	Peatiness – 5	Price – ✱✱✱✱

Colour – Pale straw with good yellow highlights. *Nose* – Woody, slightly sweet and flora. *Palate* – Medium-sweet, slightly spicy, oaky and quite heavy. *Finish* – Oaky, of reasonable length. *Notes* – Gordon & MacPhail bottling.

1966, 57.6% *abv*

Sweetness – 7	Peatiness – 5	Price – ✱✱✱✱✱

Colour – Quite deep amber with old-gold highlights. *Nose* – Big-bodied, unctuous, creamy oak and medium-sweet with a light peat note. *Palate* – Rich and round with sweet oaky vanilla, medium-sweet and quite delicately peated. *Finish* – Long, with gently chewy tannins and a slight hint of coffee on the tail. *Notes* – Gordon & MacPhail bottling from cask nos. 3410 filled 31 March 1996 and 11690 filled 15 November 1966.

GLENCRAIG, 1970, 40% *abv*

Sweetness – 3	Peatiness – 1	Price – ✱✱✱

Colour – Mid-amber with yellow/gold highlights. *Nose* – Light, fresh, fruity, medium-sweet with a greenness. *Palate* – Light, clean, medium-dry, very lightly peated with a fresh greenness. *Finish* – Clean and fresh. *Notes* – Produced from the Lomond stills and bottled as Glencraig by Gordon & MacPhail.

Glencadam

BRECHIN, ANGUS [H] [V] EST. 1825
Website: *www.glencadam.com*

Said to have been founded in 1825, the distillery passed through a number of owners before being purchased, in July 1954, by Hiram Walker from Harry Southwell and Andrew Stevenson for £83,400. Bought by Angus Dundee Distillers in 2003. Two stills.

Location – Situated half a mile to the east of the town of Brechin in the cleft of a hill. It is also about half a mile from the River Esk.

Notes – The lyne arm rises to the condenser from the top of the narrow swan neck instead of dropping as is normal. The result is that heavier alcohols fall back down into the still in a form of reflux and this gives the make an elegance and delicacy.

Water – Springs in the Unthank Hills.

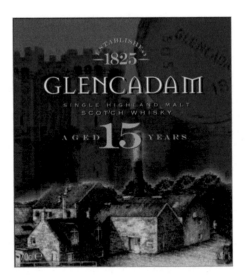

15 *yrs*, 40% *abv*

Sweetness – 4	Peatiness – 5	Price – ✱

Colour – Mid-amber with old-gold highlights. *Nose* – Quite big and dark with notes of coffee, spice, honey and orange; water brings out Olde English marmalade, a peat note akin to spent fireworks, some treacle and a meaty character. *Palate* – Medium-dry with soft oak and quite delicate peat, smooth, slightly unctuous and malty. *Finish* – Long and clean with a touch of spice. *Notes* – D.o.b.

16 yrs, 43% abv

Sweetness – 4	Peatiness – 4	Price – ✱✱

Colour – Amber with old-gold highlights. *Nose* – Quite big-bodied with waxy dried fruits – apricot and raisin, slightly unctuous with some spice and citrus; water brings out light hazelnuts, honey and some cocoa maltiness. *Palate* – Medium-dry with heather honey, silkily smooth and creamy vanilla. *Finish* – Long, dryish, spicy with some smoke coming through on the end. *Notes* – Macleod's Chieftain's Choice bottling.

1973, 46% abv

Sweetness – 4	Peatiness – 4	Price – ✱✱✱

Colour – Amber with old-gold highlights. *Nose* – Medium-bodied and rich with notes of vanilla, acacia honey, melon and pear; with water it becomes fuller and rounder with tablet/toffee, sherbet and citrus notes. *Palate* – Soft, quite full, medium-dry and round with juicy, rich citrus and peach and quite delicately peated. *Finish* – Long, rich, really fruity and complex with fresh, juicy sweetness. *Notes* – Berry's Own Selection bottling from cask no. 706.

1972, 28 yrs, 55.4% abv

Sweetness – 6	Peatiness – 4	Price – ✱✱✱

Colour – Amber with yellow highlights. *Nose* – Big, slightly medicinal with cloves; water rounds it out and brings out soft, ripe fruit, honey, beeswax and vanilla. *Palate* – Dark, mature and quite delicate with sweet oak, gently chewy tannins and softly smoky. *Finish* – Long, quite ethereal and elegant with a touch of perfume, some violets and a hint of boiled sweets. *Notes* – Blackadder bottling from cask no. 7633.

Glendronach

FORGUE, BY HUNTLY, ABERDEENSHIRE [H] [V] EST. 1826
Website: *www.theglendronach.com*

Glendronach's founder, James Allardyce, was a frequent guest of the 5th Duke of Gordon, who was largely responsible for the Excise Act of 1823. This was instrumental in creating the modern Scotch whisky industry. The distillery has had various owners over the years, including Captain Charles Grant, younger son of Willam Grant of Glenfiddich fame, who purchased it from the Crown in an auction for £9000 in February 1920. It remained in that branch of the Grant family until 1960, when George Grey Grant sold it to Wm Teacher & Sons Ltd. Extended from two to four stills in 1966–67. Now part of Pernod-Ricard and operated by Chivas Brothers.

Location – Situated straddling the Dronach Burn in the valley of Forgue, which supplies the cooling water. The distillery is set amongst tall trees in which an established colony of rooks is said to bring good luck.

Notes – Distilling was undoubtedly carried out in the area in the days before legal distilling came to Glendronach and the noisy rooks would have provided a useful alarm to warn of approaching strangers – especially excise officers. Built in the form of a square and covering four acres, Glendronach is one of the few distilleries where barley is still malted on a malting floor, providing about 15% of the distillery's requirements. It also has coal-fired stills.

Water – "The Source" – a spring four miles east of the distillery.

15 yrs, 40% abv

Sweetness – 7	Peatiness – 4	Price – ✱✱

Colour – Deep amber with ruby-tinted bronze highlights. *Nose* – Full-bodied, rich, quite creamy, nutty and medium-sweet with lovely, soft, sweet vanilla, notes of dried fruits – raisins, prunes and apricots and a slight fresh, citrus touch. *Palate* – Full, round, smooth, medium-sweet, rich, creamy and quite delicately peated. *Finish* – Long, sweet and quite ethereal with characters of sweetmeal biscuits, toffee and hazelnuts. *Notes* – Allied Distillers' bottling: "100% matured in Sherry casks".

33 yrs, 40% abv

Sweetness – 7	Peatiness – 3	Price – ✱✱✱✱

Colour – Deep amber with bronze highlights. *Nose* – Dark and warming, quite full-bodied and rich with sherried oak; water brings out Olde English Marmalade, mahogany and stewed fruits and raisins and a little chocolate. *Palate* – Big-bodied, medium-sweet, rich and mature with raisins and creamy toffee, some honey and a little fresh citrus, gently chewy, leathery oak. *Finish* – Long, sweet and decadently mature with some brazil nuts cropping up at the end. *Notes* – D.o.b

TRADITIONAL, 12 yrs, 40% abv

Sweetness – 5	Peatiness – 6	Price – ✱✱✱

Colour – Straw with golden highlights. *Nose* – Quite full-bodied, medium-sweet, rich and soft, almost honeyed with a slight oily note. *Palate* – Medium-dry, quite rich, full and smooth with a touch of spice, buttery and delicately smoky. *Finish* – Soft, smooth and long with some smokiness on the tail. *Notes* – Caledonian Distillers bottling.

Glendullan

DUFFTOWN, BANFFSHIRE [S] EST. 1897

The last distillery to be built in Dufftown in the 19th century and the distillery which prompted the "Dufftown is built on seven stills" line. The location was chosen not just for its beauty, but also for its practical convenience. It was sited to take advantage of water power and was also able to share neighbouring Mortlach's private railway siding. Two stills. Acquired by DCL in 1926 and managed by SMD/UMGD/Diageo from 1930, the licensees are Macdonald Greenlees & Co. Ltd. Rebuilt 1962. An additional distillery with six stills was built on the field between "Old Glendullan" and the employees' homes in 1971–72. The distance between the two units was defined as "a short one when the weather's good and a long one when it isn't". The old distillery was closed in 1985 and is now used as Diageo's maintenance workshops.

Location – Close by the junction of the A941 and A920.

Notes – Glendullan's process water comes from the River Fiddich. Glendullan was a favourite whisky of King Edward VIII and plays an important part in the Old Parr blend.

Water – Springs in the Conval Hills.

SPEYSIDE
SINGLE MALT
SCOTCH WHISKY

GLENDULLAN

distillery, located in a beautiful *wooded valley* was built in 1897 and is one of seven *established* in *Dufftown* in the 19th. The *River Fiddich* flows past the *distillery*; originally *providing power* to drive machinery, it is now used for cooling. *GLENDULLAN* is a firm, mellow *single MALT SCOTCH WHISKY* with a fruity bouquet and a smooth *lingering* finish.

AGED 12 YEARS

43% vol

Distilled & Bottled in *SCOTLAND*.
GLENDULLAN DISTILLERY.
Dufftown,Keith, Banffshire, *Scotland*.

70 cl

12 yrs, 43% abv

Sweetness – 8	*Peatiness* – 4	*Price* – ✳✳

Colour – Pale straw with a touch of green and lemon/yellow highlights. *Nose* – Quite full, rich, appley, slightly spirity with a hint of cereals and lightly peated. *Palate* – Medium-dry, rich, sweet oaky vanilla, a touch of greenness, spirity and malty. *Finish* – Long, smooth, oaky with a delicately smoky tail. *Notes* – D.o.b.

1994, 11 yrs, 58.7% abv

Sweetness – 4	*Peatiness* – 4	*Price* – ✳✳

Colour – Mid-amber with old-gold highlights. *Nose* – Rich, unctuous, sherried; with water, it becomes very oily, round and velvety smooth with notes of apple and honey. *Palate* – Rich, sweet, quite full-bodied with a good, medium-weight peat note and flavours of fruitcake, toffee, cream and coffee. *Finish* – Long, decadently rich and luscious with a slight youthful edge and muscovado sugar on the tail. *Notes* – Blackadder bottling.

1978, 26 yrs, 56.5% abv

Sweetness – 8	*Peatiness* – 3	*Price* – ✳✳✳

Colour – Mid-amber with pale bronze highlights. *Nose* – Rich, quite full-bodied and zesty with some spice; water brings out toffee apples, dried fruit – raisins and apricots, ginger and butterscotch. *Palate* – Gorgeously rich, crème brulée, digestive biscuits and toffee/coffee with a delicate peat underlay. *Finish* – Long, full, rich, malty and subtly oaked. *Notes* – D.o.b. from the Rare Malt series.

Glen Elgin

Built between 1898 and 1900 by a partnership of William Simpson, a former manager of Glenfarclas and James Carle, the local agent for the North of Scotland Bank. Production began on 1 May 1900. Acquired by SMD in 1930. Extended from two to six stills when rebuilt in 1964. The distiller's licence is held by White Horse Distillers Ltd. Now part of Diageo plc.

Location – Situated on the A941, the main Elgin to Rothes road.

Notes – A very compact distillery, due to a shortage of capital when it was built. The architect, Charles Doig of Elgin, said at the time that Glen Elgin would be the last to be built on Speyside for sixty years. He was right! The next was Glen Keith in 1957. Glen Elgin is an important constituent of the White Horse blend.

Water – Springs near Millbuies Loch.

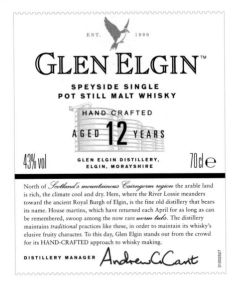

12 yrs, 43% abv

Sweetness – 8	Peatiness – 4	Price – **

Colour – Pale gold with peaty depths. *Nose* – Sweet, slightly green with fine, soft oak and hints of honey; water softens it and brings out peaches, apricot and some spicy vanilla. *Palate* – Soft, sweet, smooth and round, good body, ripe fruit – tangerines and honey, well-balanced, oaky vanilla and beeswax. *Finish* – Long, smooth, butterscotch and liquorice, fruity and distinguished. *Notes* – D.o.b.

1974, 26 yrs, 57.3% abv

Sweetness – 8	Peatiness – 4	Price – **

Colour – Quite pale amber with pale gold highlights. *Nose* – Quite full, soft, sweet, rich, honeyed with a touch of beeswax and perfume; water brings out fruit notes of citrus, orange, ripe melon and delicate peat. *Palate* – Soft, smooth, sweet and rich with gently chewy oak, good body and delicate peat. *Finish* – Long, with notes of ripe apples and peaches and gloriously rich on the tail. *Notes* – Adelphi bottling from cask no. 3.

32 yrs, 42.3% abv

Sweetness – 9	Peatiness – 4	Price – *****

Colour – Mid-amber with old-gold highlights. *Nose* – Round, sweet and quite full-bodied, deliciously, decadently rich and honeyed; water brings out nuttiness – hazelnuts, toasted oak, fruit – apples, oranges, plums and butterscotch. *Palate* – Big, with heather honey, a citrus tang of juicy tangerines, peaches and a background of delicate peat. *Finish* – Long, honeyed, cocoa and chocolate, sweet toffee and coffee. *Notes* – D.o.b.

Speyside in all her beauty

Glenesk

Glenesk distillery was originally known as Highland Esk when converted from a former flax-spinning mill in 1897 by Septimus Parsonage & Co. and James Isles of Dundee. Its name was changed to North Esk in 1899 when acquired by J. F. Caille Heddle. Closed during the First World War. Reopened in 1938 and re-equipped by new owners Associated Scottish Distillers Ltd to produce grain whisky under the name Montrose distillery. Acquired by DCL in 1945 and operated off and on by SGD until 1964 when it was transferred to SMD and converted back to a malt distillery. A large drum malting was built in 1968. Renamed Glenesk in 1980.

Location – Two miles north of Montrose, half a mile west of the A92 on the south bank of the River Esk.

Notes – Glenesk has also been known as Hillside. Now closed and unlikely to reopen, however the maltings are in full production for Diageo.

Water – The River North Esk.

17 yrs, 61.8% abv

Sweetness – 4	Peatiness – 6	Price – ***

Colour – Quite full amber with old-gold highlights. *Nose* – Quite full, dark and smoky, quite fresh, creamy and malty with a hint of toffee and a slight green vegetal note. *Palate* – Medium-sweet and quite full-bodied with a zingy, fresh, green note and a good peatiness. *Finish* – Long, fresh and hedgerow-like. *Notes* – Wm Cadenhead bottling.

1970, 25 yrs, 60.1% abv

Sweetness – 3	Peatiness – 7	Price – ***

Colour – Pale straw with pale yellow highlights. *Nose* – Medium-dry, quite rich with a lemon sherbet touch, firm peatiness at the back and a slight cereal note on the end. *Palate* – Quite good body and medium-dry with chewy tannins and a burnt peat character. *Finish* – Long with a dry cereal note and a chewy burnt smokiness. *Notes* – D.o.b. from the Rare Malts series.

Glenfarclas

MARYPARK, BALLINDALLOCH, BANFFSHIRE [S] [V] EST. 1836
Website: *www.glenfarclas.co.uk*

836 is the first recorded licence for Glenfarclas, but John Grant, the current chairman, has a painting of the distillery dated 1797. Robert Hay, a tenant farmer at Rechlerich Farm was the original licensee. It came into the ownership of the Grant family when Hay died in 1865 and John Grant took over the tenancy of the farm – and distillery. It was leased to John Smith until 1870, when he left to run his new Cragganmore distillery. The distillery was then taken over by John Grant himself and has been run by successive generations of the Grant family ever since. The present John Grant is the fifth generation to be in charge and his son, George, the sixth generation, is also involved in the business. Extended from two to four stills in 1960 and to six stills in 1976.

Location – South of the A95, almost midway between Grantown-on-Spey and Craigellachie, lying in quite desolate moorland at the foot of Ben Rinnes.

Notes – Glenfarclas means "valley of the green grass". The whisky ages very well. "Whisky Tom" Dewar waxed most lyrical of a 30-year-old he tasted in 1912, although John Grant considers the 21-year-old to be perfection – all a matter of personal taste. Glenfarclas has been the pioneer of cask strength whiskies, the company's Glenfarclas 105, bottled at 60% abv, long setting the benchmark for such whiskies and having a loyal following worldwide. Glenfarclas used to use a variety of casks, but all new Glenfarclas spirit is now aged in 100% Sherry wood at the distillery. Glenfarclas have an excellent visitor reception centre.

Water – Springs on Ben Rinnes.

10 yrs, 40% abv

Sweetness – 9	Peatiness – 5	Price – ✳

Colour – Straw with good gold highlights. *Nose* – Sightly rubbery, delicately light and sweet, leafy oak with a slight tang of coffee. *Palate* – Sweet, malty, full, rich and round. *Finish* – Sligthly spicy, long and characterful. *Notes* – D.o.b.

12 yrs, 43% abv

Sweetness – 9	Peatiness – 4	Price – ✳

Colour – Mid-amber with gold highlights. *Nose* – Round, medium-sweet, quite full-bodied with peach, honey and cloves; water softens and rounds it and brings out a creamy note with sweet red apples, beeswax and a quite delicate peat note. *Palate* – Medium-sweet and round, with a touch of spice, rich with good body, a delicate peat note and fruity – citrus, orange. *Finish* – Long, honeyed, elegant and polished with velvety smooth toffee and a little smoke on the tail. *Notes* – D.o.b.

15 yrs, 46% abv

Sweetness – 9	Peatiness – 4	Price – ✳✳

Colour – Gold/peaty with very bright, rich golden highlights. *Nose* – Full, rich and sweet with a luscious, unctuous oily-oak character and delicately peated. *Palate* – Sweet, rich and creamy, very intense, full-bodied and smooth with hints of burnt peat. *Finish* – Gloriously sweet, gently smoky – long and distinguished. *Notes* – D.o.b.

17 yrs, 43% abv

Sweetness – 8	Peatiness – 4	Price – ✳✳

Colour – Amber with old-gold highlights. **Nose** – Warm and big-bodied, richly sherried butterscotch and dried fruits; water pulls out tangerines, apples, raisins and honey and a little peat smoke. **Palate** – Big-bodied, sweet, citrus peaches and dark fruits – plums, damsons, vanilla oak and beeswax with a touch of peat at the back. **Finish** – Long, smooth, complex and elegant with a little spice popping up. **Notes** – D.o.b.

21 yrs, 43% abv

Sweetness – 9	Peatiness – 4	Price – ✳✳

Colour – Quite dark amber with rich gold highlights. **Nose** – Full, rich, sweet vanilla oak with hints of mint. **Palate** – Rich, big, full-bodied, delicately smoky. **Finish** – Lightly smoky, rich and long-lasting. **Notes** – D.o.b.

25 yrs, 43% abv

Sweetness – 9	Peatiness – 5	Price – ✳✳✳

Colour – Amber with old-gold highlights. **Nose** – Full, ripe, sweet and round, finely peated with aromas of orange marmalade, honey, coffee and a sherried nuttiness. **Palate** – Full-flavoured, smooth, sweet with oaky vanilla tannins and coffee and toffee flavours. **Finish** – Fresh with a smoky nuttiness and long lasting. **Notes** – D.o.b.

30 yrs, 43% abv

Sweetness – 6	Peatiness – 4	Price – ✸✸✸

Colour – Quite full amber with old-gold highlights. *Nose* – Big-bodied, medium-sweet, mature and quite fresh, intense and very rich with notes of lemon/honey, cough linctus, manadarin oranges, citrus oil and honeyed oak. *Palate* – Big-bodied, almost dry, but with a good rich edge, gently oakily chewy, a velvety smooth unctuousness and citrus character. *Finish* – Long, quite delicately perfumed and complex – honey, beeswax and chocolate. *Notes* – D.o.b., possibly the driest of Glenfarclas's bottlings.

40 yrs, 43% abv

Sweetness – 8	Peatiness – 4	Price – ✸✸✸✸✸

Colour – Quite deep, dark amber with dark bronze/ruby highlights. *Nose* – Quite full-bodied, rich and quite buttery with a hint of liquorice and good background peat, slight honey, clove and dried apricot notes, a dark walnut character, a hint of turmeric and a creamy toffee note. *Palate* – Medium-sweet, quite malty, a good, fresh greenness, a touch of spice and a nice, delicate peatiness. *Finish* – Long, fresh, very good oak integration, liquorice and very complex with a lovely malty tail. *Notes* – D.o.b. Bottle no. 56 of 600.

GLENFARCLAS 105, No age statement, 60% abv

Sweetness – 7	Peatiness – 6	Price – ✸✸

Colour – Deep, peaty amber with gold highlights. *Nose* – Very spirity, slightly astringent, slightly sweet. *Palate* – Spirity, malty, a little oily-oak character, quite austere. *Finish* – Long, flavoursome and, surprisingly, quite dry. *Notes* – D.o.b.

Glenfiddich

DUFFTOWN, BANFFSHIRE [S] [V] EST. 1887
Website: *www.glenfiddich.com*

When Alfred Barnard published his *Whisky Distilleries of the United Kingdom* in 1887, the home of the world's best-selling malt was just being built. Owned by William Grant & Sons Ltd, it today boasts no fewer than 28 stills: 10 wash and 18 spirit. No mean achievement for a distillery founded with £120 capital and using second-hand equipment from Cardow distillery; but such has been the success of the family enterprise founded by William Grant of Glenfiddich, the son of a soldier who had served under Wellington.

Location – Situated near the junction of the A941 and the B975 to the north of the centre of Dufftown.

Notes – One of only three malt whiskies to be bottled at the distillery. The first distillery to open a visitor centre, Glenfiddich now attracts in excess of 125,000 visitors a year. It welcomed its one millionth visitor, Mr Ronald Pederson from Albany in New York State, on 4 August 1987.

Water – The Robbie Dubh springs.

12 yrs, 40% abv

Sweetness – 8	Peatiness – 5	Price – ✱

Colour – Straw/amber with pale gold highlights. *Nose* – Fresh, clean and softly malty with a delicately fresh peatiness, medium-sweet and fresh with fruity notes of apples and peaches. *Palate* – Quite full-bodied, smooth and fruity with a firm, smoky peat character, obvious apples and a touch of cocoa and vanilla. *Finish* – Long, fresh, rich, smooth and quite creamy, cocoa and apples. *Notes* – D.o.b.

CAORAN RESERVE, 12 yrs, 40% abv

Sweetness – 4	Peatiness – 7	Price – *

Colour – Mid-amber with old-gold highlights. *Nose* – Rich, with notes of coconut, banana and green fruit with quite a dark peat character; water pulls out aromas of coal, honey, citrus – limes. *Palate* – Medium-dry with a darkly smoky peat character, good weight, a touch of menthol and an edge of sweetness. *Finish* – Long, spicy, dry and gently chewy with a note of mint. *Notes* – D.o.b.

TOASTED OAK RESERVE, 12 yrs, 40% abv

Sweetness – 8	Peatiness – 5	Price – *

Colour – Amber with pale gold highlights. *Nose* – Fresh and quite malty with wood aromas; water brings out tangerines, apricots and peaches, some mint and softens the wood aromas. *Palate* – Medium-bodied, sweet apples and vanilla, toffee with a light nuttiness – almonds and tail of apple crumble. *Finish* – Quite delicate and ethereal with a rich spiciness. *Notes* – D.o.b.

SOLERA RESERVE, 15 yrs, 40% abv

Sweetness – 7	Peatiness – 5	Price – **

Colour – Amber with pale gold highlights. *Nose* – Quite full-bodied and relatively solid with a slight dark nuttiness, medium-sweet, a touch of honey and rich orange/lime marmalade. *Palate* – Quite big, rich, medium-dry and a good, delicate peat character. *Finish* – Long, nutty, rich with a dark peat note and a touch of chocolate orange. *Notes* – D.o.b.

ANCIENT RESERVE, 18 *yrs*, 43% *abv*

Sweetness – 8	*Peatiness* – 3	*Price* – ✹✹

Colour – Straw with pale gold highlights. *Nose* – Rich and medium-bodied, with notes of orange and apples; water brings out grapes, tangerines, coffee and soft smoke. *Palate* – Medium-sweet, with notes of spice, Sherry, honey and dried fruits – sultanas and raisins and a slight green leafiness. *Finish* – Good, clean, very gently chewy and smooth with a touch of cappuccino. *Notes* – D.o.b.

GRAN RESERVA, 21 *yrs*, 43% *abv*

Sweetness – 9	*Peatiness* – 5	*Price* – ✹✹✹

Colour – Quite pale amber with good yellow/gold highlights. *Nose* – Rich and quite full-flavoured, biscuity – digestives, banana and citrus; with water, the citrus becomes rich tangerines, chocolate, butterscotch and some spice. *Palate* – Sweet, toasty vanilla oak, a bit of buttery brioche, juicy tangerines, malty with raisins. *Finish* – Enormously rich and full, chocolate and cocoa with coffee/toffee and satsumas. *Notes* – D.o.b.

Glen Garioch

OLD MELDRUM, ABERDEENSHIRE [H] EST. 1785
Website: *www.glengarioch.co.uk*

Established by one Thomas Simpson, the first spirit was announced on 1 December 1785 in the *Aberdeen Journal*. Glen Garioch is one of Scotland's oldest distilleries. In two centuries, ownership has passed through several hands, including SMD who acquired it in 1937. Closed by SMD in 1968 and sold to Stanley P. Morrison who extended it from two to three stills in 1978. Now operated by Morrison Bowmore Distillers, who are wholly owned by Japanese company Suntory.

Location – The distillery is situated in Old Meldrum village, just off the A947 Banff to Aberdeen road, close by the historic Meldrum House.

Notes – Garioch is pronounced "Geerie". The distillery's waste heat was used to heat greenhouses which grew tomatoes between 1978 and 1993. The Garioch valley, an 18-mile or so stretch of highly fertile land is known as the granary of Aberdeenshire. Glen Garioch was indeed a canny place to build a distillery. Other dates have been given elsewhere for the opening of this distillery, but the *Aberdeen Journal* announcement of December 1785 clearly pre-dates them. This source refers to a "licensed distillery", making it Scotland's longest licensed on the same site. Glen Garioch is housed in a very attractive cluster of old buildings with the pagoda heads of the floor maltings adding to its appeal. The floor maltings supply about half of the distillery's requirements, the rest being brought in from outside maltsters. Pitsligo Moss peat is used for the malt drying which is finished by gas firing. Glen Garioch was the first distillery in Scotland to convert its stills to gas-firing.

Water – The silent spring of Coutens Farm.

12 yrs, 40% abv

Sweetness – 4	Peatiness – 5	Price – *

Colour – Mid-amber with gold/green highlights. *Nose* – Medium-bodied, delicately peated and floral (almost violets), dry with a light edge of sweetness. *Palate* – Medium-dry, slightly spicy, floral and fresh with good body. *Finish* – Quite long, spicy and tangy with a green edge. *Notes* – D.o.b.

15 yrs, 43% abv

Sweetness – 3	Peatiness – 6	Price – ✳

Colour – Straw/light amber with yellow/gold highlights. *Nose* – Medium-bodied, malty and round; water brings out cereals, mint, some toffee and a heather note. *Palate* – Quite big-bodied and smooth with a rich edge and a smoky character. *Finish* – Long, almost pungent, a gentle heathery smokiness and softly chewy. *Notes* – D.o.b.

21 yrs, 43% abv

Sweetness – 4	Peatiness – 5	Price – ✳✳✳

Colour – Pale amber with yellow/green highlights. *Nose* – Medium-sweet and quite smoky; water brings out a mintiness and heathery toffee character. *Palate* – Full-bodied, rich and medium-dry, toffee and honey arise with a floral note to the delicate peat. *Finish* – Smoky, heathery, violets, slightly spicy and quite long with gently chewy oak. *Notes* – D.o.b.

1988, 52.8% abv

Sweetness – 4	Peatiness – 5	Price – ✳✳✳

Colour – Amber with gold highlights. *Nose* – Medium-bodied and quite rich with vanilla oak and mixed sweet spice; water brings out tobacco and a charred note to the oak. *Palate* – Medium-dry and rich with oaky vanilla and notes of pasta, cereal and caramel. *Finish* – Long and quite tangy with a little touch of citrus. *Notes* – Duncan Taylor bottling.

LIMITED EDITION BOTTLING		
DATE DISTILLED	BOTTLE NUMBER	DATE BOTTLED
01.05.1958		07.09.2004

MORRISON'S GLEN GARIOCH DISTILLERY
OLD MELDRUM
ABERDEENSHIRE SCOTLAND

700ml   DISTILLED & BOTTLED IN SCOTLAND   43%Vol

1958, 46 yrs, 43% abv

Sweetness – 3	Peatiness – 4	Price – ✳✳✳✳

Colour – Amber with old-gold highlights. *Nose* – Quite delicate and rich, showing vanilla and a wee bit of spice, buttery and creamy; water brings out soft, ripe apples and pears, Demerara sugar, a leafy note, some pepper and citrus. *Palate* – Medium-dry, quite vinous, fresh and spicy with soft, sweet vanilla oak and a minty touch. *Finish* – Long, very elegant, quite ethereal, pepper reprises, herby – basil, mint; wonderfully complex, there is a lot going on here. *Notes* – D.o.b.

Glenglassaugh

NR PORTSOY, BANFFSHIRE [H] EST. 1875

Founded by the Glenglassaugh Distillery Company. Acquired by the Highland Distilleries Co. Ltd in the 1890s. Glenglassaugh was silent from 1907 to 1931 and again from 1936 until it was extensively rebuilt in 1959–60. Closed again in 1986, but reopened. Since closed again. Two stills.

Location – Sited on the slope of a steep hillside in the Glassaugh Glen close to the sea at Sandend Bay, approximately two miles west of Portsoy.

Notes – During the period 1907 to 1960, Glenglassaugh only produced for a handful of years in all. When rebuilt, the distillery managed to double its output simply by doubling the size of its stills.

Water – The Glassaugh Spring.

1983, 40% *abv*

Sweetness – 5	Peatiness – 4	Price – *

Colour – Mid-amber with gold highlights. *Nose* – Quite full, smoky with an oily-oaky character, medium-dry. *Palate* – Medium-dry with good richness in the middle, smooth and round with good body. *Finish* – Long, medium-dry and rich with a nice spiciness. *Notes* – Gordon & MacPhail bottling

1977, 13 *yrs*, 59.8% *abv*

Sweetness – 8	Peatiness – 4	Price – **

Colour – Straw/pale amber with yellow/gold highlights. *Nose* – Quite full-bodied, fresh and clean with a touch of cereal and green apple, medium-sweet with a hint of perfume. *Palate* – Fresh, green, medium-peated and medium-sweet. *Finish* – Long and fresh, sweet with a touch of spice and a soft, peaty backdrop. *Notes* – Wm Cadenhead bottling distilled November 1977.

Glengoyne

OLD KILLEARN, DUMGOYNE, STIRLINGSHIRE   [H] [V]   EST.   1833
Website: *www.glengoyne.com*

Originally known as Burnfoot, Glengoyne was owned by Lang Brothers from 1876, that company becoming a part of the Robertson & Baxter Group in 1965. Acquired by Ian Macleod Distillers Ltd in April 2003. Rebuilt 1966/67, when it was extended from two to three stills.

Location – About twelve or so miles from the centre of Glasgow and about seven from Loch Lomond, Glengoyne nestles in a truly delightful setting at the foot of Dumgoyne Hill, at the north end of the Campsie Hills.

Notes – The distillery is sited on the Highland Line, but, as its water supply comes from north of the Line, it is classified as a Highland malt. The West Highland Way, the long-distance footpath which runs from Glasgow to Fort William, runs past the distillery. Although first licensed in 1833, the distillery is believed to be somewhat older. The make was triple distilled in Victorian times, but is now double distilled. It is reduced using natural spring water. Not far from the distillery is a hollow tree in which Rob Roy MacGregor, immortalised by Sir Walter Scott – and Hollywood – is reputed to have hidden while fleeing from the English king's men. The malt used to produce Glengoyne is unpeated. This, coupled with the lack of peat in its source water, makes Glengoyne the least peated of all whiskies. The excise officer at Glengoyne at the turn of the 20th century was Arthur Tedder, who later became the Chief Inspector of Excise and was knighted. His son, who had grown up at Glengoyne, was eventually to become Air Chief Marshal of the Royal Air Force. When he was later made a baron, he chose as his title Baron Tedder of Glenguin, the old spelling of Glengoyne. The distillery has an excellent visitor centre which sits at the bottom of the 50-foot waterfall which cascades down the side of Dumgoyne Hill.

Water – A burn which falls down Dumgoyne Hill and is known locally as "the Distillery Burn".

10 yrs, 40% abv

Sweetness – 5	Peatiness – 0	Price – *

Colour – Pale straw with lemony–gold highlights. *Nose* – Round, fresh and medium-sweet, quite light and rich with a slight floral note and a touch of greenness at the back. *Palate* – Round, smooth, creamy, medium-dry, fresh and clean with good body. *Finish* – Quite long with a smooth, buttery vanilla character and a touch of greenness on the tail. *Notes* – D.o.b.

PRODUCT OF SCOTLAND

GLENGOYNE

HIGHLAND SINGLE MALT
SCOTCH WHISKY

TEN YEARS

*L*ike all Glengoyne malts, the
Ten Years Old is distilled from air-dried barley
untainted by the harshness of peat smoke.
A natural bright gold in colour it has a clean,
smooth, warming taste with delicate flavours
of fresh green apples, oak, toffee, a hint of
almonds and liquorice all leading to a
sweet, malty finish. A subtle complex whisky
with the *'Real Taste of Malt'.*

700ml ℮   Distilled, Matured & Bottled by   40%vol
Lang Brothers Ltd, Dumgoyne, Scotland.

I guarantee that this malt
whisky has been maturing in
oak casks for a duration of
at least TEN years

AGED
10
YEARS

---

12 yrs, 40% abv

Sweetness – 5	Peatiness – 0	Price – *

Colour – Pale straw with lemony-gold highlights. *Nose* – Medium-bodied, round and fresh, medium-dry with a sweet oily-oak character and hints of buttery toffee. *Palate* – Medium-dry, round, smooth and clean, fresh and medium-bodied with a touch of the toffee character. *Finish* – Long and fresh, buttery, smooth and clean with a touch of oaky vanilla. *Notes* – D.o.b. Available in export markets.

SCOTTISH OAK, 16 yrs, 53.5% abv

Sweetness – 4	Peatiness – 0	Price – ***

Colour – Pale amber with pale golden highlights. *Nose* – Quite sweet with hazelnut, leafy, apple and banana fruit notes with dark, burnt tablet and toffee. *Palate* – Drier than Glengoyne's usual, with a touch of spice and a solid, smoky note with definite brazil nut and walnut characters. *Finish* – Dark, long, quite solid and dry. *Notes* – D.o.b. Aged for 15 years in ex-Bourbon and finished in Scottish oak for 13 months.

---

17 yrs, 43% abv

Sweetness – 6	Peatiness – 0	Price – **

Colour – Pale peaty with yellow/golden highlights. *Nose* – Rich, sweet oak, light fruit and toffee with an almost liquorice-like character. *Palate* – Soft, rich and smooth with sweet oaky vanilla. *Finish* – Spicy, malty and of nice length, quite chewy. *Notes* – D.o.b.

19 yrs, 55.8% abv

Sweetness – 6	Peatiness – 0	Price – ✱✱✱✱

Colour – Amber with old-gold highlights. *Nose* – Sweet, quite big-bodied and fruity with tangerines and honey; water brings out apples, sultanas, vanilla and croissants with butter and some beeswax. *Palate* – Quite solid, medium-sweet and rich with orange, some spice, banana, honey, toffee apples and creamily smooth. *Finish* – Long, spicy, gently chewy, elegant and complex. *Notes* – D.o.b.

21 yrs, 43% abv

Sweetness – 6	Peatiness – 0	Price – ✱✱✱

Colour – Deep amber with old-gold highlights. *Nose* – Round, dark and medium-dry, fruity, richly nutty with unctuous oaky vanilla and notes of mint and toffee. *Palate* – Full-bodied, medium-sweet, rich, round and velvety smooth. *Finish* – Long, clean and sweet with a slight hint of mint on the tail. *Notes* – D.o.b.

1969, 25 yrs, 47% abv

Sweetness – 6	Peatiness – 0	Price – ✱✱✱✱✱

Colour – Straw/mid-amber with gold/yellow highlights. *Nose* – Fresh, clean, quite full-bodied and rich with a good unctuous oaky underlay, a hazelnut character, a touch of tarry rope and green apple fruit. *Palate* – Quite fresh with a good malty character and a touch of chocolate, firm oaky tannins. *Finish* – Medium-dry and rich, quite spicy with a note of liquorice on the tail. *Notes* – D.o.b.

Glen Grant

ROTHES, MORAY [S] [V] EST. 1840
Website: *www.glengrant.com*

Founded by the brothers James and John Grant, who had previously been distillers at nearby Aberlour. Amalgamated with George & J. G. Smith of The Glenlivet in 1953. Owned by the Seagram Company of Canada from 1977 until 2001 when it was purchased by Pernod-Ricard. They, in turn, sold it to Gruppo Campari of Italy on 17 March 2006.

Location – At the northern end of Rothes.

Notes – The Glen Grant stills are direct-fired gas and all have purifiers which are said to add extra finesse to the style of spirit produced. It is now generally recognised that Glen Grant is the world's second best-selling single malt, thanks to its dominant position in Italy, where, as a 5-year-old, it has around 70% of the considerable single malt market. It is also Italy's best-selling whisky. A supply of over-proof Glen Grant is kept in a whisky safe built into the rock at the burnside above the distillery. It is reached through the award-winning Glen Grant gardens. Taste it cut with water from the burn if you get the chance. Glen Grant was the first distillery to be established in Rothes and the first industrial building in the north of Scotland to have electric lighting. Although a best-seller through its younger expressions, Glen Grant ages particularly well.

Water – The Glen Grant Burn.

5 yrs, 40% abv

Sweetness – 4	Peatiness – 4	Price – *

Colour – Light gold/copper. *Nose* – Light, grapey and a little nutty, but somewhat hard and astringent. *Palate* – Drier than most Speyside malts, spirity, slightly peppery. *Finish* – Of reasonable length with a strange heathery-perfumed tang. *Notes* – D.o.b.

10 yrs, 40% abv

Sweetness – 5	Peatiness – 4	Price – ✳

Colour – Pale amber with pale gold highlights. *Nose* – Medium-bodied, medium-sweet with apples and a little vanilla; water softens it, some black tea, a little toffee and a strange smoked ham note. *Palate* – Solid, medium-sweet, some oaky vanilla and a hint of fruit. *Finish* – Dryish, delicate peat, and a bit hard. *Notes* – D.o.b.

15 yrs, 40% abv

Sweetness – 6	Peatiness – 4	Price – ✳

Colour – Peaty/gold with good highlights. *Nose* – Sweet, lightish, nutty and with a slight fruitiness. *Palate* – Medium-sweet, nutty, smooth, slightly smoky. *Finish* – The smokiness comes through on the finish, which is smooth and mellow. *Notes* – Gordon & MacPhail bottling.

18 yrs, 46% abv

Sweetness – 5	Peatiness – 4	Price – ✳✳

Colour – Full amber with gold highlights. *Nose* – Full, quite rich, slightly green and a little austere, soft, oaky vanilla with a little smokiness at the back and hints of apricots and apples. *Palate* – Medium-dry, quite full, round and rich with a touch of toffee and maltiness. *Finish* – Long and rich with a nice edge of greenness. *Notes* – Wm Cadenhead bottling.

21 yrs, 40% abv

Sweetness – 5	Peatiness – 4	Price – ✳✳

Colour – Amber with good gold highlights. *Nose* – Fruity, slightly astringent with a note of green wood. *Palate* – Medium-sweet, peppery and oaky. *Finish* – Smooth, well-balanced, of medium length with good oaky vanilla. *Notes* – Gordon & MacPhail bottling.

1984, 46% abv

Sweetness – 5	Peatiness – 3	Price – ✳✳

Colour – Amber with old-gold/green highlights. *Nose* – Big-bodied and rich with an oily texture and a slightly off/over-ripe aroma; with water, this almost disappears and adds hessian sacks. *Palate* – Medium-sweet and quite rich with an oily unctuousness and notes of poppadums, spice and lemon. *Finish* – Long and clean with the peat coming out. *Notes* – John Milroy Selection bottling from cask no. 4006.

1972, 46% *abv*

Sweetness – 5	Peatiness – 3	Price – ✳✳✳

Colour – Amber with old-gold/green highlights. *Nose* – Medium-bodied and mature with orange and vanilla notes; water brings out honey, apple and pear, a sharp, spirity note and some American Cream Soda. *Palate* – Medium-sweet with an edge of sugar, some floral notes – lavender and violets and gently chewy tannins. *Finish* – Long, quite ethereal and drying with soft peat. *Notes* – Berry's Own Selection bottling from cask nos. 1983, 1954 and 1978.

1972, 29 *yrs*, 57.3% *abv*

Sweetness – 5	Peatiness – 4	Price – ✳✳✳

Colour – Deep, dark amber with bronze highlights. *Nose* – Big-bodied, dark, mature and medium-dry with a charred oak note; with water, it is drier, is quite rich and has a nutty overlay with autumnal flavours and a smoky bonfire character. *Palate* – Big-bodied with quite chewy tannins, smooth with dark oak flavours and a slightly medicinal note to the quite solid peat flavours. *Finish* – Long, chewy and complex with notes of cough linctus, citrus and a touch of spice. *Notes* – Blackadder Raw Cask bottling from cask no. 696.

1969, 31 *yrs*, 53.9% *abv*

Sweetness – 6	Peatiness – 4	Price – ✳✳✳✳

Colour – Very deep amber with ruby-tinted bronze highlights. *Nose* – Quite big-bodied with sweet oak and a slight hedgerow greenness, a burnt mahogany aroma, almost cough-linctus and rich toffee/coffee/ burnt Christmas-cake notes. *Palate* – Big-bodied, medium-dry. Medium-peated with chewy tannins and quite imposing. *Finish* – Long, chewy with a touch of spice and chocolate and good sweetness on the end. *Notes* – Adelphi bottling from cask no. 1772.

1965, 31 *yrs*, 58.4% *abv*

Sweetness – 6	Peatiness – 4	Price – ✳✳✳✳

Colour – Pale amber with pale gold highlights. *Nose* – Quite full-bodied, sweet and rich with a slightly green, nutty, peaty character, smooth with a note of honeyed beeswax. *Palate* – Full and medium-sweet with chewy tannins. *Finish* – Long, with characters of vanilla and oak. *Notes* – Signatory bottling from cask no. 5849 distilled 1 November 1965.

Glen Keith

KEITH, BANFFSHIRE [S] EST. 1957

Originally part of an oat mill of uncertain age, it was converted into a distillery by Chivas Brothers (at that time, a subsidiary of the Seagram Company of Canada) between 1957 and 1960. It was originally designed for triple distillation, but converted to the more normal double distillation in 1970. Bought by Pernod-Ricard in 2001. The distillery is currently mothballed; Chivas Brothers operate their Technical Centre from the site.

Location – By the Linn Pool in the River Isla near the centre of Keith.

Notes – The first distillery to be founded in Scotland since the boom years of the late 19th century. It was also the first distillery in Scotland to have a gas-fired still and the first to use a micro-processor to control the whole operation.

Water – The Balloch Hill springs.

Before 1983, 43% *abv*

Sweetness – 6	*Peatiness* – 3	*Price* – *

Colour – Pale amber with lemon highlights. *Nose* – Medium-bodied and medium-sweet with firm peat and soft, rich lanolin, a touch mashy and an unctuous oakiness. *Palate* – Medium-sweet, soft oak, rich, creamy and smooth. *Finish* – Rich and smooth with a slight toffee touch. *Notes* – D.o.b.

1967, 22 yrs, 45.6% *abv*

Sweetness – 7	*Peatiness* – 3	*Price* – ***

Colour – Bright straw with gold/green highlights. *Nose* – Quite full, rich, oily, nutty and oaky with a slight citrus note. *Palate* – Rich, medium-sweet, gently peated and with an oily creaminess. *Finish* – Long and sweet with a touch of vanilla. *Notes* – Wm Cadenhead bottling.

Glenkinchie

PENCAITLAND, EAST LOTHIAN [L] [V]   EST. 1837
Website: *www.malts.com/en-gb/Malts/summary/GlenKinchie*

Established by John and George Rate, Glenkinchie was disused between 1853 and 1890, when it was revived by the Glen Kinchie Distillery Co. Owned by SMD since 1914, Glenkinchie was one of the founding distilleries in SMD, and licensed to John Haig & Co. Now a part of Diageo plc. Two stills.

Location – Due south of Pencaitland, the distillery is in a hollow in the hills and, although the chimney can be seen from some distance, the road end can easily be missed, as the sign was traditionally overgrown.

Notes – The distillery has a unique museum of distilling which was originated by Alistair Munro, a former manager, the work being continued by his successors. This includes an enormous model of a Highland malt distillery which was built to a scale of one-sixth of actual size for the Empire Exhibition in 1924–25. Glenkinchie has also been known as Kinchie and is probably the same distillery as Milton, of which records exist as being operated by John and George Rate from 1825 to 1834. Glenkinchie has long been an important malt in the Haig blend.

Water – Reservoirs in the Lammermuir Hills.

10 yrs, 43% abv

Sweetness – 2	*Peatiness – 5*	*Price – **

Colour – Pale straw/golden with yellow highlights. *Nose* – Fresh, dry, pleasantly peated and slightly spirity. *Palate* – Dry, malty, quite spicy, full and smooth. *Finish* – Long, lingering, delicately smoky and quite rich. *Notes* – D.o.b.

DISTILLER'S EDITION, 1988, 43% *abv*

Sweetness – 4	*Peatiness* – 5	*Price* – ✳

Colour – Honeyed amber with old-gold highlights. *Nose* – Sweet, rich, honeyed and herby; water pulls out toffee, butterscotch and a herby – oregano or bay? – note. *Palate* – Medium-dry, very rich, nutty – hazelnuts, malty, full-bodied, fruity – cooked fruits, smooth and round. *Finish* – Long, clean, fruity again, delicately peated, muscovado sugar and with a creamy tail. *Notes* – D.o.b. Finished in an Amontillado cask.

Casks ready for bottling at Craigton Packaging, Paisley

The Glenlivet

MINMORE, BALLINDALLOCH, BANFFSHIRE   [S] [V]   EST. 1824
Website: *www.theglenlivet.com*

George Smith established his distillery in 1824 at Upper Drummin Farm, being the first distiller in the Highlands to take out a licence after the passing of the Excise Act of 1823. In 1858, after the original distillery had been destroyed by fire, a new one was built on land obtained from the Duke of Gordon. The Glenlivet was amalgamated with J & J Grant of Glen Grant in 1953 and later with Longmorn-Glenlivet Distilleries Ltd in 1970. The enlarged Glenlivet group of companies was purchased by the Seagram Company of Canada in 1977 and subsequently sold to Pernod-Ricard in 2001. Now operated by Chivas Brothers. Eight stills.

Location – Situated on an unclassified road looping south off the B9136 on the slopes of the Braes of Glenlivet, the local hills.

Notes – The very district of Glenlivet is rich in history. It was here that, in 1594, the king's army under the Earl of Huntly defeated the Covenanters commanded by the Duke of Argyll. The real name of the very English-sounding Smiths was Gow. They had been supporters of the Jacobites and Bonnie Prince Charlie, but, after his defeat at Culloden in 1746, the family apparently changed their name to avoid the oppression which followed. Although many others have laid claim to the "Glenlivet" appellation, following legal action taken by the Glenlivet distillery's then owners in the 1880s there is only one whisky which can rightly be called "The Glenlivet". So famous had the name Glenlivet already become by then that the wags of the day christened it "the longest glen in Scotland". Such was the reputation for quality that The Glenlivet had gained that whiskies that had not been distilled anywhere near the Livet glen were claiming its provenance on their labels. When King George IV visited Edinburgh in 1821, he insisted on drinking nothing but The Glenlivet – three years before The Glenlivet became a legalised distillery!

Water – Josie's Well.

Sweetness – 8	*Peatiness* – 4	*Price* – ✳

Colour – Straw with a definite greenness to its edge. *Nose* – Leafy, malty, honey and floral with heather; water brings out beeswax, marzipan, sweet vanilla oak, apricots, apples and creamy crème brulée. *Palate* – Sherry nuttiness, honeyed shortbread, quite full and medium-sweet with minty fruit. *Finish* – Rich, nutty – hazelnuts, quite long-lasting with notes of marzipan and pineapple. *Notes* – D.o.b.

AMERICAN OAK FINISH, 12 yrs, 40% abv

Sweetness – 8	*Peatiness* – 4	*Price* – ✳

Colour – Amber with old-gold highlights. *Nose* – Sweet, quite full-bodied, fresh and medium-peated with notes of rich shortbread and green apples. *Palate* – Medium-sweet, quite soft, round, gently peated and of nice weight with touches of honey, toffee and butterscotch. *Finish* – Long, clean, quite ethereal and rich. *Notes* – D.o.b.

FRENCH OAK RESERVE, 15 yrs, 40% abv

Sweetness – 8	*Peatiness* – 4	*Price* – ✳✳

Colour – Deep amber with old-gold highlights. *Nose* – Sweet, round, quite fresh, rich, soft and fruity; water brings out notes of banana and grapefruit, shortbread and toffee with a delicate, liquorice-flavoured peat. *Palate* – Soft, round and medium-sweet, rich and slightly unctuous, oily oaked beeswax, of good weight, gently peated with flavours of toffee/coffee/chocolate. *Finish* – Long and quite ethereal with notes of cappuccino, hazelnut, tobacco and cocoa. *Notes* – D.o.b.

18 yrs, 43% abv

Sweetness – 6	*Peatiness* – 5	*Price* – ✳✳

Colour – Quite deep amber with bronze highlights. *Nose* – Quite full-bodied, medium-sweet with a dark, soft nuttiness, a good peaty character with a lightly honeyed, almost Christmas-cake richness and a gentle, peaty fruitiness. *Palate* – Big-bodied, smooth, round, soft, rich and medium-sweet, slightly toffeeyed and gently peated. *Finish* – Rich, with a touch of spice, a light, elegant, smoky touch to the tail and surprisingly dry. *Notes* – D.o.b.

THE GLENLIVET ARCHIVE, *21 yrs*, 40% *abv*

Sweetness – 7	*Peatiness* – 4	*Price* – ✹✹

Colour – Mid-amber with bronze highlights. *Nose* – Quite full-bodied, round and sweet with notes of citrus, honey and mature vanilla; water pulls out beeswax, coconut, dried fruit – raisins and apricots, Olde English marmalade, mahogany and marzipan. *Palate* – Medium-sweet, honeyed, beeswax, very gently chewy, with notes of toffee, butterscotch, ginger and with a slight green edge to the peat. *Finish* – Long, surprisingly fresh, softly chewy hazelnuts and liquorice, complex. *Notes* – D.o.b.

1968, 49.4% *abv*

Sweetness – 7	*Peatiness* – 2	*Price* – ✹✹✹✹

Colour – Amber with gold highlights. *Nose* – Quite fresh, medium-bodied with oak and orange notes; water brings out beeswax and floor polish and the citrus character becomes more of lemons. *Palate* – Medium-bodied, rich and gently peated, honeyed with apple and lemon. *Finish* – Long and spicy with mouth-wateringly juicy citrus. *Notes* – Duncan Taylor bottling from cask no. 5242.

CELLAR COLLECTION, 1964, 45.1% *abv*

Sweetness – 4	*Peatiness* – 3	*Price* – ✹✹✹✹✹

Colour – Deep amber with bronze highlights and a ruby hue. *Nose* – Quite big-bodied, rich and mature with mahogany, honey and citrus characters; water brings out toast, bergamot, cinnamon and beeswax. *Palate* – Quite big-flavoured with mature tannins, gently chewy nuttiness with beeswax and honey. *Finish* – Very long, complex and wood-dominated, but with soft, floral notes and a good citrus and honey tail. *Notes* – D.o.b.

Glenlochy

Glenlochy was always very up-to-date. All the fittings in 1898 were "arranged throughout with a view to saving labour". A visitor reported, in 1907, that Glenlochy possessed "every modern facility for enabling it to be worked with a minimum of labour". Joseph Hobbs of Associated Scottish Distillers sold it in 1940. Eight years later, he established the Great Glen Cattle Ranch, an area of 54 square kilometres where beef cattle fend for themselves, as they do on the US prairies. The ranch is still in operation. Glenlochy was silent from 1917 to 1924 and again from 1926 to 1937. It was bought by DCL in 1953 when the unit was transferred to SMD. It had two stills.

Location – Situated within Fort William on the north bank of the River Nevis, to the west of the A82.

Notes – The distillery closed for good in 1983 and the site was sold, in 1992, to a local hotel group which has developed a hotel and restaurant on the site, retaining the pagoda roof on the former maltings.

Water – The River Nevis.

22 yrs, 61.4% abv

Sweetness – 7	Peatiness – 4	Price – ✱✱✱✱

Colour – Amber with pale old-gold highlights. *Nose* – Quite light, fresh, rich and medium-sweet with notes of citrus and Demerara sugar. *Palate* – Quite big-bodied, round, rich and smooth, medium-sweet with gently chewy tannins, quite delicately peated with coffee/cocoa characters and a touch of toffee. *Finish* – Long and quite tangy with an apple note, a touch of perfume and a good, soft, peat note. *Notes* – Wm Cadenhead bottling.

1963, 30 yrs, 52.2% abv

Sweetness – 3	Peatiness – 6	Price – ✱✱✱✱

Colour – Mid-amber with gold highlights. *Nose* – Light, quite fresh with a cooked-apple character and quite dry. *Palate* – Quite dry with a smoky oak and coffee character. *Finish* – Good length and delicately smoky. *Notes* – Signatory bottling.

Glenlossie

Built in 1876 by John Duff, tenant of the Fife Arms, Lhanbryde and previously manager of the Glendronach distillery. A controlling interest was obtained by SMD in 1919 and the distillery was taken over completely by DCL in 1930. Extended from four to six stills in 1962. The make is important to John Haig's blends, the distillery being licensed to that company. Now part of Diageo plc.

Location – Sited at Thomshill on an unclassified road to the west of the A941, two miles south of Elgin.

Notes – A purifier has been installed between the lyne arm and the condenser on each of the three spirit stills. Electricity only replaced steam as late as 1960 as the means of power generation at the distillery. A fire at the distillery in 1929 caused some damage. One of the appliances that fought the blaze was the distillery's own engine. Dating from the 1860s and originally horse-drawn, it can now be seen at Dallas Dhu. The site now houses two distilleries, the other being the much newer Mannochmore, built in 1971.

Water – The Bardon Burn.

SPEYSIDE
SINGLE MALT *SCOTCH WHISKY*

The three *spirit stills* at the

GLENLOSSIE

distillery have *purifiers* installed between the *lyne arm* and the *condenser*. This has a bearing on the *character* of the *single MALT SCOTCH WHISKY* produced which has a *fresh, grassy* aroma and a *smooth*, lingering flavour. Built in 1876 by *John Duff*, the *distillery* lies four miles *south* of ELGIN in *Morayshire*.

AGED **10** YEARS

43% vol   Distilled & Bottled in *SCOTLAND*. GLENLOSSIE DISTILLERY, Elgin, Moray, *Scotland*.   70 cl

---

10 yrs, 43% abv

Sweetness – 6	Peatiness – 3	Price – **

Colour – Quite pale straw with lemon/yellow highlights. **Nose** – Fresh, cerealy and green, fragrant with a touch of perfume. **Palate** – Fresh with a touch of oaky tannin, quite green and gently smoky, medium-dry with richness in the middle of the palate. **Finish** – Lasts quite well, clean, fresh and spicy. **Notes** – D.o.b.

Glen Mhor

INVERNESS, INVERNESS-SHIRE [H] EST. 1892

Founded by John Birnie, a former Lord Provost of Inverness and James Mackinlay of Charles Mackinlay & Co., Glen Mhor began production on 8 December 1894. It became a part of DCL in 1972, John Walker & Co. having long had a large shareholding in the company, from which date it was operated by SMD. Closed in 1983 and subsequently demolished in 1986 to make way for a shopping complex.

Location – The distillery was situated at the north end of the Caledonian Canal where it intersects with the Great North Road (the A9) to the north-west of Inverness, across the road from Glen Albyn.

Notes – The name Glen Mhor means "great Glen". It was the first distillery in Scotland to introduce mechanical maltings. Neil Gunn, the celebrated Highland novelist and whisky writer, spent his early working life there as an exciseman and was a great fan of Glen Mhor's whisky. Mackinlay's sold Glen Mhor as a single malt long before the category became fashionable.

Water – Loch Ness.

8 yrs, 57% abv

Sweetness – 4	Peatiness – 4	Price – ✳✳✳

Colour – Straw/amber with good gold highlights. *Nose* – Lightly peated with an edge of sweetness. *Palate* – Medium-sweet, slightly woody and quite full-bodied. *Finish* – Spicy, creamy, long and almost leafy. *Notes* – Gordon & MacPhail bottling.

24 yrs, 50% abv

Sweetness – 1	Peatiness – 6	Price – ✳✳✳

Colour – Pale amber with yellow highlights. *Nose* – Medium-bodied with a slight toffee note; water pulls out a vegetal touch, medium-dry. *Palate* – Dry (very), chewy tannins and medium peated. *Finish* – Long, but drying, woody, chewy. *Notes* – Douglas Laing Old Malt Cask bottling.

Glenmorangie

TAIN, ROSS-SHIRE [H] [V] EST. 1843
Website: *www.glenmorangie.com*

Converted from the Morangie Brewery of McKenzie & Gallie by William Mathieson. Rebuilt in 1887, in 1979, when it was extended from two to four stills, and again in 1990 when it was extended to eight stills. Glenmorangie has been owned by Macdonald & Muir (who were renamed Glenmorangie plc in 1996), the Leith blenders since 1918. They were acquired by Moët Hennessy (the Wine and Spirits Division of Louis Vuitton Moët Hennessy) in January 2005 and, in March 2005, the company became known as The Glenmorangie Company Ltd.

Location – Sited on the Dornoch Firth, on the A9 between Tain and Edderton looking across the firth towards the hills of Sutherland.

Notes – All of the make is used by the owners, none being made available as fillings. When William Mathieson established the distillery, his stills were second-hand gin stills. Glenmorangie has retained this shape of still, with the result that the stillhouse is populated by very tall (16 ft 101/4 in., or 5.14 metres), slim and elegant stills, the tallest in Scotland.

Water – The Tarlogie Spring above the distillery.

10 yrs, 43% abv

Sweetness – 4	Peatiness – 2	Price – *

Colour – Pale straw with pale gold highlights. *Nose* – Medium-bodied, fresh and floral; water brings out the malt and some orange notes, some nuttiness and some delicate peat. *Palate* – Fresh, delicate, creamily unctuous with honey, citrus and a delicate smokiness. *Finish* – Good length, with sweet and softly toffeeyed almonds. *Notes* – D.o.b.

Sweetness – 4	Peatiness – 4	Price – ✱✱

Colour – Amber with old-gold highlights and an edge of bronze. *Nose* – Quite full-bodied and honeyed with a really distinctive lemon-curd tang, medium-dry and smooth with notes of vanilla, beeswax and apple blossom. *Palate* – Dry, round and smooth with a nice, chunky peatiness, good body and a slightly green citrus bite. *Finish* – Long, dry and complex, with notes of honey, vanilla and cocoa. *Notes* – D.o.b.

ARTISAN CASK, 1995, 46% *abv*

Sweetness – 4	Peatiness – 2	Price – ✱

Colour – Quite pale amber with pale gold highlights. *Nose* – Quite delicate and medium-dry with a smoky, new-sawn oak character and rich with soft, sweet vanilla and delicately peated; with water, the clean, new-sawn nature of the oak is emphasised, with orange fruit and a little honey. *Palate* – Medium-dry and rich, the flavour creeps up on you, lots of oak, chewy tannins, some spice, coconut and beeswax with a fine structure. *Finish* – Long, elegant, quite ethereal butterscotch notes with delicate peat, the oak tannins mask the richness. *Notes* – D.o.b. Matured in casks constructed from Glenmorangie's own forest in the Ozarks.

MADEIRA WOOD FINISH, No age statement, 56% *abv*

Sweetness – 6	Peatiness – 2	Price – ✱✱

Colour – Amber with old-gold and ruby highlights. *Nose* – Medium-bodied, rich, warm and a touch peppery; water brings out a meaty, steak-pie seasoning, spicy character, some citrus and cherry fruit notes. *Palate* – Sweet, rich, peppery and spicy, medium-sweet with good body. *Finish* – Long, warm and quite delicate. *Notes* – D.o.b.

FINO SHERRY WOOD FINISH, 43% *abv*

Sweetness – 5	Peatiness – 4	Price – ✳✳✳

Colour – Mid-amber with almost old-gold highlights and a slight hint of lemon. *Nose* – Quite fresh, fruity, rich and full-bodied with hints of tangerine, apple and sweet vanilla, medium-sweet with a slight hint of dark peat at the back and spicy with a Christmas-cake grapiness. *Palate* – Medium-dry, soft, sweet oaky vanilla, almost biscuity (digestives), spicy, delicate and with a subdued peatiness. *Finish* – Long, winey, elegant, biscuity and complex. *Notes* – D.o.b. Finished for 3 years in a Fino butt.

COTE DE NUITS WOOD FINISH, 1975, 43% *abv*

Sweetness – 4	Peatiness – 6	Price – ✳✳✳✳✳

Colour – Quite full amber with a wonderful rosé, almost salmon-pink hue and old-gold/onion-skin highlights. *Nose* – Rich, perfumed, delicate with an almost hazelnut note, a fresh, green note to the peat and a sensuous pinot noir aroma of strawberries; water brings out the aromas of children's confections and bubble-gummy cherries. *Palate* – Soft, medium-dry and gently chewy with vanilla oak tannins, good body and a hint of toffee and cherry fruit. *Finish* – Long, fruity, round and magnificently scented. *Notes* – D.o.b. Finished in a Grand Cru Burgundy cask.

BURGUNDY WOOD FINISH, 43% *abv*

Sweetness – 4	Peatiness – 2	Price – ✳✳

Colour – Amber gold with a hint of rosé-pink highlights. *Nose* – Delicate, quite full and tight with strawberry hints, apple blossom, toffee and honey and a little charred oak; water expands the nose to soft, sweet vanilla oak toffee, strawberry, sandalwood, farmyardy truffle aromas. *Palate* – Medium-dry, of good body, softly chewy tannins, round, warm and rich. *Finish* – Long, with a touch of spice, rich, quite ethereal, quite decadent and relaxing. *Notes* – D.o.b.

COGNAC FINISH, 1985, 43% *abv*

Sweetness – 5	Peatiness – 3	Price – ✳✳✳

Colour – Mid-amber with pale old-gold highlights. *Nose* – Fresh and youthful with a slightly green toffee apple character, the peat note is slightly darker with the addition of water. It is very sweet (for Glenmorangie) with notes of pear drops, acid drops and almost Fox's glacier mints. *Palate* – Dry with a quite burnt smoky character and a cooked, Madeira-like fruitiness, a Calvados-like apple note and a touch of spice. *Finish* – Lasts well with notes of toffee/green coffee, a gently chewy note and a nice touch of oaky tannin. *Notes* – D.o.b.

GOLDEN RUM CASK, 12 yrs, 40% abv

Sweetness – 3	Peatiness – 2	Price – ✳✳✳

Colour – Pale amber with pale gold highlights. *Nose* – Rich and medium-sweet with a note of fennel/aniseed; with water, it is rounder, with ripe citrus – lime and marmalade, liquorice and a little spice. *Palate* – Medium-dry, rich, clean, quite fruity with citrus – tangerines, a slight floral note, some ginger and velvety smooth. *Finish* – Long, orangey Olde English marmalade with a slight floral note, some ginger and dried fruits – raisins and apricots. *Notes* – D.o.b.

TAIN L'HERMITAGE FINISH, 46% abv

Sweetness – 7	Peatiness – 2	Price – ✳✳✳✳

Colour – Deep amber with bronze highlights. *Nose* – Big-bodied, rich and round with leather, beeswax and honey; water brings out a charred oak note, some stone fruits, toffee and black tea. *Palate* – Medium-sweet, rich and round, smooth with a little spice and some toffee and butterscotch. *Finish* – Long, rich, gently chewy and elegant, complex and quite ethereal. *Notes* – D.o.b.

SAUTERNES FINISH, 15 yrs, 46% abv

Sweetness – 6	Peatiness – 2	Price – ✳✳

Colour – Mid-amber with old-gold highlights. *Nose* – Quite big-bodied, quite powerful, rich, and warm with honeyed, botrytised and beeswax aromas; with water, citrus leaps out, Seville orange marmalade, intense and rich apricots and lemon meringue pie. *Palate* – Medium-sweet, botrytised with soft, gentle peat, very rich with soft tannins and quite full-bodied. *Finish* – Long, rich and ethereal with notes of citrus and eucalyptus bouncing over the top of the palate. *Notes* – D.o.b. Finished in a Premier Grand Cru Sauternes barrique.

Glen Moray

ELGIN, MORAY   [S]   [V]   EST. 1897
Website: *www.glenmoray.com*

Like its sister distillery, Glenmorangie, a former brewery, having been built in 1815. It was closed in 1910 and, in 1923, passed into the ownership of Macdonald & Muir, which is now known as The Glenmorangie Company Ltd., and is a part of the Louis Vuitton Moët Hennessy group. It was rebuilt in 1958 when it was increased from two to four stills.

Location – Situated in a hollow on the banks of the River Lossie, on the western outskirts of Elgin.

Notes – Close by the distillery is Gallowcrook Hill, which was, as its name implies, the scene of public hangings in days gone by. Some of the make goes into Macdonald & Muir's *Highland Queen* blend. The old steam engine that formerly powered the distillery is still in place.

Water – The River Lossie.

CLASSIC, 40% *abv*

Sweetness – 7	Peatiness – 3	Price – ❋

Colour – Pale amber with pale gold highlights. *Nose* – Quite fresh and malty with a floral note and a little citrus; water expands it to lemon meringue pie with a youthful mashy note and some heather honey. *Palate* – Sweet and quite rich with a touch of spice and some juicy citrus notes. *Finish* – Quite delicate, soft and spicy with a touch of almonds and ginger nuts. *Notes* – D.o.b.

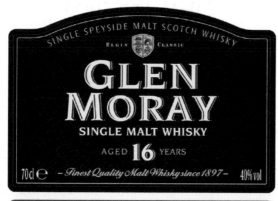

16 yrs, 43% abv

Sweetness – 7	Peatiness – 2	Price – **

Colour – Amber with gold highlights. *Nose* – Fresh, medium-bodied with an appley character, sweet, soft, bubblegummy vanilla, good richness and a hint of perfume. *Palate* – Round with oaky tannins, quite a rich fruity character and good body. *Finish* – Smooth, spicy and medium-sweet with a rich, chewy tail. *Notes* – D.o.b.

SHERRY BUTT, 1981, 57.7% abv

Sweetness – 6	Peatiness – 3	Price – ****

Colour – Deep amber with bronze and ruby highlights. *Nose* – Medium-bodied, medium-sweet, citrus – tangerines, a floral touch, honeyed and a gentle dark peat note; water softens it, pulling in rich toffee, coffee and cocoa. *Palate* – Big and sweet with chewy tannins, a dark, charred oak note and cocoa flavours. *Finish* – Long and woody with chewy oaky tannins, possibly too old. *Notes* – D.o.b. from cask no. 3661.

MELLOWED IN CHENIN BLANC BARRELS, 12 yrs, 40% abv

Sweetness – 6	Peatiness – 4	Price – *

Colour – Quite pale amber with yellow highlights tinged with lemon. *Nose* – Medium-bodied, medium-dry with a touch of honeyed oak, quite delicate, but chunky peat, a creamy toffee character opens up with water, as does a slight hazelnut note. *Palate* – Medium-dry, round, quite soft toffee and honey with a firm backbone of peat. *Finish* – Rich, smooth, honeyed and long. *Notes* – D.o.b. Finished in Chenin Blanc casks.

Glenrothes

ROTHES, MORAY [S] EST. 1878
Website: *www.glenrotheswhisky.com*

Built by William Grant & Co. Amalgamated in 1887 with the Islay Distillery Company (owners of Bunnahabhain distillery) to form Highland Distilleries Ltd. Now licensed to Berry Brothers. Enlarged in 1963 from four to six stills, to eight in 1980 and to ten stills in 1989.

Location – A short way up the glen formed by the Burn of Rothes, which flows from the Mannoch Hills.

Notes – The first spirit ran from the stills on the night of the Tay rail bridge disaster – Sunday, 28 December 1879. The distillery experienced "one of the most disastrous distillery fires" on 15 May 1922, when the no. 1 bonded warehouse was destroyed, along with 2,500 casks (800,000 litres of maturing spirit); a stream of burning whisky flowed out of the stricken building and into the burn. An old angler told a wonderful story of how the trout that evening were easily reeled in, being docile from the Glenrothes "spirit". The whisky is now called "The Glenrothes".

Water – The Ardcanny Spring in the hills above the distillery.

1994, 43% *abv*

Sweetness – 7	Peatiness – 3	Price – ✸✸

Colour – Quite pale amber with pale golden, honeyed highlights. *Nose* – Fruity, sweet and rich, with citrus and a floral note; water brings out lemon and tangerines and a yeasty character. *Palate* – Cooked apples, some cloves, quite full-bodied and sweet, some honey, a malty note and hazelnuts with some Chinese spices. *Finish* – Long, rich, sweet with some lemon curd on the tail. *Notes* – D.o.b. The bottle, label and carton for the company's vintage bottlings have been lauded and received many prizes in industry awards.

Sweetness – 8	*Peatiness* – 3	*Price* – ✳✳

Colour – Mid-amber with gold highlights. *Nose* – Very rich and sweet, with fruity notes of banana and apple; water brings out a rich Christmas cake, some honey, toffee, beeswax and delicate peat. *Palate* – Quite big-bodied and sweet with a spicy touch and some ginger underlaid by some dark nuttiness. *Finish* – Long, rich and soft with fennel and toffee-wrapped coconut. *Notes* – D.o.b.

1979, 15 *yrs*, 43% *abv*

Sweetness – 7	*Peatiness* – 3	*Price* – ✳✳

Colour – Mid-amber with old-gold highlights. *Nose* – Rich, soft and round with an unctuous sweetness, a slight nutty character and a touch of fresh citrus. *Palate* – Full-bodied, soft, round and medium-sweet withj gentle tannins. *Finish* – Long, quite fresh, delicately peated, rich and smooth. *Notes* – D.o.b.

1978, 40% *abv*

Sweetness – 7	*Peatiness* – 4	*Price* – ✳✳✳

Colour – Straw/pale amber with yellow highlights. *Nose* – Light to medium-bodied, sweet with a honeyed nuttiness, delicately peated and a little spirity. *Palate* – Quite full-bodied, medium-sweet and quite smooth with a good smoky character. *Finish* – Good length, quite fresh, clean and rich. *Notes* – Gordon & MacPhail Centenary Reserve bottling.

1966, 27 *yrs*, 51.3% *abv*

Sweetness – 7	*Peatiness* – 3	*Price* – ✳✳✳

Colour – Very dark amber with an almost black heart and bronze/ruby highlights. *Nose* – Big-bodied, dark, nutty oak with spirit at the back, almost a beeswax note, rich and medium-dry. *Palate* – Big and dark with quite gentle tannins, full-bodied and smooth. *Finish* – Long, quite spirity and rich. *Notes* – Signatory bottling – butt no. 13512 distilled 13 November 1966.

Glen Scotia

CAMPBELTOWN, ARGYLL   [C]   EST. 1832

Since it was founded as Scotia in 1832 by Stewart, Galbraith & Co., Glen Scotia has gone through many changes of ownership, the most recent being when Gibson International, who had owned it since 1987, went into receivership in 1994. It has two large stills of classic swan neck design. The distillery and all maturing stocks were bought by Glen Catrine Bonded Warehouses Ltd in 1994. The distillery recommenced production in 1999 and has distilled irregularly since then, being now operated by Loch Lomond Distillery Co. Ltd, an associate company of Glen Catrine.

Location – To the north of the town centre, at the junction of High Street with Saddell Street.

Notes – One of only three distilleries remaining in Campbeltown; somewhat fewer than the 19 which were in operation at the start of the economic recession of the 1920s and 30s, during which time all were closed. Glen Scotia, Springbank and now Glengyle were the only three to reopen. After £1,000,000 had been spent upgrading the distillery between 1979 and 1982, it was closed again until 1989. It is currently operational for five days per week. Looking at the distillery today, one wonders where that £1,000,000 went.

Water – The Crosshill Loch and two wells bored 24 metres down into the rocks below the distillery.

12 yrs, 40% abv

Sweetness – 7	Peatiness – 6	Price – *

Colour – Mid-amber with gold highlights *Nose* – Quite dark with a hint of greenness and charred oak; water brings out a definite tarry rope character, a steely note and elements of the aroma of the old linoleum factories in Fife. *Palate* – It is medium-sweet with a quite full, dark peaty note, very much in-your-face and tangy. *Finish* – Long and rich with gently chewy tannins and the slight edge of a floral note. *Notes* – D.o.b. Glen Catrine seem more careful in their cask selection for the single malt than were the previous owners.

Sweetness – 4	Peatiness – 3	Price – ✱✱

Colour – Straw with yellow/gold highlights. *Nose* – Clean, medium-bodied with a slight bubblegummy sweetness, a touch of perfume and a hint of greenness. *Palate* – Round, smooth and gentle, quite good body and medium-dry with the bubblegummy note and a soft peatiness. *Finish* – Long, clean and slightly tangy with a hint of smokiness. *Notes* – D.o.b.

1991, 15 *yrs*, 62.1% *abv*

Sweetness – 4	Peatiness – 6	Price – ✱✱

Colour – Pale amber with pale lemon highlights. *Nose* – Fresh, medium-dry, medium-bodied with citrus and floral notes; water brings out green apple and mash tun/potato aromas with quite soft peat. *Palate* – Medium-dry, rich and medium-bodied with vegetal and fruity notes. *Finish* – Long with quite solid peat and a touch of spice. *Notes* – Clydesdale Original bottling from cask ref. 0233/1080.

1977, 16 *yrs*, 57.6% *abv*

Sweetness – 5	Peatiness – 6	Price – ✱✱✱

Colour – Pale amber with yellow/gold highlights. *Nose* – Medium-bodied, fresh and off-dry with hints of Orange Pekoe tea and a light, earthy peatiness. *Palate* – Quite rich, medium-dry with a touch of spice, gentle tannins, a firm peatiness and a flavour of tea. *Finish* – Quite tangy, softly smoky and of good length. *Notes* – Wm Cadenhead bottling.

1966, 27 *yrs*, 51.5% *abv*

Sweetness – 4	Peatiness – 2	Price – ✱✱✱✱

Colour – Pale straw with yellow/lemon highlights. *Nose* – Fresh and medium-dry with a leafy greenness, a delicate nuttiness and a slight oaky unctuousness. *Palate* – Medium-dry, fresh and clean with a good richness and an almost chocolatey maltiness. *Finish* – Clean, quite crisp and lightly tangy with good length and concentration. *Notes* – Signatory bottling – cask nos. 1271–2 distilled April 1966.

Glen Spey

Established by James Stuart & Co. Owned by W. & A. Gilbey since 22 September 1887 and now part of Diageo plc. Rebuilt in 1970 when it was extended from two to four stills.

Location – The distillery stands just below the ruins of Castle Rothes, the ancient seat of the Leslie family, the earls of Rothes.

Notes – James Stuart & Co. once also owned the Macallan distillery, a short distance away at Archiestown. Like Knockando, Glen Spey is an important constituent of the J & B blends. The original unit covered an area of two acres, the distillery beginning life as an extension to a mill which was the company's original business as a grain merchant. The maturation warehouse was very innovative for its day – 10,000 square feet covered by two arched corrugated iron spans and supported by decorative iron pillars. Regrettably, on 10 January 1892, there was an exceptionally heavy snowfall and the roof collapsed under the weight of a covering of two feet of snow.

Water – The Doonie Burn.

12 yrs, 43% abv

Sweetness – 7	Peatiness – 3	Price – **

Colour – Amber with pale gold highlights. *Nose* – Quite light and delicate, medium-sweet, grassy and hay-like with a soft smokiness; water gives red apples, honey and beeswax and some cereal notes. *Palate* – Medium-sweet with quite good body, fragrant, nutty with a heathery floral note, quite fresh and smooth with an oily oak unctuousness. *Finish* – Rich and enjoyable, if quite light, with a bit of spice. *Notes* – D.o.b.

Glentauchers

The foundation stone was laid on 29 May 1897, on one of the fields belonging to Tauchers Farm, and the first brew was made on 16 June 1898. One of the original owners was James Buchanan, later Lord Woolavington, of Black & White fame. Merged with DCL in 1925, the distillery came under SMD's wing in 1930. Rebuilt in 1965–66, when it was increased from two to six stills. Closed in May 1983. Sold to Allied Distillers in 1989 and reopened in 1992. Now part of Pernod-Ricard and operated by Chivas Brothers.

Location – On the A95, four miles to the west of Keith.

Notes – Experimentation into continuous distillation was carried out here in 1910 and, during the Allied years, an automated cleaning system which is used for their wash stills, yeast tanks, wort lines and various other tanks was piloted at Glentauchers.

Water – Springs in the local hills.

1990, 40% *abv*

Sweetness – 6	Peatiness – 3	Price – *

Colour – Light amber with pale gold highlights. *Nose* – Medium-bodied, rich and nutty with Sherry rubber notes; water brings out a note of oriental spices and some citrus and dried apricots and a floral peat character. *Palate* – Medium-sweet, round and with quite good body, chocolate digestive biscuits, a charred oak note and a soft maltiness. *Finish* – Quite delicate, hazelnuts and smooth. *Notes* – Gordon & MacPhail bottling.

1979, 40% *abv*

Sweetness – 7	Peatiness – 3	Price – ***

Colour – Light amber with gold highlights. *Nose* – Medium-weight with good richness, nutty, medium-sweet with an aroma of dried apricots and delicately peated. *Palate* – Nutty, oaky, medium-sweet with a touch of spice. *Finish* – Fresh, smooth, good length with a nice light nuttiness. *Notes* – Gordon & MacPhail bottling.

Glenturret

THE HOSH, CRIEFF, PERTHSHIRE [H] [V] EST. 1775
Website: *www.famousgrouse.co.uk*

Glenturret, previously called Hosh, is the second to take that name. It was renamed Glenturret in 1875, some 20 or so years after the nearby distillery of the same name closed. The distillery, which, with two stills, is one of Scotland's smallest, was silent from 1923 to 1959. It was revived by James Fairlie who, with the later assistance of his son, Peter, established Glenturret as one of the world's most sought-after single malts and the Glenturret distillery as a superb tourist attraction. Now a part of the Edrington Group and the home of The Grouse Experience.

Location – On the banks of the River Turret, north-west of Crieff on a secondary road which leads from the A85 round Crieff to Monzie and Gilmerton.

Notes – Although the present buildings were erected in 1775, illicit distilling took place at least as early as 1717. The Drummond Arms Hotel in Crieff was the building in which Prince Charles Edward Stuart (Bonnie Prince Charlie) held his stormy council of war on 3 February 1746. Apart from being possibly the oldest distillery in Scotland, Glenturret has another claim to fame in the *Guinness Book of Records*. A legend even in her own lifetime, Towser, the distillery's rodent operative, was credited with catching a world record 28,899 mice. Born at the distillery on 21 April 1963, Towser died on 20 March 1987, not far short of her 24th birthday – a very good age for a cat! As well as the mice, Towser was also more than a match for rats, baby rabbits and even pheasants.

Water – Loch Turret.

10 yrs, 57.1% abv

Sweetness – 6	Peatiness – 4	Price – *

Colour – Very pale straw with pale yellow/green highlights. *Nose* – Full-bodied, slightly sweet, floral and slightly meaty. *Palate* – Quite full-bodied, round, smooth, creamy, slightly meaty and medium-dry. *Finish* – Smooth, dry and quite long with soft edges. *Notes* – D.o.b.

12 yrs, 40% abv

Sweetness – 7	Peatiness – 3	Price – ✳

Colour – Straw/amber with good greeny-gold highlights. *Nose* – Rich and sherried with oaky vanilla, medium-sweet. *Palate* – Rich, medium-sweet, oaky vanilla, full-bodied and smooth. *Finish* – Long and sherried. *Notes* – D.o.b.

15 yrs, 40% abv

Sweetness – 7	Peatiness – 3	Price – ✳✳✳

Colour – Golden/copper coloured with good yellow highlights. *Nose* – Big-bodied, full, spicy and medium-sweet with oaky vanilla and characters of liquorice, citrus and mint. *Palate* – Full, rich, sweet and slightly peppery with hints of mint and liquorice – very complex. *Finish* – Smooth, spicy, long and memorable. *Notes* – D.o.b.

18 yrs, 40% abv

Sweetness – 7	Peatiness – 3	Price – ✳✳✳

Colour – Straw/amber with yellow/gold highlights. *Nose* – Rich, medium-bodied and slightly perfumed with characters of honey, toffee and green coffee. *Palate* – Round, smooth, medium-sweet with a slight apple and coffee tang. *Finish* – Smooth, sweet and rich with a slight tang of fennel. *Notes* – D.o.b.

21 yrs, 40% abv

Sweetness – 7	Peatiness – 3	Price – ✳✳✳✳✳

Colour – Light mid-amber with old-gold highlights. *Nose* – Rich and quite full-bodied, a greenness and liquorice/aniseed, medium-sweet. *Palate* – Medium-sweet, lightly peated, rich aniseed and creamily smooth with a touch of oaky vanilla. *Finish* – Fresh, clean and long with a touch of sweetness. *Notes* – D.o.b.

Sweetness – 6	Peatiness – 3	Price – ✹✹✹✹

Colour – Straw with yellow/gold highlights. *Nose* – Quite fresh, medium-bodied and medium-sweet, a slight oaky oiliness and a nice citrus character. *Palate* – Quite full-bodied and sweet with touches of vanilla and tannin. *Finish* – Long and sweet, tannic and quite fresh. *Notes* – D.o.b.

1980, 21 yrs, 51.7% abv

Sweetness – 6	Peatiness – 4	Price – ✹✹✹

Colour – Straw with pale gold highlights. *Nose* – Rich, medium-to-full-bodied, quite fresh with sweet vanilla, a green, leafy character and a hint of Darjeeling tea; water opens up the toffee character, sweetness and a hint of coffee. *Palate* – Smooth, round, medium-dry with gently chewy tannins, quite lightly peated with a toffee-apple character. *Finish* – Long, quite fresh, quite tangy, fruity and complex. *Notes* – Blackadder Raw Cask bottling from cask no. 4915.

1968, 40% abv

Sweetness – 6	Peatiness – 3	Price – ✹✹✹✹✹

Colour – Straw with yellow/lemon highlights. *Nose* – Medium-sweet, grapey and rich with slight chocolate and nutty characters, caramel toffee and bubble-gummy notes. *Palate* – Medium-sweet, quite good body, rich and smooth with a coffee/toffee tang. *Finish* – Long, tangy with a coffee/toffee note, quite rich and clean. *Notes* – D.o.b.

1966, 40% abv

Sweetness – 6	Peatiness – 3	Price – ✹✹✹✹✹

Colour – Pale to mid-amber with gold highlights. *Nose* – Rich and quite full-bodied, medium-sweet oaky vanilla with a tang of orange and delicately peated. *Palate* – Medium-dry, quite full-bodied, oaky, spicy with characters of liquorice and vanilla, quite round. *Finish* – Quite long and complex, with rich liquorice/aniseed and a tail of oaky tannin. *Notes* – D.o.b.

Glenugie

Built by Donald McLeod & Co., Glenugie passed through the hands of a number of different owners over the years. More recently, in 1970, it was owned by Long John International, which was purchased by Whitbread & Co. Ltd in 1975, who were also at the time owners of Laphroaig distillery. Unlike many distilleries which had originally been breweries, Glenugie was converted into a brewery for a while before being turned back to distilling. Two stills.

Location – About three miles south of Peterhead, Glenugie sat below the A92, close to the sea.

Notes – The distillery buildings, with their cast-iron frames, were of an unusual and interesting design. Closed in 1983, the buildings have since been sold for use other than as a distillery.

Water – Springs in the local hills.

1966, 40% *abv*

Sweetness – 7	Peatiness – 4	Price – ∗∗∗

Colour – Quite full amber with old-gold highlights. *Nose* – Full and rich, quite sweet and delicately peated with a ripe fruitiness. *Palate* – Medium-sweet, rich and oaky with a green tang. *Finish* – Clean and lightly smoky with oaky characters. *Notes* – Gordon & MacPhail bottling.

Glenury

Built to provide a market for barley in a period of agricultural depression by Barclay, McDonald & Co. It was closed from 1925 to 1937, having been sold for £7500 to Joseph Hobbs the preceding year. He, in turn, sold it to Associated Scottish Distilleries Ltd in 1938 for £18,500. Glenury acted as the "Control Office" for all of ASD's distilleries and the site was landscaped and roads were built into the unit, making it a showpiece. ASD was bought by DCL in 1953 and Glenury was worked from that date by SMD. The licensees were John Gillon & Co. Ltd. Glenury was extensively rebuilt between 1965 and 1966, at which time it was doubled from two to four stills. Glenury was closed in 1985, its licence was cancelled in 1992 and the site was sold for development.

Location – On the north bank of the Cowie Water, on the northern outskirts of Stonehaven.

Notes – The water supply was also that of the town of Stonehaven. Glenury's founder, Captain Robert Barclay, was the local Member of Parliament. Through influence, he was given permission by King William IV to call his whisky "Glenury-Royal".

Water – The Cowie Water.

1978, 15 yrs, 62.3% abv

Sweetness – 4	Peatiness – 2	Price – ✱✱✱

Colour – Very pale with hints of watery-green and lemon-green highlights. *Nose* – Quite full-bodied, malty and almost dry with an apple hint and fresh lanolin characters. *Palate* – Medium-dry, round and smooth with a touch of spice and greenness, gentle tannins and lightly peated. *Finish* – Long, smooth and quite sweet. *Notes* – Signatory bottling from cask no. 9770.

12 yrs, 40% abv

Sweetness – 2	Peatiness – 7	Price – ✱✱✱

Colour – Mid-amber with gold highlights. *Nose* – Medium-bodied, quite dry, dark and smoky with a dry, burnt character. *Palate* – Dry, peaty, quite smooth and fragrant with a slight floral character at the back. *Finish* – Long, smoky and quite fresh. *Notes* – Gordon & MacPhail bottling.

1978, 14 yrs, 43% abv

Sweetness – 6	Peatiness – 3	Price – ✱✱✱

Colour – Very pale straw with pale lemon highlights. *Nose* – Light and fresh, medium-dry with a touch of richness and an appley character. *Palate* – Medium-sweet, good body, a slightly green character with good richness. *Finish* – Lasts well: good, rich and delicate with a dry tail. *Notes* – Blackadder International bottling.

1968, 36 yrs, 51.2% abv

Sweetness – 4	Peatiness – 6	Price – ✱✱✱✱✱

Colour – Mid-amber with honeyed old-gold highlights. *Nose* – Quite big-bodied, medium-dry and rich with a delicate heathery peat note; water pulls out a rubbery, almond-scented, Sherry note and some citrus. *Palate* – Big-bodied, quite rich and medium-dry, heather honey and tangerines, gently chewy with a firm nuttiness. *Finish* – Long and elegant with leathery, malty vanilla and some cardamom. *Notes* – D.o.b. in the Rare Malt series.

Highland Park

KIRKWALL, ORKNEY [H] [V] EST. 1798
Website: *www.highlandpark.co.uk*

Said to have been founded by David Robertson, Highland Park is Scotland's most northerly distillery. It had several different owners before coming into the hands of James Grant and family in March 1895. Enlarged from two to four stills in 1898 and operated by James Grant & Co. until 1935, when the company was purchased by Highland Distilleries Co. Ltd. Now a part of The Edrington Group.

Location – Sited on a hillside overlooking Scapa Flow to the south and Kirkwall to the north.

Notes – The distillery is built on the spot where the legendary 18th-century smuggler Magnus Eunson's bothy stood. A local beadle and preacher as well as a distiller, he apparently kept a stock of whisky under his pulpit. Hearing that his church was about to be searched by the excisemen, he had the kegs removed to the manse where a coffin lid was placed on top of them and they were shrouded in white cloth. Eunson and his "mourners" knelt in prayer next to it. When the excisemen entered, the whispered word "smallpox" quickly ended any idea of a search. Highland Park produces 35 tonnes of malt from its own malting floor every week, which supplies 20% of the distillery's requirements.

Water – The Crantit Spring and springs to the east which feed Cattie Maggie's quarry. Unusually, Highland Park's water supply is hard water which is rich in carbonates.

12 yrs, 40% abv

Sweetness – 3	*Peatiness – 6*	*Price – ✳*

Colour – Mid-amber with gold highlights. *Nose* – Creamy cereal, quite delicately peated and medium-sweet, the addition of water rounds it out and brings out a slightly green, vegetal edge. *Palate* – Medium-dry, clean with a cereal note, a touch of spice, quite tangy with a slightly unctuous oily character and a dark peat note with chocolate at the back. *Finish* – Long, leafy, medium-sweet, showing beeswax and honey. *Notes* – D.o.b.

15 yrs, 40% abv

Sweetness – 6	*Peatiness – 6*	*Price – ✳✳✳*

Colour – Mid-amber with gold highlights. *Nose* – Much sweeter than the 12 y.o., quite full-bodied, elegant, water reduces the sweetness and brings out liquorice/fennel notes. *Palate* – Medium-dry, a hit of oak, medium-bodied, less tangy than the 12 y.o., but a definite citrus note. *Finish* – Long, quite ethereal and elegant. *Notes* – D.o.b.

15 yrs, 46% abv

Sweetness – 6	*Peatiness – 6*	*Price – ✳✳*

Colour – Straw with pale lemon highlights. *Nose* – Quite full-bodied with creamy peat and coconut; water softens it, with a medium-sweet and very rich Muscat grapey character. *Palate* – Quite big-bodied, rich and medium-sweet with good peat and vanilla oak notes. *Finish* – Long, rich and quite ethereal. *Notes* – Alchemist bottling.

Sweetness – 4	Peatiness – 6	Price – ✳✳

Colour – Mid-amber with mid-gold highlights. *Nose* – Medium-sweet and rich with notes of chocolate and cocoa and dried fruits – apricots and raisins; with water, the wood characters of honey, vanilla and beeswax are more obvious. *Palate* – Quite big-bodied, medium-dry, gently chewy oaky vanilla, chocolate, beeswax and honey and a touch tangy. *Finish* – Long, big-bodied and elegant, drier than the younger expressions, with soft peat. *Notes* – D.o.b.

HIGHLAND PARK DISTILLERY KIRKWALL, ORKNEY ISLANDS

HVF006

PRODUCT OF SCOTLAND

HIGHLAND
PARK
ESTD 1798

SINGLE MALT SCOTCH WHISKY

HIGHLAND PARK 25 YEAR OLD HAS A RICH AMBER GLOW & TASTE OF SMOKINESS & HEATHER HONEY, WITH A HINT OF PEAT

48.1% vol.   DISTILLED IN KIRKWALL, ORKNEY ISLANDS, SCOTLAND   700ml

25 yrs, 48.1% abv

Sweetness – 5	Peatiness – 6	Price – ✳✳✳✳

Colour – Mid-amber with old-gold highlights. *Nose* – Oak, with almost a barbeque smoke character, water brings out slight honey, apple and beeswax notes with a touch of tarry rope and a slight oily fruitiness. *Palate* – Big-bodied, very rich and medium-dry, with oaky vanilla and coffee notes and dark peat at the back. *Finish* – Long, full-flavoured, a touch tangy, very, *very* elegant with a final note of chocolate ice cream. *Notes* – D.o.b.

27 yrs, 50% abv

Sweetness – 4	Peatiness – 4	Price – ✳✳✳

Colour – Amber with old-gold highlights. *Nose* – Medium-bodied, rich and toffeeyed with quite a dark peat note; water pulls out citrus oil and lime with a spirity character. *Palate* – Medium-dry and rich with a wee touch of spice, some citrus and red apple and delicately peated. *Finish* – Very long, clean and lingering with red apple skins, complex. *Notes* – Douglas Laing Old Malt Cask bottling.

AGED 30 YEARS

WHISKY MAKER

DISTILLERY MANAGER

SINGLE MALT SCOTCH WHISKY

48.1%vol. PRODUCT OF SCOTLAND 700ml

30 yrs, 48.1% abv

Sweetness – 4	Peatiness – 6	Price – ✱✱✱✱

Colour – Mid-amber with old-gold highlights. *Nose* – Rich, soft, medium-sweet and round showing chocolate orange, water brings out more orange/tangerine of a softer, riper aroma and peat. *Palate* – Medium-dry and of good weight, with fennel and chocolate peat characters and a slight green freshness underpinned by oaky vanilla. *Finish* – Long, very elegant, quite tangy with chocolate, tangerine, toffee and beeswax notes coming in on the tail. A very complex glassful. *Notes* – D.o.b.

1989, 51.7% abv

Sweetness – 5	Peatiness – 6	Price – ✱✱

Colour – Pale amber with pale gold highlights. *Nose* – Rich espresso coffee and chocolate, quite soft and delicate; water brings out perfume, violets and winey apples with hazelnuts and toffee. *Palate* – Smooth, medium-dry, softly peated, rich, perfumed with gently chewy, medium-sweet, toffeeyed oak. *Finish* – Long, quite full and ethereal, elegant and slightly tangy. *Notes* – Blackadder Raw Cask bottling from cask no. 10042 distilled 1 March 1989.

1984, 56.6% abv

Sweetness – 3	Peatiness – 6	Price – ✱✱✱

Colour – Pale amber with yellow highlights. *Nose* – Quite big and a solid peat note; water brings out the richness, roundness and fruit and softens the peat. *Palate* – Dry, quite big-bodied with an edge of richness and notes of caramel and citrus. *Finish* – Long, quite powerful and unctuous with quite rich oak and a hint of tablet. *Notes* – Duncan Taylor bottling.

1977, 19 yrs, 43% abv

Sweetness – 3	Peatiness – 5	Price – ✱✱

Colour – Very pale, watery straw with pale lemon highlights. *Nose* – Fresh, clean and medium-sweet with a note of rich mint, round with a delicate peatiness. *Palate* – Fresh, quite dry and smooth with good body. *Finish* – Long, elegant and ethereal. *Notes* – Signatory bottling from cask nos. 5778/9 distilled 29 December 1977.

Imperial

CARRON, MORAY [S] EST. 1881

Built by Thomas Mackenzie in 1897, ownership was transferred to Dailuaine-Talisker Distilleries the following year. It closed in 1899 and was silent until 1919. Became a part of DCL in 1925 and closed again. Reopened under the control of SMD when rebuilt in 1955. Doubled to four stills in 1965. Closed again in 1985 and sold to Allied Lyons in May 1989, who reopened it in 1991. Mothballed again in 1998 and sold to Pernod-Ricard in 2005, since when the site has been managed by Chivas Brothers.

Location – On an unclassified road between the A95 and B9012, some two miles south west of Aberlour in a hollow on the banks of the Spey and next to the former Carron railway station.

Notes – The distillery was designed by Elgin architect Charles Doig of red Aberdeen bricks within a framework of iron beams and frames. One of the malt kilns was surmounted by an enormous imperial crown which flashed and glittered in the sun. The crown, which by then had rusted, was taken down in 1955. It was one of the distilleries where experimentation on the technique of drying distillery effluent for use as cattle fodder was pioneered.

Water   The Ballintomb Burn.

1994, 46% abv

Sweetness – 7	Peatiness – 5	Price – ✱✱

Colour – Straw with pale yellow highlights. *Nose* – Fresh, medium-bodied and malty with toffee and a slight green edge; water softens and rounds with notes of crème caramel, oranges and a little tobacco. *Palate* – Rich vanilla ice-cream, quite full-bodied and medium-sweet with an orangey tang. *Finish* – Long, clean and sweet with a shortbread character and a little spice. *Notes* – Duncan Taylor bottling.

Inchgower

BUCKIE, BANFFSHIRE [S] EST. 1871

Built by Alexander Wilson & Co. as "the great distillery of Inchgower" to replace Tochineal which had become outdated and cramped. The company celebrated its centenary on 12 July 1922. It was purchased by Buckie Town Council for £1000 in 1936 and sold on to Arthur Bell & Sons in 1938, reputedly for £4000. Doubled to four stills in 1966. Now part of Diageo plc.

Location – On the north side of the A98 between Fochabers and Buckie.

Notes – A farm on the hill above the distillery was once the home of a noted local smuggler by the name of Macpherson. His still, well hidden at the back of the hill, was only discovered when some stray cattle dislodged a large piece of turf, thus exposing the still to the farmer driving his cattle home. Sad to say for Macpherson, the farmer was quick to tip off the excisemen and claim his reward.

Water – Springs in the Mendip Hills.

SPEYSIDE
SINGLE MALT
SCOTCH WHISKY

The *Oyster Catcher* is a common *sight* around the

INCHGOWER

distillery, which stands *close* to the *sea* on the mouth of the *RIVER SPEY* near *BUCKIE*. Inchgower, established in 1824, produces *one* of the most *distinctive single* malt whiskies in *SPEYSIDE*. It is a malt for the *discerning drinker* ~ a *complex* aroma precedes a *fruity, spicy* taste with a hint of *salt*.

AGED **14** YEARS

43% vol   Distilled & Bottled in SCOTLAND. INCHGOWER DISTILLERY. Buckie, Banffshire, Scotland   70 cl

14 yrs, 43% abv

Sweetness – 7	Peatiness – 3	Price – **

Colour – Straw with lemon-yellow highlights. *Nose* – Medium-sweet, quite light and fresh; water brings out citrus and apple, a richness and some honey, with lemon meringue pie on the end. *Palate* – Smooth, with creamy vanilla, medium-sweet, good body with juicy citrus. *Finish* – Long and clean, some espresso and some ginger and spice. *Notes* – D.o.b.

Inverleven

GLASGOW ROAD, DUMBARTON [L]   EST. 1938

Inverleven was built in 1938 by Hiram Walker & Sons within the site of the Dumbarton grain distillery and Ballantine's offices complex. It was licensed to George Ballantine & Son Ltd and closed in 1991. The distilling equipment has been dismantled and shipped out to Islay where the innovators at Bruichladdich are going to use them to rebuild the Port Charlotte distillery. The full complex was mothballed in 2002 and demolished in 2006.

Location – Next to the River Clyde in the centre of Dumbarton.

Notes – Two pot stills for malt whisky production at Dumbarton. There was also a third Lomond-type still which produced a heavier style of spirit known as Lomond.

Water – Loch Lomond.

INVERLEVEN, 1986, 40% *abv*

Sweetness – 6	*Peatiness* – 2	*Price* – ✱✱✱

Colour – Mid-amber with gold highlights. *Nose* – Delicate, light, mashy and medium-dry with apple and a floral note; water gives peaches and apple blossom with almost a touch of orange. *Palate* – Rich and medium-sweet with a dark fruit note, quite creamy with liquorice on the end. *Finish* – Light, very delicate, shortish even with a herby note. *Notes* – Gordon & MacPhail bottling.

LOMOND, 30 *yrs*, 60% **approx.**

Sweetness – 2	*Peatiness* – 3	*Price* – N/A

Colour – Pale star/amber with yellowy green highlights. *Nose* – Quite full-bodied with good richness and still with a touch of fresh greenness. *Palate* – Full, spirity, dry, but with a richness at the back, the greenness of the aroma is still present. *Finish* – Long, quite light and spicy. *Notes* – A cask sample supplied by Whyte & Mackay for a tasting tutored by Richard Paterson held at Christie's, Glasgow.

Isle of Arran

LOCHRANZA, ISLE OF ARRAN [A] [V] EST. 1995
Website: *www.arranwhisky.com*

Harold Currie had a dream. When he retired as managing director of Chivas Brothers, he wanted to create his own distillery. He found a site at Lochranza in the north of the island of Arran and built a modern distillery with the architectural appearance and feel of much older buildings. Very small, it dovetails perfectly with the rest of the island which is described as "Scotland in miniature".

Location – Immediately to the east of the village of Lochranza in the north of the island.

Notes – The only distillery on the Isle of Arran – the last (legal) distillery, at Lagg, in the south, closed in 1837. The manager, Gordon Mitchell, who had been there since the opening in 1995 till his retirement in September 2007, established a flock of ducks which swim in the water-cooling pond. The area is also home to a pair of eagles, which nest on the crags above the distillery and caused the initial building works to stop while they tended their young.

Water – Loch na Davie.

10 yrs, 46% abv

Sweetness – 6	Peatiness – 5	Price – *

Colour – Straw with gold and lemon highlights. *Nose* – Medium-bodied and malty with a green cereal note and a touch floral; water brings out a leafy note and notes of pine and cypress, some liquorice and ripe oranges. *Palate* – Medium-dry with good body, very clean and quite soft with a nice richness, a touch of spice, delicately peated and some citrus. *Finish* – Long, very clean, rich and fresh with hints of lemon/orange and honey on the tail. *Notes* – D.o.b.

100° PROOF, 57% *abv*

Sweetness – 5	Peatiness – 5	Price – ∗∗

Colour – Straw with pale gold and green highlights. *Nose* – Quite light, delicate, fresh and cerealy with apple and leafy notes; water brings out touches of mint and perfume with a soft, quite dark peat note. *Palate* – Medium-dry, rich and quite full with a stewed apple fruitiness, fresh and delicately peated. *Finish* – Long, clean, fruity and slightly floral. *Notes* – D.o.b.

AMARONE FINISH, No age statement, 55% *abv*

Sweetness – 5	Peatiness – 4	Price – ∗∗

Colour – Mid-amber with a rosé hue and rose-tinted gold highlights. *Nose* – Medium-bodied, herby – fennel and meaty; water draws out the richness, round, black fruits, black cherry and raisins with sweet vanilla. *Palate* – Very rich, medium-sweet, round, quite full-bodied and gently chewy with a touch of spice. *Finish* – Long, spicy, quite ethereal with cherries and red fruits bouncing up at the end. *Notes* – D.o.b. Finished in an Amarone della Valpolicella cask.

1995, 11*yrs*, 50% *abv*

Sweetness – 4	Peatiness – 4	Price – ∗∗

Colour – Pale straw with pale lemon highlights. *Nose* – Medium-bodied, quite rich with notes of green apple and liquorice; water brings out a warm, dark peat note and a herby character. *Palate* – Medium-dry, quite chewy, round and herby – oregano with a quite soft peat character. *Finish* – Long, clean, quite ethereal and with a slight fresh-baked bread character. *Notes* – Douglas Laing Old Malt Cask bottling from hogshead no. 3341 distilled November 1995.

Isle of Jura

CRAIGHOUSE, ISLE OF JURA, ARGYLL   [H] [V]   EST.   1810
Website: *www.isleofjura.com*

After passing through a number of owners in its early years, Jura blossomed in the late 1800s when it came into the hands of James Ferguson & Sons in 1875, being rebuilt at a cost of £25,000. However, it closed in the early 1900s because, it is said, of an argument over the rent, after which the distiller upped and went, taking his stills and equipment with him. Jura was abandoned until the late 1950s when it was championed by William Delme-Evans and a rebuilding programme was begun. The first spirit for more than 50 years flowed in 1963. Enlarged from two to four stills in 1978, it is now owned by Whyte & Mackay.

Location – Across from Islay, on the leeward east coast of Jura, on a bay where a string of islands forms a natural breakwater.

Notes – Records are said to trace distilling on Jura as far back as 1502. After the distillery had been rebuilt in the 1870s, it gained a reputation for being one of the most efficient in Scotland. However, it was once discovered that the spent wash from the stills was finding its way into a local cattle trough. The effect on the animals, it is said, was most interesting.

Water – Loch a'Bhaile Mhargaidh (Market Loch).

10 *yrs*, 40% *abv*

Sweetness – 3	Peatiness – 7	Price – *

Colour – Amber with pale gold highlights. *Nose* – Medium-bodied, fresh and delicately peated with a rich touch of fresh greenness to the peat and a slight toffee note. *Palate* – Quite big-bodied, rich, warm and round with quite a solid fresh peatiness. *Finish* – Long, rich, round and quite fresh with a nice belt of peat on the tail. *Notes* – D.o.b.

<h2 style="text-align:center">16 yrs, 40% abv</h2>

Sweetness – 4	Peatiness – 6	Price – **

Colour – Amber with old-gold highlights. *Nose* – Quite full-bodied, rich and quite buttery with floral notes of honey, citrus and a herbal (oregano) touch, the peat has an edge of liquorice. *Palate* – Quite full and rich with flavours of vanilla and toffee and a good belt of dry peat. *Finish* – Long, spicy and rich with a touch of liquorice and rich toffee on the tail. *Notes* – D.o.b.

<h2 style="text-align:center">25 yrs, 50% abv</h2>

Sweetness – 4	Peatiness – 7	Price – ****

Colour – Amber with old-gold highlights. *Nose* – Medium-bodied, dry and a wee bit austere; water rounds it out with richness, a dark peat note, some nuttiness and liquorice. *Palate* – Rich, full-bodied and medium-sweet with well-integrated peat, softly chewy tannins and a vegetal note at the back. *Finish* – Very long, tangy, elegant and well-balanced with tangerine on the tail. *Notes* – Douglas Laing Old Malt Cask bottling.

<h2 style="text-align:center">40 yrs, 46% abv</h2>

Sweetness – 3	Peatiness – 5	Price – *****

Colour – Deep amber with bronze and ruby highlights. *Nose* – Quite big and rich with hazelnut characters; fruit comes out with water, a touch of citrus – tangerines and apricots, quite delicate. *Palate* – Medium-dry, tangy and quite big-bodied with a dark, nutty flavour. *Finish* – Very long, surprisingly delicate with beeswax notes and a fresh, green edge to the peat. *Notes* – D.o.b.

<h3 style="text-align:center">SUPERSTITION, No age statement, 45% abv</h3>

Sweetness – 5	Peatiness – 7	Price – **

Colour – Amber with old-gold highlights. *Nose* – Big-bodied, rich with a dried fruity note and lots of peat; water gives rich nuttiness, toffee, marzipan, cocoa, heather honey with an earthy peat note. *Palate* – Quite big-bodied, medium-dry, but very rich and smooth with honey and a creaminess underpinned by solid, approachable peat. *Finish* – Long and impressively rich with a sweet edge, some liquorice and tideline notes with a note of pine needles on the end – complex. *Notes* – D.o.b. A vatting of young, heavily peated spring whisky and more mature whiskies.

Knockando

Built by the Knockando-Glenlivet Distillery Co. Owned by J. Thomson & Co. from 1900 to 1903. Acquired by W. & A. Gilbey in 1904. Now part of Diageo plc.

Location – South of the B9102 between Knockando and Archiestown, sited on the bank of the River Spey.

Notes – Much of the make is used in the J. & B. blend. An individual feature of the malt is that its bottle states the year of distillation and date of bottling. If you believe that whisky, like wine, has vintage years, then Knockando is worthy of a close study. Knockando is "cnoc an dhu" in the Gaelic, which means "little black hillock".

Water – The Cardnach Spring.

1992, 40% abv

Sweetness – 7	Peatiness – 3	Price – *

Colour – Pale amber with pale gold highlights. *Nose* – Medium-bodied with newly-sawn oak and a green, leafy note; water brings out fruit – sweet and ripe apples and peaches, a malty touch and some grassiness. *Palate* – Smooth, of good body, quite sweet and creamy with soft peat and a chocolate nuttiness. *Finish* – Long, clean, smooth and sweet with a slight nutty toffee end to the tail. *Notes* – D.o.b

1980, 46% abv

Sweetness – 7	Peatiness – 2	Price – **

Colour – Straw with pale yellow highlights. *Nose* – Quite fresh and rich with a slight hint of fresh green fruit and blossom; with water it opens out offering apples, honey, orange marmalade and a soft maltiness. *Palate* – Sweet, quite rich with notes of apple, vanilla, toffee and coffee. *Finish* – Long, soft and decadent with vanilla ice cream. *Notes* – Duncan Taylor bottling from cask no. 1912 distilled in July 1980.

Knockdhu

KNOCK, BANFFSHIRE [H] EST. 1893
Website: *www.inverhouse.com/distilleries-knockdhu*

Knockdhu, as the distillery is known, was the first to be built by the DCL, being licensed to John Haig & Co. Closed in 1983. Sold late 1988 to the Knockdhu Distillery Company Ltd, a subsidiary of Inver House Distillers plc and reopened in 1989. Two stills.

Location – West of the B9022, seven miles north of Huntly.

Notes – Built of local grey granite by Gordon & Macbey, architects of Elgin. The water supply, owned by the company, is piped from Knock Hill and is also supplied to the villagers of Knock. The distillery was occupied by a unit of the Indian Army from 1940 to 1945. As Inver House want to avoid confusion with, or suggestion of another brand of malt whisky, the single malt from Knockdhu is now marketed under the Gaelic name An Cnoc.

Water – A spring on the southern slopes of Knock Hill.

12 yrs, 43% abv

Sweetness – 6	Peatiness – 7	Price – *

Colour – Straw/amber with gold highlights. *Nose* – Fresh, medium-bodied, malty and medium-sweet with a touch of greenness. *Palate* – Sweet, round, quite full-bodied and lightly peated. *Finish* – Long, smooth and sweet with a green smokiness. *Notes* – D.o.b.

21 yrs, 57.7% abv

Sweetness – 7	Peatiness – 3	Price – ***

Colour – Pale amber with gold highlights. *Nose* – Quite full-bodied and medium-sweet, a quite creamy vanilla touch with notes of leafy apple. *Palate* – Medium-sweet, quite rich and gently chewy with quite a delicate peatiness and hints of toffee and coffee. *Finish* – Long, fresh toffeeyed and popcorn. *Notes* – D.o.b.

Ladyburn

Opened in 1966 by William Grant & Sons Ltd, Ladyburn has not produced any spirit since 1976. Four stills.

Location – Ladyburn is part of the complex which includes the Girvan grain distillery, between the A77 and the B741 to the north of the town of Girvan.

Notes – William Grant & Sons are also the proud owners of the Speyside malts Glenfiddich and The Balvenie, but Ladyburn is much harder to come by. William Grant have just announced (2007) that they are to reinstate malt whisky production at Girvan.

Water – Penwapple reservoir.

1973, 50.4% *abv*

Sweetness – 3	Peatiness – 4	Price – ✽✽✽✽✽

Colour – Mid-amber with old-gold highlights. *Nose* – Dry, spirity, earthy; with water, some beeswax comes out and a floral (violets) note, but with an overwhelming woodiness. *Palate* – Medium-dry and drying, some citrus attempting to come out but beeswax and drying oaky tannins are dominant, light peat character with some orange at the end. *Finish* – Long, but lots of drying oak with just a wee hint of fruit. *Notes* – D.o.b.

20 yrs, 46% *abv*

Sweetness – 4	Peatiness – 4	Price – ✽✽✽✽✽

Colour – Pale straw with lemon/gold highlights. *Nose* – Malty, lightly peated, leafy and slightly rich with an oily character. *Palate* – Almost dry, smooth, round, soft and peaty; quite simple, but with good body. *Finish* – Slightly smoky, a touch of spice and of reasonable length. *Notes* – Wm Cadenhead bottling.

Lagavulin

NEAR PORT ELLEN, ISLAY, ARGYLL   [I]   [V]   EST. 1816
Website: *www.malts.com/en-gb/Malts/summary/Lagavulin*

Originally two legal distilleries were set up on the site; the first, in 1816, was Lagavulin, founded by John Johnson. The second, the following year, was established by Archibald Campbell and is believed to have been known as Kildalton. In Alfred Barnard's report on his visit of 1886, he stated that the make was "principally sold in Glasgow, England and the Colonies". Lagavulin has long been an important constituent in the White Horse brand, becoming part of DCL in 1927 and managed by SMD/UMGD from 1930. Rebuilt in 1962 when the stills from Malt Mill (see below) were incorporated. Four stills. Now part of Diageo plc.

Location – Occupying a site of six acres, Lagavulin stands at the head of a small bay. The ruins of Dunyvaig castle are on the eastern mouth of the bay and an ancient fort is at the western side.

Notes – Lagganmhouillin, or Lagavulin, means "mill in the valley". Distilling on the site is thought to date from as early as 1742, when there were ten small bothies there. Mackie & Co., owners at the turn of the 20th century, were also the agents from neighbouring Laphroaig. When they lost the agency in 1907, they built a new distillery within the Lagavulin site to produce a similar style of whisky to Laphroaig. Called Malt Mill, it had its own maltings, which had a haircloth-floored kiln fired only with open peat fires. The Lagavulin mash tun was utilised, but there were two independent washbacks and two pear-shaped stills. Malt Mill closed in 1960.

Water – The Solan Lochs.

12 yrs, 40% abv

Sweetness – 2	Peatiness – 10	Price – ✱✱✱✱✱

Colour – Amber with old-gold highlights. *Nose* – Big, pungent, very peaty and tarry; water brings out a black-tea character, a bit of black pepper, a medicinal, maritime note – germolene, iodine and hospital wards. *Palate* – Powerful and pretty immense, seaweed as the tide starts to ebb, shellfish and carbolic soap with a hint of sweetness, all underpinned by a huge peat character. *Finish* – Peat, peat and more peat overpowering everything else and lasting a good two days. *Notes* – D.o.b.

16 yrs, 43% abv

Sweetness – 3	Peatiness – 10	Price – ✱✱

Colour – Deep amber with rich gold highlights. *Nose* – Distinctive, pungent, burnt heather, very peaty and full-bodied. *Palate* – Big, peaty, dry, very smooth and powerfully complex. *Finish* – Long and smoky with an almost burnt character, very persistent. *Notes* – D.o.b.

DISTILLER'S EDITION, 1979, 43% abv

Sweetness – 1	Peatiness – 9	Price 3 – ✱✱✱

Colour – Deep amber with bronze highlights. *Nose* – Dark, dry, quite powerful and tarry with a burnt stick and dried seaweed character. *Palate* – Dry, full-bodied, powerful, tangy seashore characters combined with wood fire. *Finish* – Long, good richness, a slight hint of sweetness and vanilla, but overpoweringly peaty. *Notes* – D.o.b. Finished in a Pedro Ximinez cask.

Laphroaig

NEAR PORT ELLEN, ISLAY, ARGYLL   [I]   [V]   EST. 1815

Website: www.laphroaig.com

Said to have been founded by Donald and Alex Johnston. Originally a farm distillery, records show distilling took place on the site in 1812. By 1815, when the forerunner of today's distillery opened, distilling had overtaken farming in importance to the Johnston family. Laphroaig remained in the Johnston family until 1954, when the then proprietor, Ian Hunter, bequeathed it to Bessie Williamson. At this time she was Company Secretary, having worked in the business for many years, and she went on to become a most important and respected figure in the Scotch whisky industry before she retired as Managing Director in 1972. Miss Williamson sold Laphroaig to Long John Distillers Ltd, part of the Seager Evans group, between 1962 and 1967. Operated by Allied from 1990 to 2005. Now part of Fortune Brands Inc. of the US.

Location – Situated on a small bay frequented by otters, swans and a pair of herons. It has been greatly influenced by the sea throughout its history.

Notes – Generally accepted as being the most individually flavoured of all single malts. Although Laphroaig, like all the distilleries on the island, is built on the coast, it has always been maintained that it is not only the sea air but the peat which accounts for the distinctiveness of the make. Laphroaig has its own floor maltings and the peat which it uses has a high proportion of moss in its content and this is said to give Laphroaig its particular flavour. Part of the site occupied by the modern Laphroaig distillery includes that of the old Ardenistle distillery (1837–c.1848).

Water – The Kilbride Dam.

10 yrs, 40% abv

Sweetness – 2	Peatiness – 10	Price – ✳

Colour – Palish amber with slightly greenish tones. *Nose* – Dry, heavy and peaty with a heathery smokiness. *Palate* – Full of character, very peaty and smoky with iodine/medicinal flavours. *Finish* – Lingering, smoky, smooth and unique. *Notes* – D.o.b.

ORIGINAL CASK STRENGTH, 10 yrs, 57.3% abv

Sweetness – 2	Peatiness – 10	Price – ✳✳

Colour – Amber with gold highlights. *Nose* – Big, full-bodied and powerful with a dark, burnt-heather peaty character, an ozone/wrack medicinal note and a slight hint of richness. *Palate* – Smooth and big-bodied with a chewy tarriness, smoky and dry, but with an edge of richness. *Finish* – Long, tangy, smoky and slightly chewy, powerful and complex. *Notes* – D.o.b.

BY APPOINTMENT TO HRH THE PRINCE OF WALES,
DISTILLER AND SUPPLIER OF SINGLE MALT SCOTCH WHISKY,
D. JOHNSTON & CO., (LAPHROAIG) ISLE OF ISLAY.

LAPHROAIG®

AGED YEARS

**ISLAY SINGLE MALT
SCOTCH WHISKY**

The most richly flavoured of all Scotch whiskies

EST'D **1815** EST'D

DISTILLED AND BOTTLED IN SCOTLAND BY
D. JOHNSTON & CO. , LAPHROAIG DISTILLERY, ISLE OF ISLAY

PRODUCT OF SCOTLAND

750 ml ℮   **43% alc./vol.**

2PBF8001

15 yrs, 43% abv

Sweetness – 2	Peatiness – 10	Price – ✳✳

Colour – Amber/peaty with good gold highlights. *Nose* – Peaty, full and medicinal with a slight fruity edge. *Palate* – Soft, smoky, round and smooth with a slightly sweet middle to the palate. *Finish* – Long, smoky and refined. *Notes* – D.o.b.

1976, 43% *abv*

Sweetness – 1	Peatiness – 10	Price – *****

Colour – Amber with old-gold highlights. *Nose* – Full-bodied, dark and pungent – an earthy coal-dust/seaweed character to the peat and notes of heather blossom/ violets and citrus oil. *Palate* – Big, dry, pungent and smoky with a nice edge of richness, vanilla, quite chewy tannins and violets. *Finish* – Long and quite elegant with a heathery softness in the middle and tangy poundings of the sea. *Notes* – D.o.b. Only available from the distillery.

30 *yrs*, 43% *abv*

Sweetness – 4	Peatiness – 8	Price – *****

Colour – Deep amber with dark-bronze highlights and a ruby hue. *Nose* – Big, powerful and rich with notes of apple and sherried rubber; water brings out more fruits, raisins, beeswax with some tar and seashore notes, some nuts – walnut and Hessian sacks. *Palate* – Big, rich, medium-dry and fruity with an underpinning of sea-soaked peat and a charred stick note. *Finish* – Long, round and impressive, some liniment and spice with almost a delicacy of peat. *Notes* – D.o.b.

LEAPFROG, 1987, 46% *abv*

Sweetness – 1	Peatiness – 10	Price – **

Colour – Straw with yellow highlights. *Nose* – Big-bodied, pungent, dry and malty with a full-bodied peat character and aromas of cornflakes. *Palate* – Powerful and sea-tainted, heather-peaty, dry and rich. *Finish* – Very long, softly perfumed, rich and intense. *Notes* – Murray McDavid bottling.

The ancient Kildalton Cross stands in the ruined churchyard at Kildalton, almost at the end of the road past Lagavulin, Laphroaig and Ardbeg distilleries.

Linkwood

Built by Peter Brown in 1821 and named after the estate on which it was built. The *Elgin Courant* of 10 April 1874 reported that the old buildings of Linkwood distillery were being pulled down and that new, more extensive buildings were being erected. By 1887, Linkwood had a 2000-gallon wash still and a 1,850-gallon spirit still, and was producing 50,000 gallons a year. It was bought by DCL in 1933 and managed by SMD/UMGD and rebuilt twice more: in 1962 and again in 1971, when a second distillery unit was built alongside the original, extending it from two to six stills. Now part of Diageo plc.

Location – On Linkwood Road, about half a mile to the east of the A941 south of Elgin.

Notes – A very picturesque distillery with a reservoir of water for cooling purposes, which is inhabited by swans, alongside the buildings. It is surrounded by woodlands, hence the name. Roderick Mackenzie, who was manager from 1945 to 1963, believed that the character of the spirit depended not just on the vessels in which it was made, but also on everything in its immediate environment. He is reputed not to have permitted even the removal of spiders' webs in case the character of the whisky were to alter as a result.

Water – Springs near Millbuies Loch.

SPEYSIDE
SINGLE MALT
SCOTCH WHISKY

LINKWOOD

distillery stands on the *River Lossie*,
close to *ELGIN* in *Speyside*. The *distillery*
has retained its *traditional atmosphere*
since its *establishment* in 1821
Great care has always
been taken to *safeguard* the
character of the *whisky* which has
remained the same through the
years. Linkwood is one of the
FINEST Single Malt Scotch Whiskies
available - *full bodied* with a *hint* of
sweetness and a *slightly smoky aroma*.

YEARS 12 OLD

43% vol   Distilled & Bottled in SCOTLAND
LINKWOOD DISTILLERY
Elgin, Moray, Scotland   70 cl

12 yrs, 43% abv

Sweetness – 7	Peatiness – 5	Price – *

Colour – Straw/amber with lemon highlights. *Nose* – Medium to full-bodied, medium-sweet with an appley character and a soft smokiness at the back. *Palate* – Good weight, medium-sweet, fruity and lightly smoky. *Finish* – Long and spicy with a nice edge of sweetness. *Notes* – D.o.b.

15 yrs, 40% abv

Sweetness – 7	Peatiness – 5	Price – *

Colour – Quite full amber with a tinge of green and gold highlights. *Nose* – Quite full-bodied, musty apples and oak, with a fresh smokiness. *Palate* – Medium-sweet and full-bodied with a touch of spice and oaky vanilla. *Finish* – Smooth and appley with a dry, smoky finish. *Notes* – Gordon & MacPhail bottling.

21 yrs, 40% abv

Sweetness – 8	Peatiness – 6	Price – **

Colour – Quite deep amber with bronze highlights. *Nose* – Smooth, dark and nutty with a touch of Demerara sugar, medium-sweet and rich with a musty apple aroma. *Palate* – Sweet, quite full-bodied and smooth with a delicate but firm peatiness. *Finish* – Long and sweet with just a hint of smokiness on the tail. *Notes* – Gordon & MacPhail bottling.

1985, 46% *abv*

Sweetness – 7	Peatiness – 5	Price – **

Colour – Amber with honeyed gold highlights. *Nose* – Quite full, rich and mature, with red apple characters; water makes it softer with honey, toffee and vanilla, a slightly meaty note and some nutmeg. *Palate* – Medium-sweet and rich with dry tannins, good body with well-integrated peat, apple and toffee. *Finish* – Long, rich and honeyed with apples lingering. *Notes* – Berry's Own Selection.

1982, 17 *yrs*, 64.2% *abv*

Sweetness – 7	Peatiness – 5	Price – **

Colour – Pale amber with yellow highlights. *Nose* – Medium-sweet, medium-bodied, quite peachy, malty and citrus-charactered, apple and a touch of vanilla with a little perfume on the tail. *Palate* – Big-bodied, rich, sweet, appley with a soft peat character. *Finish* – Long, fresh and appley with a touch of bubble-gummy fruitiness. *Notes* – Adelphi bottling from cask no. 4592.

1979, 14 *yrs*, 58.5% *abv*

Sweetness – 3	Peatiness – 6	Price – **

Colour – Deep, treacly amber with deep bronzeruby highlights. *Nose* – Big-bodied, burnt-wood peatiness, a dark nuttiness, medium-dry with the soft aroma of one of Leith's old tea warehouses. *Palate* – Big, burnt and almost dry with chewy tannins. *Finish* – Soft, rich, long, chewy and off-dry. *Notes* – Wm Cadenhead bottling.

Littlemill

BOWLING, DUNBARTONSHIRE   [L]   EST. 1772

The distillery has had numerous owners over its two centuries of operation, although its origins are somewhat obscure. Littlemill could have been Scotland's oldest distillery. It is possible that whisky was distilled on the site as long ago as the 14th century, when the Colquhouns built Dunglas Castle to guard the crossing of the Clyde. Around 1750 George Buchanan, a wealthy maltster from Glasgow, bought Littlemill when he purchased the Auchterlonie estate and in 1772 he had to build houses for the excise officers. Annual production in 1821 is recorded as 20,000 gallons. Rebuilt in 1875, Littlemill used triple distillation until the 1930s. The distillery closed in 1984 and was reopened by Gibson International in 1989. Following that company's failure late in 1994, Littlemill was taken over by Loch Lomond Distillery Co. Ltd. The distillery buildings have now been demolished.

Location – Between the main road, the A82 and the River Clyde at the foot of the Kilpatrick Hills, 19 km (12 miles) from Glasgow city centre, towards Dumbarton.

Notes – Although strictly speaking a Lowland distillery, this was another which took its water from north of the Highland Line. The stills were of an unusual design, with a rectifier attached to the spirit still.

Water – A spring in the Kilpatrick Hills.

8 yrs, 40% abv

Sweetness – 6	Peatiness – 1	Price –✹✹✹✹

Colour – Straw with yellow/gold highlights. *Nose* – Quite young, slightly mashy, with an unpeated green, new-mown grassiness, medium-dry and with quite good body. *Palate* – Fresh, quite mashy, medium-sweet and clean with good body. *Finish* – Quite rich and clean, of good length with just a suggestion of darkness at the end. *Notes* – D.o.b.

Loch Lomond

ALEXANDRIA, DUNBARTONSHIRE   [H]   EST. 1957

Built in 1965–66 by the Littlemill Distilling Co. Ltd. Barton Distilling (Scotland) operated it from 1971 until closure in 1984. It was bought by Glen Catrine Bonded Warehouse Ltd in 1986 and reopened in 1987. Now operated by a sister company, Loch Lomond Distillery Co. Ltd. It has three sets of stills, two sets with traditional bulbous bases, but with a rectifying column instead of a swan's neck, and one pair of traditional pot stills.

Location – Alexandria is at the southern end of Loch Lomond on the A82 Glasgow to Fort William road.

Notes – Produces no fewer than seven different malts, three of which are marketed as singles, the remaining four used solely for blending. There is also a continuous still on the site producing grain whisky (which has been lauded as the finest grain spirit in Scotland).

Water – Loch Lomond.

No age statement, 40% *abv*

Sweetness – 7	Peatiness – 4	Price – *

Colour – Amber with pale gold highlights. *Nose* – Quite full-bodied, malty, round and medium-dry with a quite soft, fresh, green peatiness and a hedgerow character. *Palate* – Quite sweet, round, smooth, quite delicately peated and fresh. *Finish* – Long, rich, clean. *Notes* – D.o.b.

OLD RHOSDHU, 10 *yrs*, 40% *abv*

Sweetness – 6	Peatiness – 4	Price – *

Colour – Amber with pale gold highlights. *Nose* – Fresh, medium-dry and youthful with a cereal note and quite gentle dark peat. *Palate* – Medium-sweet with a touch of richness, of good body, with delicate peat and a cereal note. *Finish* – Long, with a slight burnt note. *Notes* – D.o.b.

OLD RHOSDHU, 1985, 9 yrs, 60.5% abv

Sweetness – 6	Peatiness – 4	Price – ✳✳

Colour – Straw with lemon-yellow highlights. *Nose* – Quite full, young, spirity and mashy, a dry earthy smokiness with just an edge of sweetness. *Palate* – Medium-sweet, mashy and vegetal, medium-bodied. *Finish* – Sweet, cerealy, of medium length and with a burnt-toffee tail. *Notes* – Wm Cadenhead bottling.

INCHMURRIN, 10 yrs, 40% abv

Sweetness – 4	Peatiness – 6	Price – ✳

Colour – Amber with old-gold highlights. *Nose* – Youthful, fresh, mashy, rich and medium-dry with a good weight of peat. *Palate* – Quite sweet and fresh with good weight and a nice green note to the peat character. *Finish* – Long, clean and rich. *Notes* – D.o.b.

INCHMURRIN, 1985, 9 yrs, 64% abv

Sweetness – 4	Peatiness – 3	Price – ✳

Colour – Pale, watery straw with lemon highlights. *Nose* – Young, mashy, vegetal and dry with just a hint of sweetness at the back. *Palate* – Medium sweet, vegetal and mashy with a citrus note, slightly harsh and austere. *Finish* – Earthy, quite short and spirity. *Notes* – Wm Cadenhead bottling.

Palletised cask storage at Loch Lomond distillery

Lochside

MONTROSE, ANGUS   [H]   EST. 1957

Established on the site of Deuchar's brewery in 1957 by Joseph Hobbs, formerly of Associated Scottish Distillers, as a grain and malt distillery and blending and bottling plant. The towered building was unique in Scotland and owed much more to the architectural traditions of German breweries than those of Scottish distilleries. It was to be run by Hobbs under the operational company MacNab Distilleries Ltd. It was sold to Destilerias y Crianza de Whisky SA of Madrid in November 1973. It originally had four pot stills and one Coffey (grain) still; the latter was closed in 1970.

Location – At the north end of Montrose, at the junction of the Aberdeen to Dundee road (the A92) and the A935 from Montrose to Brechin.

Notes – All of the make used to be bottled at the distillery by MacNab Distilleries. A small loch once existed opposite the distillery, hence the name. The stills ceased production in the mid-1980s and the brauhaus building, which many locals regretted had never been listed, has been demolished to make way for a DIY store.

Water – A bore well beneath the distillery.

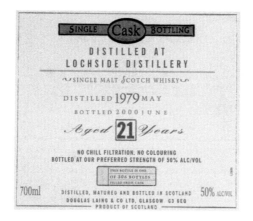

21 yrs, 50% abv

Sweetness – 4	Peatiness – 4	Price – **

Colour – Amber with pale gold highlights. **Nose** – Quite light and cerealy with a touch of perfume; water brings out gentle touches of honey and toffee, a hint of citrus and gunpowder. **Palate** – Medium-dry, quite soft and fresh with notes of oranges and cloves. **Finish** – Long, very clean and ethereal with quite a delicate peat note. **Notes** – Douglas Laing Old Malt cask bottling.

Longmorn

Built by the Longmorn Distillery Company, which was amalgamated with the Glenlivet and Glen Grant Distilleries and Hill, Thomson & Co. Ltd to form The Glenlivet Distilleries Ltd. Bought by Seagram in 1977 and sold to Pernod-Ricard in 2001. Extended from four to six stills in 1972 and eight in 1974.

Location – On the A941 Elgin to Rothes and Craigellachie road.

Notes – Professor R. J. S. McDowall considered Longmorn to be one of the four finest malts. The name Longmorn comes from the Gaelic "Llanmorgund", meaning "place of the holy man", the distillery reputedly being on the site of an ancient abbey. The distillery houses an old steam engine which is occasionally used, and it also has a disused water wheel. This malt is much favoured by blenders as a "top dressing" for their blends.

Water – Local springs.

15 yrs, 45% abv

Sweetness – 6	Peatiness – 4	Price – **

Colour – Mid-amber with gold highlights. *Nose* – Rich, full-bodied with soft oak and a cooked apples/grapey fruitiness, slightly peppery. *Palate* – Quite full-bodied, round, soft and smooth, medium-sweet with a delicate edge of smokiness and gentle tannins. *Finish* – Rich, smooth and elegant with just a touch of smokiness. *Notes* – D.o.b.

12 yrs, 40% abv

Sweetness – 6	Peatiness – 5	Price – *

Colour – Amber with old-gold highlights. *Nose* – Medium-bodied, a light, sweet smokiness, a touch of creamy toffee and an almost menthol character. *Palate* – Medium-dry, round, slightly creamy and smooth with a dark nuttiness. *Finish* – Long and nutty with a slight fragrant smokiness and a floral tail. *Notes* – Gordon & MacPhail bottling.

12 yrs, 58.6% abv

Sweetness – 8	Peatiness – 3	Price – *

Colour – Pale/mid-amber with pale yellow/gold highlights. *Nose* – Sweet, unctuous banana fruitiness with quite good body and delicately peated. *Palate* – Sweet, round, soft and full-flavoured, gently tannic with a good, clean, chocolatey peatiness. *Finish* – Long, sweet, rich and lingering with a smooth, oaky vanilla background. *Notes* – Blackadder Limited Editions bottling.

30 yrs, 50% abv

Sweetness – 8	Peatiness – 3	Price – ****

Colour – Amber with pale gold highlights. *Nose* – Warm and rich with a touch of perfume and hazelnuts; water pulls out apple/peach and a fresh touch of greenness. *Palate* – Medium-bodied, medium-sweet, soft and creamy with a medium peat character. *Finish* – Rich, long, elegant and velvety smooth. *Notes* – Douglas Laing Old Malt Cask bottling.

1990, 16 yrs, 58.3% abv

Sweetness – 8	Peatiness – 4	Price – **

Colour – Pale amber with yellow highlights. *Nose* – Round and medium-bodied with notes of apple and vanilla with a medium peat character; water brings out an aroma of vegetable broth, some acetone, sweet vanilla and cigar tobacco. *Palate* – Smooth, medium-sweet, quite rich and gently chewy with a soft peat character. *Finish* – Long and medium-sweet with a touch of richness and a note of honeycomb. *Notes* – Blackadder Raw Cask bottling from cask no. 30051.

1988, 46% abv

Sweetness – 9	Peatiness – 3	Price – **

Colour – Pale amber with lemon highlights. *Nose* – Sweet with a spirity apple aroma and some liquorice; with water, the fruit becomes tangerines, ripe apples and peaches with rich honey. *Palate* – Rich, round, sweet muscovado sugar, honey, toffee and wet cardboard. *Finish* – Long, rich and sweet with a little hit of peat on the end. *Notes* – Berry's Own bottling from cask no. 010.

1972, 31 yrs, 45% abv

Sweetness – 7	Peatiness – 3	Price – ****

Colour – Dark amber with deep bronze highlights and a ruby hue. *Nose* – Mature and dark, Olde English marmalade and beeswax; water softens it, bringing out brazil nuts, dark syrup, treacle, ripe banana and coconut. *Palate* – Rich, medium-sweet, of good body with gentle peat, honey and a creamy note. *Finish* – Long, rich with a backbone of oak which is not too dominant, banana, even pineapple and dark chocolate – very complex. *Notes* – Blackadder bottling.

Longrow

Longrow is a particular type of malt produced occasionally from two of the stills within Springbank distillery.

Location – In the centre of Campbeltown.

Notes – Although the current brand was introduced only in 1973, the name was originally given to a distillery that once stood next door to Springbank and was said to have been founded in 1824. It had closed by 1896. The old Longrow site is now Springbank's car park. Historically, very little *Longrow* has been released.

Water – Crosshill Loch and a spring on the premises.

10 yrs, 46% abv

Sweetness – 4	Peatiness – 7	Price – ✳

Colour – Amber with gold highlights. *Nose* – Big-bodied, fresh and smoky with a fresh, green peatiness, creamy, rich and medium-sweet. *Palate* – Big, quite pungent and smoky, yet soft with a liquorice character and medium-dry. *Finish* – Long, tangy and peaty, finishing with a note of cocoa. *Notes* – D.o.b.

25 yrs, 46% abv

Sweetness – 3	Peatiness – 7	Price – ✲✲✲✲✲

Colour – Amber with pale old-gold highlights. *Nose* – Quite big-bodied, fresh and rich with a slightly green edge to a quite heavy peat character. *Palate* – Medium-dry, quite full-bodied, round and creamily smooth with flavours of vanilla and honey and a solid peatiness. *Finish* – Long, fresh and quite pungent with a green edge. *Notes* – D.o.b.

LONGROW SHERRY, 1974, 10 yrs, 46% abv

Sweetness – 4	Peatiness – 7	Price – ✲✲✲✲✲

Colour – Amber with old-gold highlights. *Nose* – Surprisingly delicate, nutty and darkly peaty with a touch of richness and hints of beeswax and citrus. *Palate* – Quite delicate, soft, medium-dry and of good body with a nice dollop of peat. *Finish* – Long, rich, round and warmly nutty. *Notes* – D.o.b.

LONGROW TOKAJI WOOD EXPRESSION, 10 yrs, 55.6% abv

Sweetness – 6	Peatiness – 5	Price – ✲✲

Colour – Quite dark amber with bronze highlights. *Nose* – Quite full, soft and round with tablet, fudge and toffee notes; water brings out the peat and a green, almost vegetal, touch. *Palate* – Rich, medium-sweet and youthful with a little spice, some citrus and a dry peat character, gently chewy. *Finish* – Long and quite ethereal with juicy ripe oranges. *Notes* – D.o.b. Matured for 8 years in Bourbon wood and 2 years in fresh Tokaji wood.

Stillhouse at Springbank distillery

The Macallan

CRAIGELLACHIE, MORAY   [S] [V]   EST. 1824
Website: *www.themacallan.com*

Until the bridge at Craigellachie was built by Thomas Telford in 1814, the ford across the Spey at Easter Elchies was one of the few on the river. It was much used by cattle drovers and whisky distilled at the old farm distillery which preceded the licensed distillery was a popular feature of the river crossing for them. The licensed distillery was founded by Alexander Reid in 1824. Macallan was, until quite recently, controlled by successors of Roderick Kemp who purchased it in 1824. The distillery was extended in the early 1950s and again in 1959, but the demand for Macallan fillings was such that it was doubled from six to twelve stills in 1965, increased to eighteen in 1974 and to twenty-one in 1975. The stills are small. In 1996, the family interests were bought out by a partnership of Highland Distillers and Suntory. Suntory were bought out when Edrington took the company back into private hands in 1999.

Location – On a hillside overlooking the Spey with the old Easter Elchies house now magnificently refurbished as corporate offices.

Notes – The company's own bottlings are sold as *The Macallan*. The makers of *The Macallan* have long championed the use of Sherry casks for maturing whisky, but more recently have released Bourbon-matured expressions in their Fine Oak range. Old vintages of *The Macallan* are much sought after and very valuable. One bottle was bought for £12,000 in 1997.

Water – From bore holes.

10 yrs, 40% abv

Sweetness – 7	Peatiness – 4	Price – *

Colour – Mid-amber with old-gold highlights. *Nose* – Full, sherried, nutty and rich with notes of honey and dried fruits – banana, pears and apricots and a hint of Demerara sugar. *Palate* – Sweet, full-bodied and rich with good peat integration. *Finish* – Long and sherried with sweet vanilla notes. *Notes* – D.o.b.

FINE OAK, 10 *yrs*, 40% *abv*

Sweetness – 7	Peatiness – 6	Price – *

Colour – Amber with gold highlights. *Nose* – Medium-dry, malty and quite darkly aroma-ed with definite notes of suet dumplings, honey and a herbal touch over the dark peat. *Palate* – Medium-sweet and quite rich, it has a surprisingly tarry (for The Macallan) peat note with secondary flavours of cinnamon, cloves and red apple. *Finish* – Long, quite elegant, clean and malty with a touch of spice on the tail. *Notes* – D.o.b. Matured in a mix of Bourbon and Sherry oak.

FINE OAK, 15 *yrs*, 43% *abv*

Sweetness – 7	Peatiness – 4	Price – **

Colour – Mid-amber with honeyed gold highlights. *Nose* – Clean and fresh with aroma notes of butterscotch, ginger, rich lemon zest, lime and orange. *Palate* – Medium-sweet with spicy syrup and apple notes. *Finish* – Long and gorgeous, richly decadent and complex. *Notes* – D.o.b. Matured in a mix of Bourbon and Sherry oak.

FINE OAK, 21 *yrs*, 43% *abv*

Sweetness – 7	Peatiness – 4	Price – ****

Colour – Mid-amber with old-gold highlights. *Nose* – Rich and full-bodied, with beeswax and floral notes – violets; water softens it to honey, toffee and butterscotch with a spicy layer, ginger and mixed spice. *Palate* – Rich and medium-sweet with velvety smooth vanilla and sticky toffee, good body with a toffee apple flavour. *Finish* – Long, spicy and elegant with a touch of cocoa on the tail. *Notes* – D.o.b. Matured in a mix of Bourbon and Sherry oak.

FINE OAK, 30 *yrs*, 43% *abv*

Sweetness – 7	Peatiness – 6	Price – *****

Colour – Mid-amber with old-gold highlights. *Nose* – Almost tarry rope smoky notes which mingle with lime, tangerine and dried apricots. *Palate* – Medium-sweet, big-bodied, soft and round with a gentle touch of oak – butterscotch, beeswax and honey. *Finish* – Long and elegant, with good grip and showing floral, fragrant and perfumed notes over butterscotch and ripe citrus fruits. *Notes* – D.o.b. Matured in a mix of Bourbon and Sherry oak.

PROVENANCE, 12 *yrs*, 50% *abv*

Sweetness – 7	Peatiness – 2	Price – ✳✳

Colour – Very pale straw with water white highlights. *Nose* – Medium-bodied and rich with notes of Sherry-rubber and a leafy greenness; it opens out with water, giving green apple, honey, citrus oil/lemon zest and a slightly unctuous, oily, rancio note. *Palate* – Very rich, round with citrus – orange marmalade and smooth, like velvet. *Finish* – Long and intense with a flavour of satsumas and a wee touch of smoky peat and cigars on the tail. *Notes* – Douglas Laing Old Malt Cask bottling.

1982, 18 *yrs*, 43% *abv*

Sweetness – 7	Peatiness – 4	Price – ✳✳✳✳

Colour – Amber with old-gold highlights. *Nose* – Big-bodied, rich, fresh, sweet and sherried with notes of honey and apple and darkly peaty. *Palate* – Quite full-bodied, sherried and medium-sweet with a honeyed character, gently chewy with quite a delicate peatiness, darkly smoky and quite elegant. *Finish* – Long, elegant, richly smoky, sherried and toffeeyed. *Notes* – D.o.b.

1946, 46.6% *abv*

Sweetness – 4	Peatiness – 5	Price – ✳✳✳✳✳

Colour – Mid-amber with gold highlights. *Nose* – Big, medium-sweet and nicely mature with full notes of oaky vanilla and quite a heavy peat note. *Palate* – Medium-dry, with an edge of richness, chewily tannic with a sweet oak character and quite delicately peated. *Finish* – Long and chewy with just a hint of sweetness; quite elegant, if a little austere. *Notes* – D.o.b.

Macduff

BANFF, BANFFSHIRE   [H]   EST. 1962

Built 1962–63 by a consortium which included George Crawford, Morty Dykes and Brodie Hepburn. Acquired by William Lawson in 1972, which became part of the General Beverage Corporation, a Luxembourg company which controls Martini & Rossi's worldwide interests. Extended from two to three stills in 1966 and to four in 1968. Now a subsidiary of Bacardi Ltd.

Location – Situated to the east of Banff on the east bank of the River Deveron, about half a mile from the Moray Firth.

Notes – William Lawson bottlings take the name *Glen Deveron* from the River Deveron valley rather than that of the distillery itself. A five-year-old version is sold in Italy. It can be obtained from independent bottlers as *Macduff.*

Water – The Gelly Burn.

GLEN DEVERON, 10 *yrs*, 40% *abv*

Sweetness – 6	Peatiness – 4	Price – *

Colour – Amber with light-gold highlights. *Nose* – Fresh, malty, quite full-bodied and medium-dry with delicate but solid peat, with a slight fresh green edge, a touch of liquorice and a hint of nuttiness. *Palate* – Medium-sweet, quite full-bodied, very clean and creamily smooth with a nice dark peaty character. *Finish* – Long, soft, very fresh and clean with a touch of spice. *Notes* – D.o.b.

MACDUFF, 32 *yrs*, 50% *abv*

Sweetness – 5	Peatiness – 5	Price – ***

Colour – Mid-amber with gold highlights. *Nose* – Big-bodied, rich and honeyed with notes of shortbread and tablet; water brings out charred oak, burnt fruitcake and burnt rope notes. *Palate* – Of good body, with notes of apple and beeswax, medium-dry and with quite chewy tannins. *Finish* – Long, medium-dry and quite ethereal with a slight green peat note. *Notes* – Douglas Laing Old Malt Cask bottling.

Mannochmore

ELGIN, MORAY   [S]   EST. 1971

Established by SMD in 1971 and licensed to John Haig & Co., Mannochmore was built on the same 25-acre (10-hectare) site as the older Glenlossie (1876). Mannochmore does not utilise a purifier between the lyne arm and condenser as Glenlossie does. Part of Diageo plc. Mothballed in 1985, but reopened in 1989. Six stills.

Location – Sited next to Glenlossie at Thomshill on an unclassified road to the west of the A941, two miles south of Elgin.

Notes – Previously not available as a single, Mannochmore is important to a number of blends, including Haig.

Water – The Bardon Burn.

SPEYSIDE
SINGLE MALT *SCOTCH WHISKY*

MANNOCHMORE

distillery stands a few miles *south* of Elgin in *Morayshire*. The nearby *Millbuies Woods* are rich in birdlife, including the Great *Spotted* Woodpecker. The *distillery* draws process *water* from the Bardon Burn, which has its source in the MANNOCH HILLS, and *cooling water* from the Gedloch Burn and the *Burn of Foths*. Mannochmore *single MALT WHISKY* has a *light, fruity* aroma and a *smooth,* mellow *taste.*

43% vol   AGED 12 YEARS   70 cl

Distilled & Bottled in *SCOTLAND*. MANNOCHMORE DISTILLERY. Elgin, Moray, *Scotland*.

12 *yrs*, 43% *abv*

Sweetness – 5	Peatiness – 3	Price – ✳✳

Colour – Vey pale, almost watery with lemon highlights. *Nose* – Quite full, cerealy and yeasty with green fruit, medium-dry and quite lightly peated. *Palate* – Medium-dry, mashy, quite fresh, clean and aromatic. *Finish* – Light and clean with a hint of coffee, lasts well. *Notes* – D.o.b.

LOCH DHU, THE BLACK WHISKY, 10 *yrs*, 40% *abv*

Sweetness – 4	Peatiness – 6	Price – ✳✳✳✳

Colour – A very deep black heart with an amber/garnet edge and a ruby hue. *Nose* – Full, rich, dark and nutty with a slight winey sweetness. *Palate* – Quite full-bodied, medium-dry and smooth with slightly chewy tannins. *Finish* – Long and gently chewy. *Notes* – D.o.b. UDV finished in heavily charred casks for this bottling. Originally derided by connoisseurs, it is now changing hands for in excess of £200.

Millburn

Said to have been founded by a Mr Welsh. The earliest recorded reference dates from 1825, when James Rose and Alexander Macdonald were named as the licence holders. Used as a flour mill in 1853, it was rebuilt and reopened on 28 December 1876. It was then remodelled internally in 1898. Owned from 1921 to 1937 by gin distillers Booth's, who were themselves taken over by DCL in that year. Management was transferred to SMD in 1943. There were two stills.

Location – Millburn was located about one mile east of the centre of Inverness, on the banks of the Mill Burn from which the distillery and the district take their name.

Notes – Fire broke out on 26 April 1922, but the local fire brigade, "greatly assisted" by the Cameronian Highlanders, saved the stillhouse and the storage warehouses. The commander of the 3rd Battalion, Lt-Col David Price Haig, had owned the distillery until 1921. The site was sold for property development in 1988 and the buildings remain as the Beefeater Distillery Restaurant.

Water – Loch Duntelchaig.

1975, 18 yrs, 58.9% abv

Sweetness – 5	Peatiness – 7	Price – ✳✳✳

Colour – Very pale amber with pale lemon highlights. *Nose* – Medium to full-bodied with a dark, deep, smoky character, quite pungent and medium-dry. *Palate* – Quite round with good peaty smokiness and a touch of bitter chocolate. *Finish* – Long and clean with an edge of richness, quite smoky with gentle oaky tannins. *Notes* – D.o.b. from the Rare Malts Collection.

1975, 25 yrs, 61.9% abv

Sweetness – 5	Peatiness – 7	Price – ✳✳✳

Colour – Mid-amber with old-gold highlights. *Nose* – Full-bodied, rich, medium-sweet and nutty; water brings out toffee and cocoa, some dusty smoke and a sweet, almost biscuity note. *Palate* – Quite big and peaty, medium-dry, some orange and vanilla, burnt, boiled potatoes and apples. *Finish* – Lasts well with some spice and some tarry smoke. *Notes* – D.o.b. from the Rare Malts Collection.

1983, 11 yrs, 59.7% abv

Sweetness – 7	Peatiness – 4	Price – ✳✳✳

Colour – Mid-amber with yellow/gold highlights. *Nose* – Medium-bodied with a slight richness, medium-sweet with a green smokiness. *Palate* – Medium-sweet, rich and round with gentle peatiness and a slight nuttiness. *Finish* – Sweet and rich, quite full and smooth. *Notes* – Wm Cadenhead bottling.

1971, 40% abv

Sweetness – 6	Peatiness – 5	Price – ✳✳✳

Colour – Mid-amber/straw with gold/yellow highlights. *Nose* – Rich, medium-sweet, delicately peated with touches of oily nuttiness. *Palate* – Medium-dry, gently smoky, medium to full-bodied, smooth and round. *Finish* – Soft with a touch of spiciness, quite long and gently smoky. *Notes* – Gordon & MacPhail bottling.

1966, 40% abv

Sweetness – 6	Peatiness – 6	Price – ✳✳✳

Colour – Deep, syrupy golden. *Nose* – Woody, spirity and dryish. *Palate* – Round and medium-sweet, slightly woody with a touch of fruit. *Finish* – A little flat spot and then finishes well and dry. *Notes* – Gordon & MacPhail bottling.

Miltonduff

Said to have been founded by Pearey & Bain, Miltonduff came into the ownership of Hiram Walker in 1936. The distillery was extended in the mid-1890s and was largely rebuilt in 1974–75. Acquired by Pernod-Ricard and operated by Chivas Brothers. Six stills. In addition, two Lomond stills were installed in 1964; the Lomond stills produced a different style of malt known as *Mosstowie* and they were dismantled in 1981.

Location – West of the B9010 to the south of Elgin. A short distance away across the River Lossie are the ruins of Pluscarden Abbey.

Notes – In the 18th and 19th centuries, the waters of the Black Burn supplied scores of illicit stills in the Glen of Pluscarden, the fertile barley-rich plain being ideal for their situation. Miltonduff is the principal malt associated with Ballantine's Scotch Whisky.

Water – The Black Burn.

12 yrs, 40% abv

Sweetness – 9	Peatiness – 3	Price – *

Colour – Straw/golden with greenish edges. **Nose** – Medium to full-bodied, fragrant, slightly floral and sweet. **Palate** – Sweet, fruity, full and round. **Finish** – Almost delicate, refined and long. **Notes** – D.o.b.

1980, 26 *yrs*, 48% *abv*

Sweetness – 7	*Peatiness* – 2	*Price* – ***

Colour – Mid-amber with gold highlights. *Nose* – Medium-bodied, quite fresh and leafy with notes of honey and green apple; water brings out beeswax and toffee. *Palate* – Soft, medium-sweet and velvety smooth, gently chewy with delicate peat and a hint of mint, some toffee, honey and apple. *Finish* – Long, quite intense and vanilla-scented with flavours of toffee and tablet. *Notes* – Dewar Rattray bottling from Bourbon cask no. 12502 distilled 16 September 1980.

MOSSTOWIE, 1975, 40% *abv*

Sweetness – 6	*Peatiness* – 4	*Price* – ***

Colour – Amber with old-gold highlights. *Nose* – Medium-bodied and medium-sweet with a touch of toffee and quite delicately peated. *Palate* – Round, smooth and medium-sweet with a slight fruitiness, a touch of spice, good weight and softly smoky. *Finish* – Long, clean and delicately smoky. *Notes* – Gordon & MacPhail bottling.

The River Spey

Mortlach

DUFFTOWN, BANFFSHIRE   [S]   EST. 1823

The first of Dufftown's seven stills. Founded by James Findlater, for a time it was owned by J. & J. Grant of Glen Grant who removed the distilling utensils. It lay unoccupied for some years, the barley granary serving as a Free Church during the Disruption until a Free Church building could be erected. Extended from three to six stills in 1897. Acquired by John Walker & Son in 1923, by which time it was the largest distillery in the area. Walker's joined DCL in 1925 and management passed to SMD in 1936. The old Mortlach was demolished and rebuilt in the early 1960s, re-opening in 1964. Now part of Diageo plc.

Location – Sited at the junction of the A941 and B9014 on the eastern outskirts of Dufftown.

Notes – In the hollow in which the distillery lies (Mortlach means "bowl-shaped valley") was fought the battle, in 1010, at which the Scots King Malcolm II defeated the Danes. Tradition has it that the distillery is on the site of an illicit still which drew its water from a spring called Highland John's Well. With the exception of 1944, Mortlach had permission to stay open during the Second World War.

Water – Springs in the Conval Hills.

SPEYSIDE
SINGLE MALT
SCOTCH WHISKY

MORTLACH

was the first of seven
distilleries in *Dufftown*. In the
(10th *farm animals* kept in
adjoining byres were fed on
barley left over from processing.
Today *water* from springs in
the *CONVAL HILLS* is used to
produce this delightful
*smooth, fruity single
MALT SCOTCH WHISKY.*

A G E D **16** Y E A R S

Distilled & Bottled in *SCOTLAND*
MORTLACH DISTILLERY
Dufftown, Keith, Banffshire, *Scotland*

43% vol   70 cl

16 yrs, 43% abv

Sweetness – 7	Peatiness – 5	Price – ✳✳

Colour – Deep amber with old-gold highlights. *Nose* – Full-bodied, deep, dark and nutty, gently peated. *Palate* – Full, dark, rich and nutty, big-bodied, smooth and round with soft, oaky vanilla notes. *Finish* – Long, full-flavoured, smooth and darkly Sherry cask-nutty. *Notes* – D.o.b.

1996, 46% abv

Sweetness – 7	Peatiness – 6	Price – ✳

Colour – Straw with pale lemon highlights. *Nose* – Big-bodied, chunky and peaty with a slight lemon tinge; water brings out quite a pungent note to the peat supported by ripe apples and honey. *Palate* – Big-bodied, chunky and rich with ripe apricots and apples, a milk chocolate note to the peat and unctuous oak. *Finish* – Long, impressive, powerful and complex. *Notes* – Berry's Own bottling from cask no. 999.

1980, 19 yrs, 59.3% abv

Sweetness – 7	Peatiness – 6	Price – ✳✳✳

Colour – Deep amber with old-gold highlights. *Nose* – Quite big-bodied with a solid, dark, charred oak peat character, medium-dry with a touch of caramel. *Palate* – Medium-sweet, quite a big peaty character, slightly medicinal and gently chewy. *Finish* – Long, quite powerful and pungent with chewy caramel/toffee. *Notes* – Adelphi bottling from cask no. 2166.

1942, 50 yrs, 40% abv

Sweetness – 5	Peatiness – 5	Price – ✳✳✳✳✳

Colour – Full amber with old-gold highlights. *Nose* – Full, rich and dark, medium-sweet, oaky vanilla with a lightly charred smoky character. *Palate* – Full-bodied, round and rich with an edge of dryness, medium-dry with oaky tannins. *Finish* – Long, spicy and delicately smoky with firm tannins. *Notes* – Gordon & MacPhail bottling.

Trains don't stop here any more . . .

North Port

BRECHIN, ANGUS   [H]   EST. 1820

Founded by David Guthrie, a local farmer, Alfred Barnard referred to it as Brechin distillery. It originally traded as Townhead Distillery Co., the company name changing to Brechin Distillery Co. in 1823. Barnard wrote: "The district around Brechin being highly cultivated, barley of the highest quality is grown and carted" to the distillery, "where nothing but the best barley is malted". Run by SMD since 1922 and licensed to John Hopkins & Co. Ltd, the distillery had two stills. It was closed in 1983 and has since been demolished.

Location – Sited north-west of the town centre of Brechin.

Notes – North Port took its name from the north gate in the ancient city walls, now long since vanished. It was very much a "family" employer, with sons following fathers into the business.

Water – Loch Lee, which is also the town's supply.

1970, 40% *abv*

Sweetness – 7	Peatiness – 6	Price – ✱✱✱

Colour – Gold with yellow highlights. *Nose* – Sweet with heather-honey aromas and rich. *Palate* – Medium-sweet, full and round. *Finish* – Strangely slightly astringent, but lasts well. *Notes* – Gordon & MacPhail bottling.

1976, 17 yrs, 64.1% *abv*

Sweetness – 4	Peatiness – 6	Price – ✱✱✱

Colour – Pale amber with yellow highlights. *Nose* – Quite light with a burnt-oak tang and a touch of perfume, a slight earthy peatiness and medium-dry. *Palate* – Quite big and medium-dry with slightly oaky tannins. *Finish* – Long with a tail of richness and toffee. *Notes* – Wm Cadenhead bottling.

Oban

STAFFORD STREET, OBAN, ARGYLL   [H] [V]   EST. 1794
Website: *www.malts.com/en-gb/Malts/summary/Oban*

Oban distillery was built, fortress-like, jammed between the cliff, on which sits McCaig's Folly, and the main street, by the Stevenson family, founders of the town of Oban. It was rebuilt between 1883 and 1887 by Walter Higgin. It became part of DCL in 1925 and has been operated by SMD/UMGD since 1930. Licensed to John Hopkins & Co. The stillhouse was rebuilt in 1969–72 and has two stills. Now part of Diageo plc.

Location – In the centre of Oban overlooking the harbour.

Notes – During enlargement in August 1890, a cave was discovered which contained bones from the Mesolithic era (4500–3000 BC). These remains are now to be found at the National Museum of Antiquities in Edinburgh. Oban's nose and flavour are reminiscent of Bowmore.

Water – Two lochs in Ardconnel, one mile inland from the town.

14 yrs, 43% abv

Sweetness – 5	Peatiness – 7	Price – ✳✳

Colour – Very pale straw with gold highlights. **Nose** – Medium-sweet and lightly peated, quite rich with a slight burnt heather character. **Palate** – Smooth, lightly sweet and creamy with a very delicate peatiness. **Finish** – Smoky, dry and delicate. **Notes** – D.o.b.

THE
Distillers
Edition

DISTILLED
1992
BOTTLED 2006

OBAN
'Little Bay of Caves'
DOUBLE MATURED
WEST HIGHLAND
SINGLE MALT
SCOTCH WHISKY

SPECIAL RELEASE
OD 155.FR
LIMITED EDITION

43% vol.   OBAN DISTILLERY OBAN ARGYLL SCOTLAND   70cl e

DISTILLER'S EDITION, 1980, 14 *yrs*, 43% *abv*

Sweetness – 4   *Peatiness* – 7   *Price* – **

Colour – Quite full amber with old-gold highlights. *Nose* – Quite full-bodied and rich, but delicate with an elegant smoked note, a hint of the sea, a touch of sweet vanilla and a slight walnut note. *Palate* – Full-bodied, medium-dry and nutty with an edge of unctuously rich fruitiness and a smoked ham/cheese flavour. *Finish* – Long, elegant and restrained with a good balance between peat and malt. *Notes* – D.o.b. Double-matured, finished in a Montilla Fino cask.

Ord

MUIR OF ORD, ROSS-SHIRE [H] [V]   EST. 1838
Website: *www.malts.com/en-gb/Malts/summary/GlenOrd*

Ord distillery was founded as the Ord Distillery Company, which was taken over by James Watson & Co. of Dundee in 1896. Watson's, in turn, was acquired by John Dewar & Sons of Perth in 1923. Dewar's joined DCL in 1925 and the management of the distillery was taken over by SMD/UMGD from 1930. The floor maltings were converted to a Saladin maltings in 1961. Extensively rebuilt and extended from two to six stills in 1966. A large drum maltings was built on the adjacent site in 1968 and this supplies malt to many other distilleries in the north of Scotland. Licensed to Peter Dawson & Co. Now a part of Diageo plc.

Location – About 15 miles to the north of Inverness on the western side of the A832, immediately to the west of Muir of Ord.

Notes – The New Statistical Account of Scotland recorded in 1840 that "distilling of aquavitae" was the sole manufacture of the district. Ord, which was built on the site of a smugglers' bothy, is the only distillery remaining in the area. There were nine other licensed distilleries operating during the 19th century. The distillery was lit by paraffin lamps until it gained access to the national electricity grid after the Second World War, but water power remained in use for some operations as late as the 1960s. Ord was used for a programme of experiments which studied the differences between batches of spirit produced respectively by heating with coal, oil and steam. A colourful local smugglers' tale tells of excisemen taking a confiscated cask of whisky upstairs to their room for safe-keeping while staying overnight in a local inn, the Bogroy Hotel, in nearby Beauly. A hole was drilled through the ceiling underneath the cask from the bar below and the whisky was liberated while the excisemen slept.

Water – Loch nan Eun and Loch nam Bonnach.

GLEN ORD, 12 yrs, 40% abv

Sweetness – 6	Peatiness – 5	Price – ✻

Colour – Mid-amber with yellow/green highlights and just a tinge of green. *Nose* – Quite fresh and lightly peated with a green fruitiness, medium-dry with a hint of creamy richness. *Palate* – Medium-dry, quite rich and fresh, full and round with a touch of pepperiness. *Finish* – Long, fresh and quite rich with a dry tail. *Notes* – D.o.b.

ORD, 12 yrs, 40% abv

Sweetness – 7	Peatiness – 5	Price – ✻✻✻✻

Colour – Gold/straw with amber tints. *Nose* – Full-bodied, slightly dry but with an overlying richness. *Palate* – Quite full, big-bodied, round and medium-sweet. *Finish* – Very smooth, long and smoky. *Notes* – D.o.b. DCL (pre-Guinness) bottling.

1962, 27 yrs, 55.4% abv

Sweetness – 7	Peatiness – 5	Price – ✻✻✻

Colour – Amber with good gold highlights. *Nose* – Full, round, medium-sweet and quite mellow with a touch of oily-nuttiness. *Palate* – Fresh. Clean, soft, a touch oaky, quite round and full. *Finish* – Dry, smooth, slightly austere and nutty. *Notes* – Wm Cadenhead bottling.

Pittyvaich

DUFFTOWN, BANFFSHIRE [S] EST. 1975

Built by Arthur Bell & Sons Ltd as a sister to Dufftown and operated in conjuction with it. Four stills. Now part of Diageo plc. Closed in 1993 and demolished in 2003.

Location – Situated in the Dullan Glen on the outskirts of Dufftown near the 6th-century Mortlach Parish Church.

Notes – The make used the same water source as Dufftown and gave a similar whisky.

Water – The distillery drew its process water from two springs: Convalleys and Bailliemore.

SPEYSIDE
SINGLE MALT
SCOTCH WHISKY

PITTYVAICH

distillery is situated in the *DULLAN GLEN* on the *outskirts* of Dufftown, near to the *historic Mortlach Church* which dates back to the 6th. The distillery draws water from two nearby

springs - *CONVALLEYS* and *BALLIEMORE*. Pittyvaich single *MALT SCOTCH WHISKY* has a *perfumed, fruity* nose and a *robust* flavour with a *hint* of *spiciness*.

AGED 12 YEARS

Distilled & Bottled in SCOTLAND.
PITTYVAICH DISTILLERY
Dufftown, Keith, Banffshire, Scotland
43% vol 70 cl

---

12 yrs, 43% abv

Sweetness – 4	Peatiness – 6	Price – ✲✲

Colour – Amber with old-gold highlights. **Nose** – Round, quite full and malty, spicy, peppery and almost meaty with a coffee tang at the back. **Palate** – Medium-dry, quite full-bodied and dark-flavoured with a touch of tannin. **Finish** – Long, chewy and quite big. **Notes** – D.o.b.

12 yrs, 56.6% abv

Sweetness – 4	Peatiness – 7	Price – **

Colour – Straw/amber with pale gold highlights. *Nose* – Quite peaty and soft with a damp oak character and a touch of green, unripe coffee. *Palate* – Medium-dry, a coffee/chocolate character and smoky peatiness with a touch of spice. *Finish* – Long, lingering, spicy, smooth and nutty. *Notes* – Wm Cadenhead bottling.

12 yrs, 54% abv

Sweetness – 5	Peatiness – 7	Price – **

Colour – Medium to pale amber with lemon highlights. *Nose* – Medium-bodied, spirity and with a hint of toffee/coffee with a greenness at the back, medium peated. *Palate* – Medium-dry with a coffee flavour, quite full-flavoured, round and smooth. *Finish* – Creamy, quite sweet, tangy and long with a soft touch of smokiness on the tail. *Notes* – James MacArthur bottling from cask no. 15096.

13 yrs, 58% abv

Sweetness – 4	Peatiness – 7	Price – **

Colour – Deep, cough-linctus-amber with bronze highlights. *Nose* – Big-bodied, dark, rich, malty, cerealy and a touch of rubber with a smoky burnt character. *Palate* – Big, dark, rich, cerealy and smoky with a little spice. *Finish* – Quite spirity, long and smoky with a rich centre. *Notes* – Wm Cadenhead bottling.

1976, 18 yrs, 53.3% abv

Sweetness – 8	Peatiness – 2	Price – **

Colour – Pale straw/amber with pale gold highlights. *Nose* – Fresh and sweet with an almost grapey richness, a slightly unctuous lanolin aroma, a ripe apple character and slightly smoky. *Palate* – Quite sweet, full and smooth with a green ripeness. *Finish* – Long, sweet and clean with a light smokiness on the tail. *Notes* – Blackadder International bottling.

Port Ellen

Founded by Alexander Ker Mackay, with the support of landowner Walter Campbell, shortly after the Excise Act of 1823. Acquired by John Ramsay and run by him, and his heirs, until 1920, when sold to John Dewar & Sons Ltd and James Buchanan & Co., both of which companies merged with DCL in 1925. Port Ellen's management was transferred to SMD in 1930. Although silent from 1929 to 1966, the maltings continued in use. The distillery was extensively rebuilt in 1967, when it was increased from two to four stills. The distiller's licence was held by Low, Robertson & Co. Ltd. A large new maltings was erected in 1973 and, although the distillery ceased production permanently in May 1983, the maltings now serves all the Islay distilleries and also nearby Jura, following an historic concordat between the producing companies in 1987.

Location – Situated about half a mile from the centre of Port Ellen, the maltings building now dominates the shoreline.

Notes – The Excise Act of 1823 enforced the introduction of the spirit safe in distilleries. Tests had to be carried out to ensure that it had no harmful effect on the make. The official experiments were carried out at Port Ellen. The maltings were visited by Her Majesty, Queen Elizabeth II on 11 August 1980 and a commemorative bottling was produced.

Water – The Leorin Lochs.

1982, 18 yrs, 50% abv

Sweetness – 2	Peatiness – 9	Price – ***

Colour – Amber with gold highlights. **Nose** – Quite full-bodied with notes of creosote and slight burnt heather roots; water increases the pungency, making it more sea-influenced, rich and malty. **Palate** – Medium-dry with a charred note and sea-flavoured. **Finish** – Long, dry and a touch burnt. **Notes** – Douglas Laing Provenance bottling.

1982, 24 yrs, 60.4% abv

Sweetness – 2	Peatiness – 8	Price – ***

Colour – Amber with pale gold highlights. **Nose** – Big, sea-influenced, with a soft peaty note; water brings out breakfast cereals and wheat. **Palate** – Medium-dry, quite rich with a burnt heather roots peat note and a touch of seaweed and creosote. **Finish** – Long, rich and slightly tangy with an earthy note. **Notes** – Bladnoch Forum bottling from cask no. 2461 distilled 13 October 1982.

1980, 16 yrs, 59% abv

Sweetness – 2	Peatiness – 9	Price – ✱✱✱

Colour – Pale straw with pale yellow/lemon highlights. *Nose* – Big-bodied and sea-influenced (ozone and salt spray) with dry notes of cereal and a dark, smoky peatiness. *Palate* – Big, powerful and dry, but with a richness, smoky and with quite chewy tannins. *Finish* – Long and smoky with just a hint of sweetness. *Notes* – Signatory bottling.

1979, 25 yrs, 57.4% abv

Sweetness – 2	Peatiness – 9	Price – ✱✱✱

Colour – Mid-amber with gold highlights. *Nose* – Big-bodied, peaty with a slight vegetal note; water brings out creosote, Germolene, bandages and tar with a hint of cereal and some black fruit. *Palate* – Big-bodied, dry and richly fruity with an edge of sweetness, quite rich with some spice, all overlaid by sea-influenced peat. *Finish* – Long, dry, smokily peaty with some cocoa and liquorice. *Notes* – D.o.b.

1979, 56.9% abv

Sweetness – 3	Peatiness – 8	Price – ✱✱✱

Colour – Pale amber with pale gold highlights. *Nose* – Raw, spirity and surprisingly youthful; water brings out a green freshness, a slight sweetness and a meaty character. *Palate* – Medium-dry, vegetal, gently chewy and with a cereal note. *Finish* – Long, spirity and smoky with burnt-heather roots riding over all. *Notes* – Blackadder Raw Cask bottling from Sherry butt no. 2015.

1977, 14 yrs, 59.7% abv

Sweetness – 0	Peatiness – 9	Price – ✳✳✳

Colour – Mid-amber with old-gold. *Nose* – Big, pungently smoky and dry with an earthy burnt peat character. *Palate* – Big, powerful dark peatiness, a real "peat reek" and dry with a slight richness. *Finish* – Long and very peaty. *Notes* – Gordon & MacPhail bottling from cask no. 2017 distilled 14 April 1977.

1971, 40% abv

Sweetness – 1	Peatiness – 9	Price – ✳✳✳

Colour – Bright gold/amber golden/yellow highlights. *Nose* – Smoky peat, ozone, burnt heather roots with a very slight hint of sweetness. *Palate* – Quite full, round, smoky, quite smooth and almost medicinal. *Finish* – Dry and smoky with the burnt-heather roots lingering. *Notes* – Gordon & MacPhail bottling.

1970, 40% abv

Sweetness – 2	Peatiness – 9	Price – ✳✳✳✳

Colour – Peaty/gold with bright highlights. *Nose* – Big-bodied, pungent and peaty with a slight rubbery character and dry. *Palate* – Big, powerful, burnt peat with an edge of sweetness, very distinctive. *Finish* – Long, pungent and smoky. *Notes* – Gordon & MacPhail bottling.

Pulteney

WICK, CAITHNESS   [H] [V]   EST. 1826
Website: *www.oldpulteney.com*

Established by James Henderson. Became part of DCL in 1925, having been purchased by John Dewar & Sons a couple of years earlier. Closed between 1930 and 1951, then revived. In 1955, it was bought by Hiram Walker, later a part of Allied Domecq, who rebuilt the distillery in 1959. Sold to Inver House Distillers in June 1995. Two stills.

Location – The most northerly distillery on the UK mainland. It is sited on the southern side of Wick, close to the North Sea coast.

Notes – The wash stills were truncated to allow the roof to fit onto the building. The lyne arm comes off below the top of the still, resulting in a high degree of reflux and an elegance in the spirit.

Water – The Loch of Hempriggs.

12 yrs, 40% abv

Sweetness – 6	Peatiness – 5	Price – *

Colour – Very pale straw with pale, watery-green highlights. *Nose* – Soft, medium-bodied and medium-dry with a fresh, gentle, east-coast touch of the sea and an almost grapey richness. *Palate* – Medium-dry, fresh, clean and smooth, with good richness and an edge of sweetness. *Finish* – Very clean and fresh; lingering with a slightly salty touch to the lips. *Notes* – D.o.b.

15 yrs, 59.9% abv

Sweetness – 7	Peatiness – 5	Price – ✸✸

Colour – Straw/yellow with yellow highlights. **Nose** – Dry, quite full-bodied, malty and quite rich with a fresh hedgerow greenness, a herbal note and a distinct character of seaweed-covered rocks. **Palate** – Rich, medium-sweet, smooth and full-bodied, intense, fruity and gently peated. **Finish** – Long, rich, complex, fruity – apricots – tangy and salty. **Notes** – D.o.b.

17 yrs, 46% abv

Sweetness – 5	Peatiness – 5	Price – ✸✸

Colour – Amber with pale gold highlights. **Nose** – Medium-bodied, slightly vegetal and nutty; water pulls out tarry rope and a soft sea influence. **Palate** – Medium-dry, of good weight, soft and easy, rich with a touch of spice and malty honey. **Finish** – Long, clean, salty and quite ethereal. **Notes** – D.o.b.

21 yrs, 46% abv

Sweetness – 6	Peatiness – 6	Price – ✸✸✸

Colour – Mid-amber with old-gold highlights. **Nose** – Quite full-bodied, rich and a touch perfumed with notes of fresh cherries and toffee; with water, this expands into a rich fruitcake character. **Palate** – Medium-sweet and rich with a touch of spice, smooth with chocolate/cocoa notes to the peat and an apple character. **Finish** – Long, elegant and rich with a slight green edge to the peat. **Notes** – D.o.b.

Rosebank

FALKIRK, STIRLINGSHIRE   [L]   EST. 1840

The distillery, established by James Rankine, was converted from the maltings of the earlier Camelon distillery. It was rebuilt by his son in 1864. It was Rankine's objective to distil a whisky which would stand comparison with his competitors' finest makes. By the 1890s, there was an extraordinary demand for Rosebank and customers were put on allocation. In 1914, the Rosebank Distillery Ltd, as it was then called, was one of the founders of Scottish Malt Distillers Ltd. Now part of Diageo plc, Rosebank was closed in May 1993.

Location – Sited on the banks of the Forth and Clyde Canal where the A803 intersects with the canal to the west of Falkirk.

Notes – The make was triple distilled with one wash still and two spirit stills. The licensees were The Distillers Agency Ltd.

Water – Carron Valley Reservoir.

LOWLAND
SINGLE MALT
SCOTCH WHISKY

Established on its present
site at *CAMELON* in 1840

ROSEBANK

distillery stands on the
banks of the *FORTH*
and *CLYDE CANAL*.
This was once
a busy thoroughfare with
boats and steamers
continually passing by;
it is still the source
of water for cooling.
This single *MALT*
SCOTCH WHISKY is
triple distilled which
accounts for its *light
distinctive nose* and *well
balanced* flavour.

A G E D **12** Y E A R S

Distilled & Bottled in *SCOTLAND*
ROSEBANK DISTILLERY
Falkirk, Stirlingshire, Scotland

43% vol   70 cl

12 yrs, 43% abv

Sweetness – 2	Peatiness – 4	Price – **

Colour – Straw/light amber with gold and lemon highlights. *Nose* – Medium-bodied and spirity with a touch of greenness, lightly oily, medium-dry with a good edge of richness. *Palate* – Light and smooth, dryish with a mashy character. *Finish* – Smooth, dry and oaky with a pleasant lightness. *Notes* – D.o.b.

21 yrs, 50% abv

Sweetness – 2	Peatiness – 4	Price – ***

Colour – Amber with old-gold highlights. *Nose* – Quite full-bodied, medium-dry with notes of beeswax and honey and a hint of lemon; water brings out quite delicate peat, it is drier and softly unctuous with some lanolin. *Palate* – Medium-dry, quite ethereal, delicate, complex, lightly peated and creamily smooth. *Finish* – Long, clean as a whistle, just a note of sweetness on the edge, complex. *Notes* – Douglas Laing Old Malt Cask bottling.

1992, 60% abv

Sweetness – 2	Peatiness – 5	Price – ***

Colour – Pale straw with pale lemon highlights. *Nose* – Fresh, clean and cerealy with medium body and dry; water brings out a fresh sherbet character and quite a maltiness. *Palate* – Dry, medium-bodied, gently chewy with a cereal and slightly vegetal note. *Finish* – Long, quite rich and with a menthol note. *Notes* – Blackadder Raw Cask bottling from cask no. 1452 distilled 25 March 1992.

1992, 62.3% abv

Sweetness – 2	Peatiness – 5	Price – ***

Colour – Straw with pale yellow highlights. *Nose* – Quite spirity with an acetone touch, dry with a touch of richness and a note of model aeroplane dope; with water, the maltiness opens out, it is softer and has some fruit – pears – and is of quite good body. *Palate* – Dry, fresh with a slight edge of richness, pears, quite delicately peated, creamy and honey. *Finish* – Long, clean and fresh. *Notes* – Blackadder bottling from cask no. 1449.

1989, 58.9% abv

Sweetness – 2	Peatiness – 5	Price – ***

Colour – Pale straw with pale lemon highlights. *Nose* – Dry, quite a fresh hedgerow character – almost nettley – a touch of menthol, medium weight peat and quite malty. *Palate* – Dry with a fresh leafy greenness, quite a dark peat character, a clean menthol note and a touch of liquorice. *Finish* – *Notes* – Blackadder bottling from cask no. 842.

1969, 51.7% abv

Sweetness – 5	Peatiness – 3	Price – ***

Colour – Pale straw/amber with pale gold highlights. *Nose* – Malty, cerealy and soft with a slight oily oakiness and quite full with an edge of richness. *Palate* – Quite full-bodied, sweet and rich, lightly peated with a green, fresh edge. *Finish* – Long, sweet and rich with a touch of chocolate. *Notes* – Signatory bottling.

Royal Brackla

CAWDOR, NEAR NAIRN   [H]   EST. 1812

Founded by Captain William Fraser of Brackla House. A map of the Cawdor estate dated 1773 shows a "malt brewhouse" on the site. The distillery was sold to John Bisset & Co. Ltd which became a part of DCL in 1943, when management was transferred to SMD. It was rebuilt between 1964–65 and the number of stills was increased from two to four in 1970. Mothballed in 1985, Royal Brackla reopened in 1991 and was sold to Bacardi in 1998.

Location – Sited to the north of the B9090, one mile south of Nairn.

Notes – Despite being regularly fined by HM Customs and Excise for irregularities, Brackla was the first distillery to be granted a Royal Warrant in 1835. It was referred to at that time as *Brackla* or "The King's Own Whisky". During the demolition, in November 1994, of the no. 4 warehouse, which had not been used for some years, a hive of wild bees was discovered in one of the warehouse walls. The hive was between 10 and 15 feet (3 and 4 metres) across and it was estimated that the bees had inhabited this site for approximately 70 years. Demolition of that wall was postponed until the spring of 1995, when the queens were temporarily moved to another site. The bees have now been returned to beehives in the shape of pagoda roofs which are sited close to the original site of the no. 4 warehouse.

Water – The Cawdor Burn.

10 yrs, 43% abv

Sweetness – 7	Peatiness – 5	Price – ✳

Colour – Pale straw with yellow/gold highlights. *Nose* – Fresh, clean and medium-sweet; water brings out fennel and oranges, a slight crème brulée note and some apple blossom. *Palate* – Medium-sweet, quite full-bodied and with a rich maltiness, some green, leafy notes and some fruit. *Finish* – Long, fresh, delicately smoky and vanilla-scented. *Notes* – D.o.b.

Sweetness – 6	Peatiness – 7	Price – *

Colour – Pale straw with pale yellow highlights. *Nose* – Medium-bodied, quite peaty and round with a slight liquorice character. *Palate* – Medium-sweet, rich and slightly spicy with a good smoky peatiness and good body. *Finish* – Quite clean and fresh with almost a hint of bitter chocolate on the end. *Notes* – United Distillers bottling.

25 yrs, 43% *abv*

Sweetness – 7	Peatiness – 4	Price – ****

Colour – Mid-amber with old-gold highlights. *Nose* – Quite full-bodied and sweet, good maltiness and some red fruit; with water, the fruit becomes ripe cherries with vanilla and crème caramel, some honey and the peat is delicate and herby. *Palate* – Sweet and full, some nuttiness – hazelnuts, toffee and custard, a rich fruitcake note, smooth and round. *Finish* – Long, rich, elegant and sweet with a gently chewy nuttiness. *Notes* – D.o.b.

1975, 46% *abv*

Sweetness – 5	Peatiness – 7	Price – ***

Colour – Amber with pale old-gold highlights. *Nose* – Big-bodied, fruity and a touch perfumed, round with a slight Christmas-cake richness and quite a dark peat note. *Palate* – Quite big-bodied and darkly peated, smooth, softly unctuous with vanilla flavours. *Finish* – Very long, quite powerful, a touch perfumed and smoky. *Notes* – Murray McDavid bottling.

1970, 40% *abv*

Sweetness – 6	Peatiness – 6	Price – ****

Colour – Pale mid-amber with yellow-gold highlights. *Nose* – Good body with oak, cold apples and a peaty smokiness. *Palate* – Medium-dry, oaky, quite mellow and smooth with a slight oiliness and a medium peatiness. *Finish* – Reasonable oaky finish with a touch of richness. *Notes* – Gordon & MacPhail bottling.

Royal Lochnagar

CRATHIE, BALLATER, ABERDEENSHIRE   [H] [V]   EST. 1845
Website: *www.malts.com/en-gb/Malts/summary/RoyalLochnagar*

Originally known as New Lochnagar, as another Lochnagar distillery had been built nearby in 1826. This had closed by 1860. Lochnagar obtained the Royal Warrant after its owner, John Begg, had invited Queen Victoria and Prince Albert to view the distillery in 1848. The distillery was rebuilt in 1906 and acquired by John Dewar & Sons Ltd in 1916, passing to DCL in 1925 and operated by SMD/UMGD from 1930. Part of Diageo plc, licensed to John Begg Ltd.

Location – On Royal Deeside overlooking Balmoral castle and about one mile from the queen's bedroom, from which the young Queen Victoria is said to have looked out at the distillery.

Notes – The story the locals tell is of John Begg looking out of the window one evening and seeing a few figures making their way towards the distillery through the gathering dusk. The figures turned out to be Queen Victoria and Prince Albert, their children and a lady-in-waiting. The royal party had just arrived for their first stay at Balmoral and Begg had delivered the Queen a note inviting her on a not-to-be-missed tour round his new distillery. Prince Albert was particularly interested, being enthusiastic about all new technology. Royal Lochnagar is now the only distillery of the several that used to operate on Deeside. There is a very popular visitor centre, converted from the old farm steading. Scottish children try to trick one another by asking how deep Lochnagar is. The catch is that Lochnagar is not a loch, but a mountain. At 3,789 ft (1,155 m), its bulk dominates the countryside around Balmoral.

Water – Springs in the foothills of Lochnagar.

12 *yrs*, 40% *abv*

Sweetness – 7	Peatiness – 4	Price – *

Colour – Mid-amber with old-gold highlights. *Nose* – Medium-bodied, quite soft and rich with a little Sherry rubber; water brings out sweet, creamy leather with a slightly burnt fruitcake character. *Palate* – Sweet, dried fruit – raisins, the fruitcake comes through again, gently peated with a green edge and some coffee. *Finish* – Fresh, medium-sweet, lightly smoky with creamy vanilla and a little Sherry nuttiness on the tail. *Notes* – D.o.b.

SELECTED RESERVE, No age statement, 43% *abv*

Sweetness – 8	Peatiness – 3	Price – ****

Colour – Deep, peaty amber with good gold highlights. *Nose* – Rich, wet oak, vanilla, sweet and lightly sherried. *Palate* – Full, round, rich, mellow, nutty and creamy. *Finish* – Long, slightly spicy and very smooth. *Notes* – D.o.b. It has no age statement because it is produced from selected casks and the age varies from bottling to bottling.

1992, 13 *yrs*, 60.2% *abv*

Sweetness – 8	Peatiness – 3	Price – *****

Colour – Full amber with bronze highlights. *Nose* – Big-bodied with notes of burnt fruitcake and apples; water brings out woody vanilla and a slightly musty character. *Palate* – Big, medium-sweet and gently peated with softly chewy tannins, notes of apples and dried fruits. *Finish* – Long, rich and softly smoky. *Notes* – Blackadder Raw Cask bottling.

St Magdalene

Said to have been founded on the lands of St Magdalene's Cross, the former site of an annual fair and of St Magdalene's Hospital. The earliest record is of Adam Dawson as distiller in 1797. It was taken over by DCL on 16 November 1912, prior to which the owning company was A. & J. Dawson Ltd. St Magdalene was one of the five founding distilleries of SMD in July 1914.

Location – Sited at the eastern end of Linlithgow, where the railway line, running alongside the Union Canal, intersects with the A706 main road to Edinburgh.

Notes – Linlithgow was a centre of milling and malting in the 17th century, and brewing and distilling in the 18th century. The distillery closed in 1983 and its buildings have been converted to housing.

Water – The town's domestic supply.

23 yrs, 58.1% abv

Sweetness – 2	Peatiness – 3	Price – ✳✳✳✳

Colour – Amber with gold highlights and a tinge of green. *Nose* – Gentle, soft and medium-dry with a bread-yeasty aroma and a slightly oaky acetone character. *Palate* – Big-bodied, quite dry, but with an edge of richness, tannic and yeasty. *Finish* – Long, quite powerful and quite tannic. *Notes* – D.o.b.

1982, 10 yrs, 62.3% abv

Sweetness – 2	Peatiness – 2	Price – ✳✳

Colour – Pale straw with lemon/yellow highlights. *Nose* – Fresh, clean, fruity and spirity, medium-dry with a slight touch of oak and a light mashy character. *Palate* – Medium-dry with good richness and round with quite good body. *Finish* – Good length, rich and smooth. *Notes* – Wm Cadenhead bottling.

1980, 40% abv

Sweetness – 3	Peatiness – 3	Price – ✱✱✱

Colour – Straw with pale lemon/pale gold highlights. **Nose** – Quite good body with a fresh, almost fruity richness, off-dry, lightly peated and green with a slight edge of sweetness. **Palate** – Smooth, mashy, malty, clean, medium-dry and quite rich. **Finish** – Quite long and rich with a slightly green freshness. **Notes** – Gordon & MacPhail Centenary Reserve bottling.

1965, 40% abv

Sweetness – 1	Peatiness – 4	Price – ✱✱✱

Colour – Light to mid-amber with gold highlights. **Nose** – Quite fresh with a light oak character, quite lightweight and dry, a little spirity. **Palate** – Dry with oaky tannins, of medium weight and lightly smoky. **Finish** – Dry, oaky and chewy with dry tannins. **Notes** – Gordon & MacPhail bottling.

Scapa

KIRKWALL, ORKNEY [H] EST. 1885
Website: *www.scapamalt.com*

Built by Macfarlane & Townsend, acquired by Hiram Walker in 1954. In 1959, the wash still was replaced by a Lomond still; this produces a heavier spirit than the more traditional long-necked stills. Mothballed in 1994 and sold to Pernod-Ricard in 2005 when a major refurbishment was carried out. Operated by Chivas Brothers. Two stills.

Location – Sited on the Lingro Burn, two miles south-west of Kirkwall on the A964 at the head of Scapa Bay.

Notes – Scapa Flow was where the German fleet was scuttled at the end of the First World War. When whisky chronicler Alfred Barnard visited the distillery in 1886, it had been open for just a year. He wrote about it as being "one of the most complete little Distilleries in the Kingdom". The stills were described as being of "the newest type and heated by steam instead of fire, and are both fitted with 'collapse' valves, which allow air to enter in the event of a vacuum being formed". *Scapa* is one of the main malts associated with Ballantine's blended Scotch Whisky.

Water – The Lingro Burn and nearby springs.

14 yrs, 40% abv

Sweetness – 4	Peatiness – 7	Price – *

Colour – Pale amber with pale gold highlights. *Nose* – Medium-bodied, medium-dry and leafy with hedgerow and cerealy notes; water brings out a winegum character with soft oak and liquorice-flavoured peat. *Palate* – Good body, soft, malty and softly chewy with a fennel note. *Finish* – Long, quite delicate and very clean with good cocoa and coffee-flavoured peat. *Notes* – D.o.b.

12 yrs, 40% abv

Sweetness – 8	Peatiness – 5	Price – ✸✸✸

Colour – Amber with old-gold highlights. *Nose* – Fresh, medium-dry, quite malty, herby and grassy with quite a dark peat note and grapey/gooseberry fruit notes. *Palate* – Sweet, quite full-bodied, rich and round with a ripe grapefruit character and a nice caress of peat. *Finish* – Long, very rich and mouth-filling with butterscotch on the tail. *Notes* – Allied bottling.

23 yrs, 50% abv

Sweetness – 4	Peatiness – 5	Price – ✸✸

Colour – Mid-amber with old-gold highlights. *Nose* – Quite delicate, round, warm and nutty with a hazelnut-oil character; water brings out creamy toffee and muscovado sugar, medium-dry. *Palate* – Medium-dry and malty, with good body, smooth and round with a quite delicate peat note. *Finish* – Very long, imposing and toffeeyed. *Notes* – Douglas Laing Old Malt Cask bottling.

1983, 40% abv

Sweetness – 4	Peatiness – 5	Price – ✸✸

Colour – Mid-amber with old-gold highlights. *Nose* – Fresh, clean, malty and slightly green with a slight nuttiness and medium-dry. *Palate* – Almost dry, quite full-bodied, slightly spicy and tangy, gently smoky. *Finish* – Long and clean with a touch of richness. *Notes* – Gordon & MacPhail bottling.

1979, 14 yrs, 43% abv

Sweetness – 6	Peatiness – 5	Price – ✸

Colour – Pale straw with yellow/lemon highlights. *Nose* – Round, smooth and medium-sweet, slightly unctuous with a fresh, floral character and rich with a maltiness at the back. *Palate* – Medium-dry, quite full and round, quite smooth and with tannic oak. *Finish* – Long and full, quite rich with a toffee tail. *Notes* – Master of Malt bottling from cask nos. 3851/2 distilled 9 May 1979.

1979, 56.3% abv

Sweetness – 8	Peatiness – 6	Price – ✸✸✸

Colour – Straw with yellow/lemon highlights. *Nose* – Full-bodied, fruity (strawberries) bubblegummy, medium-sweet and finely peated. *Palate* – Sweet, round, quite spicy, smooth, almost grapey. *Finish* – Long, sweet and clean. *Notes* – Scotch Malt Whisky Society bottling, cask no. 17.13 bottled May 1994.

Speyburn

ROTHES, MORAY [S] EST. 1897
Website: *www.speyburndistillery.com*

Built by John Hopkins & Co. for the Speyburn-Glenlivet Distillery Company Ltd. Local tradition has it that the walls were built of stones "extracted by man and beast" from the bed of the River Spey. DCL bought John Hopkins & Co. in 1916, but the Speyburn-Glenlivet Distillery Company Ltd was not wound up until 1962, when Speyburn's management was transferred to SMD and the licensees became John Robertson & Son Ltd. It was the first distillery to install a drum maltings, which is still in operation. The distillery has two stills and is now owned by Inver House Distillers, who purchased it in 1991.

Location – Situated about a quarter of a mile north west of the B9105 on the northern outskirts of Rothes.

Notes – The Charles Doig-designed Speyburn started up in the last week of December 1897. Doors and windows had not yet been fitted to the stillhouse and, as a severe snowstorm was sweeping the district, employees had to work in overcoats. Just one butt of spirit was bonded with 1897 on its head. The two storage warehouses each have two floors and use wooden rails and tables to store casks two and three high. The distillery's alcohol vapours are condensed in over 100 metres of copper pipe in its worm tubs.

Water – The Granty (or Birchfield) Burn.

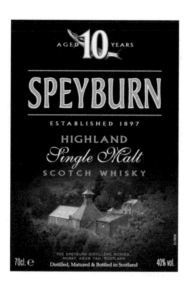

10 yrs, 40% abv

Sweetness – 8	Peatiness – 2	Price – *

Colour – Very pale straw with lemon highlights. *Nose* – Fresh, clean and aromatic with a rich, lemony fruitiness, medium-bodied and quite lightly peated. *Palate* – Fresh, clean, rich and medium-sweet; quite full-bodied. *Finish* – Long and sweet with a touch of spice. *Notes* – D.o.b.

21 yrs, 61.9% abv

Sweetness – 7	Peatiness – 6	Price – **

Colour – Deep, dark mahogany with ruby/crimson highlights. *Nose* – Full-bodied, round, medium-sweet, sherried and nutty; almost vinous with a quite solid smoky peat note at the back. *Palate* – Big-bodied, mature, medium-sweet, quite powerful and rich, with chewy tannins and a touch of spice. *Finish* – Long, sherried, smoky, a serious sippin' whisky. *Notes* – D.o.b.

SPEYBURN SOLERA, 25 yrs, 46% abv

Sweetness – 7	Peatiness – 3	Price – ***

Colour – Amber with pale gold highlights. *Nose* – Delicate, rich and honeyed with an orange note; water opens it out to quite full-bodied, medium-sweet with toffee and tablet, sweet vanilla and juicy tangerines, altogether zingy. *Palate* – Medium-bodied with delicate peat, rich, zesty, medium-sweet and honeyed, mouth-watering. *Finish* – Long, very fresh and mouth-wateringly juicy with citrus notes of orange and lime. *Notes* – D.o.b.

1971, 40% abv

Sweetness – 8	Peatiness – 5	Price – ****

Colour – Rich, peaty amber with good gold highlights. *Nose* – Sweet, fruity and slightly spirity. *Palate* – Medium-sweet, quite light and smooth. *Finish* – Mellow, of reasonable length with oak on the end. *Notes* – Gordon & MacPhail bottling.

Speyside

KINGUSSIE, INVERNESS-SHIRE   [S]   EST. 1990
Website: *www.speysidedistillery.co.uk*

Speyside was conceived in 1956 opposite the site of the former distillery of the same name (1895–1911) on land purchased by the Christie family. In the previous year, they had formed the Speyside Distillery & Bonding Co. The driving force behind the project, whisky blender George Christie, gradually built the new distillery, starting in 1962 and finally completing the work in 1987. The first spirit ran from the distillery's two stills on 12 December 1990. In September 2000, Speyside was taken over by a consortium of shareholders.

Location – At the confluence of the Tromie and Spey rivers, to the east of Kingussie.

Notes – The distillery is said to have a maximum capacity of 200,000 gallons a year, although it is planned to produce no more than 100,000, all of which is intended for the company's own use. Other than *The Speyside*, the company produces a young single malt called *Drumguish* and a single malt under the *Glentromie* label.

12 yrs, 40% abv

Sweetness – 7	Peatiness – 5	Price – ✲

Colour – Amber with bright gold highlights. *Nose* – Quite big-bodied with dark peat and cocoa notes and slightly perfumed; with water, the cocoa note broadens to dark chocolate and there is a slightly medicinal/tarry and aniseed note to the peat. *Palate* – Full-bodied, round and smooth with beeswax and gently chewy with honey and toffee notes. *Finish* – Long and rich with a quite delicate peat note. *Notes* – D.o.b.

DRUMGUISH, No age statement, 40% abv

Sweetness – 7	Peatiness – 4	Price – ✲

Colour – Rich amber with old-gold highlights. *Nose* – Quite full, malty and fresh, medium-sweet and quite youthful with a hint of orange and honey. *Palate* – Medium-dry, of good body, malty, quite rich with a sweet edge, soft vanilla and slight creamy toffee/tablet notes. *Finish* – Long, smooth and creamily rich with lingering toffee vanilla. *Notes* – D.o.b.

Springbank

CAMPBELTOWN, ARGYLL   [C]   EST. 1828
Website: *www.springbankdistillers.com*

Said to have been originally licensed to the Reid family. It was acquired by John and William Mitchell in 1837 and run by various members of the family until 1897 when the present owning company, J. & A. Mitchell & Co., was incorporated. Springbank's stillhouse contains three stills, which has created endless rumours that it is triple distilled. It is, in fact, distilled two and a half times. The whiskies *Hazelburn* and *Longrow* are also produced from the same stills, *Hazelburn* being conventionally triple distilled.

Location – The distillery is in the centre of the town.

Notes – The family owners of Springbank are direct descendants of the illicit distillers who established the once-numerous Campbeltown distilleries, and the present chairman is the great-great-great-grandson of its founder. The Campbeltown area once boasted around 30 legal distilleries, but the years of Depression after the First World War and Prohibition in the USA almost brought the total demise of Campbeltown's whisky industry. Springbank is now one of only three survivors. It is the only distillery where everything, from malting through to bottling, is carried out on the premises for all of the distillery's own production.

Water – Crosshill Loch.

MARSALA WOOD EXPRESSION, 9 yrs, 58% abv

Sweetness – 7	Peatiness – 6	Price – **

Colour – Mid-amber with old-gold highlights. *Nose* – Quite big-bodied and full-flavoured, sweet, rich and fruity with crème brulée; water brings out oranges and lemons with creamy cappuccino and just a hint of cocoa-aroma-ed peat. *Palate* – Medium-sweet, rich, full and smooth with an unctuous oily oak and hazelnut character, some fruit cocktail and charred oak peat. *Finish* – Long, elegant and fruity with cocoa reprising and salt on the tail. *Notes* – D.o.b.

10 yrs, 46% abv

Sweetness – 7	Peatiness – 6	Price – *

Colour – Amber with pale gold highlights. *Nose* – Big-bodied, medium-dry and fresh with quite a solid and gently earthy peat note, a slight tarry character and a light melon touch. *Palate* – Big-bodied, medium-sweet and rich with quite a dark peaty touch. *Finish* – Long, fresh, rich and salty. *Notes* – D.o.b.

100° PROOF, 10 yrs, 57% abv

Sweetness – 6	Peatiness – 6	Price – **

Colour – Amber with pale gold highlights. *Nose* – Quite full-bodied, rich and leathery with a creamy toffee note; water brings out a fruitiness – dried apricots and some banana, sea spray on the harbour wall and a hint of marzipan. *Palate* – Quite sweet, rich, vanilla and honey with a hint of toffee-apple. *Finish* – Long, and some (unusually) definite smoke with the tang of salt on the end. *Notes* – D.o.b.

Sweetness – 7	Peatiness – 5	Price – ✳✳

Colour – Light, honeyed mid-amber with lemony highlights. **Nose** – Medium weight, rich, oily oak with a touch of greenness, quite lightly peated. **Palate** – Clean, smooth, medium-dry with good, creamy oak and a touch of sweetness and greenness. **Finish** – Long, and smooth with a touch of tannin and hints of richness and saltiness on the tail. **Notes** – D.o.b.

21 yrs, 46% abv

Sweetness – 8	Peatiness – 5	Price – ✳✳✳✳✳

Colour – Deep amber. **Nose** – Definite fruity notes, stickily sweet in their richness, also floral notes and a suggestion of coconut and medicinal cloves. **Palate** – Silkily smooth, full-bodied and creamy with a salty tang. **Finish** – Very fine, long, dark and oaky. **Notes** – D.o.b.

25 yrs, 46% abv

Sweetness – 7	Peatiness – 6	Price – ✳✳✳✳✳

Colour – Full, peaty amber with bronze highlights. **Nose** – Rich, ripe, sweet and full-bodied, smoky with a touch of ozone and oak. **Palate** – Full, round, smoky and medium-sweet with oaky tannins and a salty tang. **Finish** – Long, smoky-oak and tangy with a touch of spiciness. **Notes** – D.o.b.

30 yrs, 46% abv

Sweetness – 8	Peatiness – 6	Price – ✳✳✳✳✳

Colour – Full amber with old-gold highlights. **Nose** – Full and rich, almost raisiny with a touch of liquorice, almost tarry and medium-dry. **Palate** – Sweet and rich with a good peaty character, a flavour of bitter chocolate and a salty tang. **Finish** – Long and tangy with good sweetness. **Notes** – D.o.b.

HAZELBURN, 8 yrs, 46% abv

Sweetness – 4	Peatiness – 0	Price – ✳✳

Colour – Straw with yellow/green highlights. **Nose** – Medium-bodied, quite rich with a hint of green fruit; water brings out orange and wider citrus, baked apples, cloves and pineapple with a soft smokiness in the background. **Palate** – Medium-dry, rich, fresh and fruity with baked apples, a touch of spice and of good body. **Finish** – Long, quite youthful, very clean and fruity. **Notes** – D.o.b.

Strathisla

KEITH, BANFFSHIRE   [S] [V]   EST. 1786

Built in 1786 as Milltown (Keith was the centre of the Scottish linen industry) and later known as Milton. Strathisla was originally the name of the make and subsequently also became that of the distillery. It was converted into a flour mill in 1838. After reconversion to distilling, the distillery was twice badly damaged in the 1870s; first by fire in 1876 and three years later by an explosion. Extensive modernisation took place after these events and again in 1965, when the distillery was enlarged from two to four stills. It is today owned and managed by Chivas Brothers Ltd, a subsidiary of Pernod-Ricard.

Location – Half a mile north from the centre of Keith on the B9116.

Notes – On 15 June 1993, Strathisla received an unexpected visitor from Louisville, Kentucky; a young black and white cat fell asleep among some Bourbon barrels in a container awaiting shipment to Scotland. On opening the container some four weeks later, the cat staggered out, weak from hunger and drunk from the Bourbon fumes in the enclosed space. After six months' quarantine the cat, for obvious reasons called Dizzy, is now employed by Chivas Brothers as a mouser.

Water – The Broomhill Spring. The reservoir which holds the distillery's water supply is said to be visited nightly by the "water kelpies", which could account for its special flavour.

8 yrs, 40% abv

Sweetness – 8	Peatiness – 3	Price – *

Colour – Amber with good gold highlights. *Nose* – Fruity, spirity and sweet with a lanolin oiliness. *Palate* – Spicy, quite smooth and medium-sweet with a touch of oak. *Finish* – Good body, although perhaps a little short because of its youth. *Notes* – Gordon & MacPhail bottling.

12 yrs, 43% abv

Sweetness – 7	Peatiness – 4	Price – *

Colour – Mid-amber with gold highlights. *Nose* – Quite big-bodied and round with a dark hazelnut note and good richness; water brings out the sweetness and citrus – oranges, beeswax and some creamy vanilla. *Palate* – Medium-dry with a smoky nuttiness, some burnt fruitcake, honey and delicate peat notes. *Finish* – Long, roasted hazelnut-flavoured and with some cooked apples. *Notes* – D.o.b.

21 yrs, 40% abv

Sweetness – 8	Peatiness – 4	Price – **

Colour – Amber with bright copper highlights. *Nose* – Medium-sweet and malty, lightly peated and oaky. *Palate* – Medium-dry, oaky and spicy and creamy. *Finish* – Long and spicy with hints of bitter chocolate. *Notes* – Gordon & MacPhail bottling.

1989, 60% abv

Sweetness – 7	Peatiness – 4	Price – ***

Colour – Straw with pale gold highlights. *Nose* – Medium-sweet and quite full-bodied with a young spiritiness, quite delicate peatiness and a slight hint of toffee richness. *Palate* – Medium-sweet and smooth with a gentle peatiness. *Finish* – Long, fresh, clean and quite sweet. *Notes* – Clydesdale Original bottling from cask no. 9408.

1974, 18 yrs, 57.8% abv

Sweetness – 6	Peatiness – 7	Price – **

Colour – Amber with old-gold highlights. *Nose* – Full-bodied with a dark nuttiness and medium-dry oaky vanilla. *Palate* – Smoky with a dark nuttiness, medium-sweet with gentle oaky tannins and a slight astringency. *Finish* – Long, creamy and smoky with a background of sweetness. *Notes* – Gordon & MacPhail bottling distilled 23 March 1974.

Strathmill

KEITH, BANFFSHIRE   [S]   EST. 1891

Originally a corn and flour mill, it was converted in 1891 as Glenisla-Glenlivet. Acquired by W. & A. Gilbey in 1895, when it was renamed Strathmill. Became part of IDV in 1962 and now absorbed into Diageo plc. Four stills.

Location – Just off the B9014 from Keith to Dufftown, to the south of the centre of Keith.

Notes – It has been rarely available as a single malt, as most of the make goes into the J&B and Dunhill blends.

Water – A spring at the distillery.

SPEYSIDE
SINGLE MALT *SCOTCH WHISKY*

STRATHMILL

distillery was established in 1891 *in a converted grain mill. The PIED WAGTAIL is a* familiar sight in the *distillery yard* and on the *banks of the nearby RIVER ISLA, which provides water for cooling. A spring on* the spring provides *processing water.* This *deep amber, single MALT* has a light, *rounded body, a creamy* sweet flavour, with a *dry finish* and *chocolaty aftertaste.*

43% vol   AGED **12** YEARS   70 cl

Distilled & Bottled in *SCOTLAND.* STRATHMILL DISTILLERY Keith, Banffshire, *Scotland.*

12 yrs, 43% abv

Sweetness – 6	Peatiness – 3	Price – **

Colour – Pale straw with lemon/gold highlights. **Nose** – Quite light and cerealy with a touch of perfume; water pulls out banana and apples, some Darjeeling tea and some hazelnuts. **Palate** – Medium-sweet, medium-bodied with some vanilla, honey and blossom and a hint of cardamom. **Finish** – Long and spicy, quite leafy and ethereal. **Notes** – D.o.b.

1980, 11 yrs, 60.6% abv

Sweetness – 7	Peatiness – 3	Price – *

Colour – Pale straw with lemon highlights. **Nose** – Fresh, young, mashy, vegetal greenness with an edge of richness, medium-sweet and lightly peated. **Palate** – Cerealy, cornflake-like, medium-sweet with soft tannins, smooth and quite round. **Finish** – Good sweetness, quite good length, clean with a mashy vegetal character and a green edge to the tail. **Notes** – Wm Cadenhead bottling.

Talisker

CARBOST, ISLE OF SKYE   [H] [V]   EST. 1830
Website: *www.malts.com/en-gb/Malts/summary/Talisker*

The distillery was originally sited at Snizort, to the north of the island, but was closed and mysteriously moved. The current buildings were founded by Hugh and Kenneth MacAskill in 1830. Rebuilt 1880-7 and further extended in 1900. Merged into Dailuaine-Talisker Distilleries Ltd in 1898, under which name it still trades, although fully absorbed into DCL in 1925. Rebuilt again 1960-2 after the stillhouse was destroyed by fire on 22 November 1960. Five stills. Now part of Diageo plc.

Location – Situated in a gentle bowl which forms a lonely, very sheltered glen on the west coast of Skye.

Notes – So far, the only (legal) distillery on the island of Skye. It took its name from a farm, about six miles distant. The make was triple distilled until 1928. Talisker retains its worm tubs.

Water – Twenty-one springs on the slopes of Cnoc nan Speireag (Hawk Hill), cooling water comes from the Carbost Burn.

10 yrs, 45.8% abv

Sweetness – 1	Peatiness – 10	Price – ✳

Colour – Straw with bright gold highlights. **Nose** – Powerfully pungent with burning heather notes; water brings out a shellfish aroma and a gentle hint of the seashore with a little citrus. **Palate** – Dry, with an earthy peatiness, a touch of spice and a creaminess with an edge of malty and citrus sweetness. **Finish** – Big and spicy, peppery and smoky with the peat smoke lingering on. **Notes** – D.o.b.

18 yrs, 45.8% abv

Sweetness – 2	Peatiness – 10	Price – **

Colour – Amber with gold highlights. *Nose* – Rich and powerful, smoky with orange, candlewax and sweet leather notes; water brings out butterscotch and rum and raisin toffee, some seaweed and shellfish. *Palate* – Dry, creamy and silky with notes of burnt marmalade and coal tar. *Finish* – Long, smoky – smoked mussels with a note of white pepper on the finish. *Notes* – D.o.b.

DISTILLER'S EDITION, 45.8% abv

Sweetness – 3	Peatiness – 10	Price – **

Colour – Deep amber with bronze highlights and a hint of ruby. *Nose* – Rich, deep, darkly peated with a sweet edge; with water, it softens with a tangerine fruit note, some vanilla toffee and some sherried brazil nuts. *Palate* – Dry, big-bodied and rich with a big peatiness, some sweet maltiness and some burnt heather roots. *Finish* – Dry with an earthy peatiness, gently chewy tannins and some cocoa on the tail. *Notes* – D.o.b.

25 yrs, 57.8% abv

Sweetness – 3	Peatiness – 10	Price – ***

Colour – Deep amber with old-gold highlights. *Nose* – Big and powerful, seashores and smoke with some Seville oranges; water pulls out a candlewax and beeswax character, charred heather roots and some smoked crab. *Palate* – Big-bodied and dry with quite juicy oranges, there is a stony character to the big peat and some creosote and tarry rope. *Finish* – Long, dry, sea-influenced and with some sweet spice. *Notes* – D.o.b.

1955, 38 yrs, 53.6% abv

Sweetness – 2	Peatiness – 9	Price – *****

Colour – Deep amber with bronze highlights. *Nose* – Deep, dark, nutty and woody with a medicinal character and just an edge of richness. *Palate* – Big, dark and tannic, quite pungent with an almost burnt peaty character and a touch of richness. *Finish* – Long, tannic, chewy and pungent. *Notes* – Gordon & MacPhail bottling, cask nos. 1257, 1310 and 1311 distilled 12 and 28 May 1955.

Tamdhu

KNOCKANDO, MORAY   [S] EST. 1897
Website: *www.edringtongroup.com/brands/tamdhu*

Built by the Tamdhu Distillery Co. Ltd which was owned by a consortium of blenders. Owned by Highland Distilleries Co. since 1898. Closed from 1927 to 1947, but extended in 1972 from two to four stills and again to six stills in 1975. A feature is Tamdhu's Saladin maltings which have been largely rebuilt.

Location – Sited on the banks of the River Spey, south of the B9102 between Knockando and Archiestown.

Notes – The old railway station at Knockando has been converted into a visitor centre for Tamdhu. Tamdhu does not have the traditional pagoda heads atop its kilns, having instead a short, square concrete chimney.

Water – A spring under the distillery.

No age statement, 40% *abv*

Sweetness – 7	Peatiness – 4	Price – *

Colour – Straw/amber with yellow highlights. *Nose* – Medium-bodied, fruity and a touch floral, medium-sweet with a greenness. *Palate* – Medium-sweet, quite light, mashy, biscuity and quite smooth. *Finish* – Quite short, spirity and sweet. *Notes* – D.o.b.

1990, 15 *yrs*, 61.7% *abv*

Sweetness – 5	Peatiness – 4	Price – **

Colour – Amber with pale gold highlights. *Nose* – Soft, fruity and ripe, showing orange and honey; with water a meaty note comes out with medium body. *Palate* – Medium-dry and gently chewy with soft peat and a touch of tobacco. *Finish* – Long, malty and quite fresh with a green edge to the peat. *Notes* – Bladnoch Forum bottling from hogshead no. 10154 distilled 20th June 1990.

Tamnavulin

TOMNAVOULIN, BANFFSHIRE   [S]   EST. 1966

Designed by William Delme-Evans and built by the Tamnavulin-Glenlivet Distillery Company, a subsidiary of Invergordon Distillers. Now owned by Whyte & Mackay. A very modern distillery, it can be operated by just a handful of technicians. Mothballed early in 1995.

Location – On the B9008 at the village of Tomnavoulin.

Notes – The only distillery actually sited on the banks of the River Livet, from which the cooling waters are drawn. "Tomnavoulin" from the Gaelic means "mill on the hill" and an old carding mill, which stood at the riverside just below the distillery, has been converted into a very attractive visitor centre. The mill machinery has been preserved inside. Equally pleasant are the grassy banks of the river which have been turned into a picnic area.

Water – Subterranean springs at Easterton in the local hills.

12 yrs, 40% abv

Sweetness – 7	Peatiness – 4	Price – *

Colour – Mid-straw with pale lemon highlights. *Nose* – A dark nuttiness and a gentle peaty character, medium-sweet with a rich, charred oak note. *Palate* – Dark and medium-dry with a nice weight and a good dollop of peat at the back. *Finish* – Smooth, long and nutty with a rich, oaky tail. *Notes* – D.o.b.

Teaninich

Founded by Captain Hugh Munro. Sold to SMD in 1933. When SMD took over, there were four stills, two of which were described as being very small. When production restarted after the Second World War, the two smaller stills were removed. Capacity was increased from two to four larger stills in 1962, and to ten when an entirely new distillation unit named "A side" began production in 1970. The milling, mashing and fermentation part of the old distillery, "B side" was rebuilt in 1973. Now owned by Diageo plc.

Location – Sited to the north of the A9 on the western outskirts of Alness and on the west bank of the River Alness, three-quarters of a mile from its outflow into the Cromarty Firth.

Notes – Alfred Barnard recorded in 1885 that Teaninich was the only distillery north of Inverness to be "lighted by electricity". In 1925, both maltings floors were of solid clay. "A side" is in production, but "B Side" was mothballed in the mid-1980s and demolished in 1999.

Water – The Dairywell Spring.

HIGHLAND
SINGLE MALT
SCOTCH WHISKY

The *Cromarty Firth* is one of the few places in the British Isles inhabited by *PORPOISE*. They can be seen quite regularly, *swimming* close to the shore *less* than a *mile* from

TEANINICH

distillery. Founded in 1817 in the *Ross~shire* town of ALNESS, the *distillery* is now one of the largest in *Scotland.* TEANINICH is an assertive *single MALT WHISKY* with a *spicy, smoky, satisfying* taste.

AGED **10** YEARS

Distilled & Bottled in *SCOTLAND.*
TEANINICH DISTILLERY,
Alness, Ross-shire, *Scotland.*

43% vol   70 cl

---

10 yrs, 43% abv

Sweetness – 7	Peatiness – 5	Price – **

Colour – Pale straw with yellow highlights and a tinge of lemon. **Nose** – Fresh and quite light with a good green peatiness, medium-sweet with an appley character. **Palate** – Medium-dry, gently smoky, smooth and round. **Finish** – Clean and fresh with a sweet tail. **Notes** – D.o.b.

Tobermory

TOBERMORY, ISLE OF MULL   [H] [V]   EST. 1798

Established by local merchant, John Sinclair. Owned from 1890 to 1916 by John Hopkins & Son & Co., when taken over by DCL. Silent from 1930 to 1972, when revived as Ledaig Distillery (Tobermory) Ltd. This company went into receivership in 1975 and the business was acquired in 1978 by the Kirkleavington Property Co. of Cleckheaton. Tobermory was in production again from 1979 to 1981, before closing again until 1989. Purchased in 1993 by Burn Stewart Distillers for £600,000 plus £200,000 for stock. Four stills.

Location – Situated in the town centre, at the head of Tobermory Bay.

Notes – The only distillery on Mull. Because the distillery was closed for several years, very little Tobermory single malt has been produced until relatively recently. *Tobermory* is now becoming more readily available. Owner Burn Stewart has decided to use only unpeated barley in the production of *Tobermory*, although a few mashes will be produced each year using peated malt. These will be reserved for whiskies marketed under the brand name *Ledaig*, which is the Gaelic name for the distillery.

Water – A small private loch close by the Mishnish Lochs.

10 yrs, 40% abv

Sweetness – 4	Peatiness – 5	Price – *

Colour – Pale amber with pale gold highlights. **Nose** – Quite soft and round with sweet vanilla, sherbet, citrus and toffee characters and a slight hint of a dark peat note. **Palate** – Medium-dry, sherbetty-sweet, medium-bodied, smooth, quite gently peated and citrus flavoured. **Finish** – Smooth, long and quite round with a limey tang. **Notes** – D.o.b.

1995, 46% *abv*

Sweetness – 3	Peatiness – 6	Price – **

Colour – Pale straw with pale lemon highlights. *Nose* – Medium-bodied, youthful and mashy with cereal and vegetal notes; water brings out melon and a cocoa peat note. *Palate* – Medium-dry, smooth, mashy and slightly vegetal with quite good body and a touch of tobacco. *Finish* – Finishes well, long and clean with perfumed peat. *Notes* – Berry's Own Selection bottling.

LEDAIG, 15 yrs, 43% *abv*

Sweetness – 6	Peatiness – 6	Price – *

Colour – Amber with pale yellow highlights. *Nose* – Quite full and fresh with a citrus lemon-juice character and a slight creamy vanilla touch. *Palate* – Quite pungent with good medium-sweet richness, round and smooth with a slightly earthy smokiness and a hint of milk chocolate. *Finish* – Long and smokily rich with a hint of cocoa and uncomplicated. *Notes* – D.o.b.

LEDAIG, 1974, 18 yrs, 43% *abv*

Sweetness – 2	Peatiness – 8	Price – ***

Colour – Medium-pale straw with lemony/gold highlights. *Nose* – Medium-bodied, woody with a slight greenness and smokiness at the back and an almost Christmas-cake yeasty character. *Palate* – Medium-bodied, oaky with a slight greenness and good richness at the back. *Finish* – Of good length with a green, smoky tail. *Notes* – D.o.b.

LEDAIG, 20 yrs, 43% *abv*

Sweetness – 4	Peatiness – 7	Price – **

Colour – Quite pale amber with yellow highlights. *Nose* – Sweet, rich toffee, dark chocolate/cocoa with quite a solid dark peat note. *Palate* – Medium-dry, quite rich and quite big-bodied with a big, earthy peat character. *Finish* – Very long and expansive, carefully peated with a hint of cocoa on the tail. *Notes* – D.o.b.

LEDAIG SHERRY FINISH, No age statement, 42% *abv*

Sweetness – 7	Peatiness – 7	Price – *

Colour – Pale straw with pale lemon highlights. *Nose* – Youthful, quite herby with a green vegetal note, a hint of vanilla and a quite smoky peat character. *Palate* – Quite big-bodied, vegetal, medium-dry with a smoky, almost burnt peat note. *Finish* – Sweet, vegetal, quite tangy and gently chewy. *Notes* – D.o.b.

Tomatin

TOMATIN, INVERNESS-SHIRE   [H]   [V]   EST.   1897
Website: *www.tomatin.com*

Founded by the Tomatin Spey District Distillery Co. Ltd. Extended from 2 to 4 stills in 1956, to 6 in 1958, to 10 in 1961, to 11 in 1964 and finally to 23 in 1974.

Location – Sited on the west of the A90 at the village of Tomatin, 12 miles south of Inverness. At 313 metres (1,028 feet) above sea level, it is one of Scotland's highest distilleries.

Notes – The first Scottish distillery to be owned by a Japanese company when purchased by the Takara and Okura Consortium following its then owner's liquidation in 1985. It has the potential for the greatest output (more than 12 million litres of alcohol per annum) of all the malt distilleries. From the Gaelic, "Tomatin" means "hill of the bushes".

Water – Allt-na-Frithe (a local burn).

12 yrs, 43% abv

Sweetness – 7	Peatiness – 2	Price – ✳

Colour – Amber with yellow-gold highlights. **Nose** – Medium-bodied, nutty and malty with notes of honey and tobacco; water softens it, bringing out citrus – ripe oranges and lemons, liquorice and some heather honey. **Palate** – Medium-sweet, of quite good body and smooth with ripe red apples and toffee. **Finish** – Long, fresh and sweet with a wee pinch of spice. **Notes** – D.o.b.

18 yrs, 43% abv

Sweetness – 8	Peatiness – 3	Price – ✷✷

Colour – Amber with gold highlights. *Nose* – Medium-bodied with mature oak and beeswax; water brings out chocolate and charred mahogany with delicate peat and a touch of perfume. *Palate* – Fresh, medium-sweet and delicately peated, softly chewy with spicy oak and notes of cocoa and leather. *Finish* – Long, quite intense and rich with some ripe green fruit. *Notes* – D.o.b.

25 yrs, 43% abv

Sweetness – 7	Peatiness – 3	Price – ✷✷✷

Colour – Pale amber with yellow-gold highlights. *Nose* – Medium-bodied and delicate with citrus and honey; water brings out lemon zest, citrus oil and honey with delicate peat. *Palate* – Medium-bodied, medium-dry, slightly vinous and grapey with some smoke in the background, some red fruit and gently chewy, drying oak tannins. *Finish* – Long and quite ethereal with the grapey character and smoke resurgent. *Notes* – D.o.b.

Tomintoul

NEAR TOMINTOUL, BANFFSHIRE [S] [V] EST. 1964
Website: *www.tomintouldistillery.co.uk*

A modern distillery, production only began in 1965 and it was not until 1972 that the make began to appear in bottle. Built by Tomintoul Distillery Ltd and bought by Scottish Universal Investment Trust (part of Lonrho) in 1973. Managed by Whyte & Mackay, which was itself bought from Lonrho by Brent Walker in February 1989 and subsequently sold to American Brands Inc the following year. Doubled from two to four stills in 1974. Sold by JBB (Greater Europe) plc to Angus Dundee plc in August 2000.

Location – Situated in the valley of the River Avon on the B9136, off the A939 Grantown-on-Spey to Tomintoul road.

Notes – Tomintoul is the highest village in the Scottish Highlands, although the distillery itself, being outside the village, is not Scotland's highest. Tomintoul, both village and distillery, are regularly cut off by snow during the winter.

Water – The Ballantruan Spring.

10 yrs, 40% abv

Sweetness – 7	Peatiness – 4	Price – *

Colour – Mid-amber with old-gold highlights. *Nose* – Soft, medium-bodied and malty with toffee and floral notes; water brings out the freshness, a cereal note and some apple and lemon. *Palate* – Medium-bodied, soft and round, medium-sweet, floral and fruity. *Finish* – Long, sweet, clean and toffeeyed with some heather honey. *Notes* – D.o.b.

16 yrs, 40% abv

Sweetness – 7	Peatiness – 4	Price – *

Colour – Mid-amber with old-gold highlights. *Nose* – Medium-bodied, rich and toffeeyed with Seville oranges; water brings out a freshness and some hazelnut character. *Palate* – Medium-sweet, of nice weight, some caramel and butterscotch with mouthwatering, zesty orange and delicately peated. *Finish* – Long, fresh and citrusy, sweet with a wee touch of spice and a hint of cocoa. *Notes* – D.o.b.

27 yrs, 40% abv

Sweetness – 6	Peatiness – 4	Price – **

Colour – Mid-amber with old-gold highlights. *Nose* – Medium-bodied, rich and malty, showing toffee, delicate peating and a little touch of perfume; water brings out the toffee and fruit – tangerines – and makes the perfume stand out. *Palate* – Of good weight, medium-sweet with bubble-gummy cherries and quite rich with a wee touch of spice. *Finish* – Long and quite citrus-tangy with good cocoa-flavoured peat. *Notes* – D.o.b.

Tormore

ADVIE, GRANTOWN-ON-SPEY, MORAY   [S]   EST. 1958
Website: *www.tormore.com*

Built 1958–60 by Long John Distillers Ltd. Sold by Allied Domecq to Pernod Ricard in 2000 and operated by Chivas Brothers. Doubled from two to four stills in 1972.

Location – South of the A95 between Grantown-on-Spey and the Bridge of Avon.

Notes – The first new Highland distillery buildings to be constructed in the 20th century. The novelist (and former exciseman) Neil M. Gunn was invited by Lord Bracken to search for a suitable site for this new distillery. The expedition is described in "An Affair of Whisky", published in *New Saltire* (Dec. 1962). Glen Keith, established the previous year, used the buildings of a former mill. Tormore and associated buildings are of a most striking design, the work of Sir Albert Richardson, a past President of the Royal Academy.

Water – The Achvochkie Burn.

12 yrs, 40% abv

Sweetness – 8	Peatiness – 3	Price – ✳

Colour – Pale amber with gold highlights. *Nose* – Light and quite delicate with a mineral tang; water pulls out some hazelnut and caramel, butterscotch, apple and orange. *Palate* – Quite sweet with notes of toffee and burnt marshmallows and crème brulée with just a wee touch of peat in the background. *Finish* – Long, soft and easy, quite decadently rich. *Notes* – D.o.b.

Tullibardine

BLACKFORD, PERTHSHIRE [H] [V] EST. 1949
Website: *www.tullibardine.com*

There was previously a distillery of the same name near Blackford which was established in 1798, although its exact location is unknown. The current distillery is the work of William Delmé Evans, who also designed Jura and Glenallachie. Owned by Invergordon Distillers since 1971 and, subsequently, Whyte & Mackay following their takeover of Invergordon in 1993, it lay mothballed from 1994 until December 2003, when it was taken over by a quartet of businessmen who formed Tullibardine Ltd.

Location – North of the A9 on the south-western outskirts of the village of Blackford, four miles south of Auchterarder.

Notes – On the site of an ancient brewery which was awarded a Royal Charter in 1503, the distillery takes its name from the nearby Tullibardine Moor, home of Gleneagles Hotel and golf courses. The area has always been famed for its water: Highland Spring and Gleneagles mineral waters are both from Blackford. Queen Helen, the wife of King Magnus of Alba (943–954), fell from her horse into a ford to the east of the village and was drowned, hence the name Blackford.

Water – The Danny Burn.

1993, 40% abv

Sweetness – 4	Peatiness – 5	Price – *

Colour – Pale amber with gold highlights. *Nose* – Fresh, malty with a cereal character and a peppery peat note; with water, rounder with an edge of sweetness and a slight green, hedgerow character. *Palate* – Medium-dry, with good body and a slight hazelnut and creamy caramel character, good richness with quite a soft peat note. *Finish* – Long, rich, fresh and quite elegant; the malt reprises on the tail. *Notes* – D.o.b.

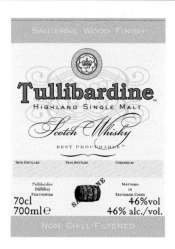

SAUTERNES FINISH, 1993, 46% *abv*

Sweetness – 5	Peatiness – 4	Price – ❋❋

Colour – Pale amber with honeyed gold highlights. *Nose* – Rich and honeyed showing aromas of tangerine and liquorice; water releases more citrus and pineapple with some crème brulée and lime marmalade. *Palate* – Soft and smooth with zesty citrus – juicy tangerines and crème caramel. *Finish* – Long and elegant with tangy lemon zest and decadent botrytis. *Notes* – D.o.b.

1988, 46% *abv*

Sweetness – 4	Peatiness – 6	Price – ❋❋

Colour – Mid-amber with old-gold highlights. *Nose* – Malty, cerealy with a slight chocolate note; with water it pulls out the cereal note, a slightly winey note and almost medicinal peat. *Palate* – Quite big-bodied, round and darkly-flavoured, quite a delicate chocolate peat character and a hint of dried apples. *Finish* – Long, notes of chocolate peat, quite ethereal and very clean with a touch of spice and digestive biscuits. *Notes* – D.o.b.

1965, 48.3% *abv*

Sweetness – 6	Peatiness – 4	Price – ❋❋❋❋❋

Colour – Very deep amber with ruby highlights. *Nose* – Quite big-bodied with a dark brazil nut character, some beeswax and honey, with a little floral perfume; water brings out a rich fruitcake aroma – dried fruit and marzipan, soft peat, warm leather and coffee. *Palate* – Big, rich, smooth, sherried and medium-sweet, gently chewy with dried fruit flavours – raisins and sultanas. *Finish* – Long, softly chewy, velvety and quite ethereal. *Notes* – D.o.b. from a Sherry hogshead.

Japan

The history of whisky distillation in Japan has very Scottish roots. In 1918, Settsu Shuzou, a spirit producer, made plans to start distilling whisky. Deciding that the best way to learn the art of distillation was to send a representative of the company to study Scotch whisky production techniques, he sent Masataka Taketsuru, who studied Applied Chemistry at Glasgow University. When he returned to Japan in 1921 (with a Scottish wife), he found the country was in the depths of a recession and Settsu could no longer finance the project. Kotobukiya (now Suntory) appointed him to develop a distillery for their company, and the Yamazaki distillery in Osaka started production in 1924. Taketsuru managed Yamazaki until he left to establish his own company (Nikka) and distillery at Hokkaido. Today there are seven working distilleries in Japan. The success of Scotch whisky in Japan and other world markets has encouraged Japanese drinks companies to produce Japanese whisky with the characteristics of Scotch.

Y A M A Z A K I   Built at the foot of Mt Tennozan outside Kyoto in 1923 by Shinjiro Torii, founder of Suntory. The area's water supply is famed for its purity. There are 12 stills producing a wide range of styles of whisky; five of the low wines stills are direct-fired by gas and the remaining one low wines still and all six spirit stills have internal steam coils. Three low wines and three spirit stills were replaced during 2006 by smaller than original stills. Owned by Suntory, who use the Japanese oak *Quercus serrata* as well as *Q. alba* and *Q. robur*. Suntory have developed a whisky museum, Yamazaki Whisky Kan, on the site, where visitors can taste from a wide range of cask samples.

10 yrs, 40% abv

Sweetness – 3	Peatiness – 7	Price – *

Colour – Amber with pale gold highlights. *Nose* – Fresh, quite intense and rich with a vegetal hint; water brings out Demerara sugar, apple and some nuttiness. *Palate* – Dry, quite full-bodied with quite solid tannins and a big peat character. *Finish* – Clean and fresh with a hedgerow character. *Notes* – D.o.b.

18 yrs, 43% abv

Sweetness – 8	Peatiness – 3	Price – **

Colour – Amber with gold highlights. *Nose* – Medium-bodied with rich fruit and a slight vegetal note; water rounds it out and emphasises the richness, with honey, apples and tangerines. *Palate* – Rich, sweet, of good body, smooth with softly chewy tannins and a gentle brush of peat. *Finish* – Long, with a vegetal touch and a wee note of spice. *Notes* – D.o.b. bottle no. 163654.

Sweetness – 2	Peatiness – 3	Price – ✳✳✳

Colour – Very deep amber with ruby-hued bronze highlights. *Nose* – Big, oaky and nutty with a dark, medicinal note; water brings out spices, liquorice and Sherry rubber. *Palate* – Medium-dry and chewy with dark mahogany flavours and a slight fruitcake character. *Finish* – Long, quite elegant, chewy and dry. *Notes* – D.o.b. bottle no. 8055.

1984, 56% abv

Sweetness – 6	Peatiness – 2	Price – ✳✳✳

Colour – Very, very dark tawny with deep bronze and dark-brown highlights. *Nose* – Quite big-bodied with notes of Chinese spices and seaweed; water brings out big, dark, nutty characters. *Palate* – Medium-sweet, sherried and fruity – plums, gently chewy. *Finish* – Long, rich, hot and spicy with delicate peating. *Notes* – D.o.b.

H A K U S H U   Built in 1973 by Suntory in a beautiful forest at Yamanashi at the southern end of the Japanese Alps, to the west of Mt Fuji. Hakushu has 24 stills. Suntory has established a bird reserve which is open to the public. There is also a fascinating whisky museum on the site. Hakushu malt is used only for blending.

H A K U S H U   H I G A S H I   This second Hakushu distillery was built in 1981 to supplement the output of the original Hakushu distillery, but with different styles. There are 12 gas-fired stills. Hakushu Higashi produces the bottled *Hakushu* malt.

10 yrs, 40% abv

Sweetness – 3	Peatiness – 3	Price – ✳

Colour – Pale amber with yellow highlights. *Nose* – Medium-bodied and malty with soft toffee and a fresh greenness; water brings out a vegetal note and a delicate mashiness. *Palate* – Off-dry with quite delicate peat and slightly astringent chewy oak. *Finish* – Quite short and dry. *Notes* – D.o.b.

12 yrs, 43% abv

Sweetness – 4	Peatiness – 5	Price – ✳✳

Colour – Pale amber with pale gold highlights. *Nose* – Medium-bodied and quite delicate with peaches and oranges; water brings out orange blossom, honey and citrus zest. *Palate* – Medium-dry, round and softly chewy with chocolate, quite delicate peat and a floral note. *Finish* – Of good length with quite smoky cocoa-flavoured peat and espresso on the tail. *Notes* – D.o.b.

1988, 61% *abv*

Sweetness – 4	Peatiness – 3	Price – ∗∗∗

Colour – Pale amber with pale gold highlights. *Nose* – Medium-bodied with a floral note and medium peat; water emphasises the peat and adds a touch of spice, brown chip sauce and varnish. *Palate* – Medium-bodied and off-dry with good richness, of nice weight with some chewy tannins, some toffee and coffee and some apple. *Finish* – Lasts well, quite elegant and rich with a green, leafy touch, some honey, toffee and citrus and delicately peated. *Notes* – D.o.b.

HAKUSHU, 12 *yrs*, 40% *abv*

Sweetness – 3	Peatiness – 3	Price – ∗

Colour – Amber with gold highlights. *Nose* – Soft and sweet with citrus and pineapple and a little floral note; water brings out woody vanilla, orange and lemon zest. *Palate* – Medium-dry and medium-bodied with a strange fishy flavour and a note of overripe fruit. *Finish* – Long and clean with notes of shellfish and lemon sherbet. *Notes* – Vatted malt from Suntory.

Y O I C H I   Founded in 1934 close to the sea at the neck of the Shakotan peninsula by Masataka Taketsuru with one pot still – he could not afford a second. The second distillation was carried out in this one still which was washed out between distillations. Taketsuru felt that the humidity and water supply were similar here to Scotland and the buildings have a very Scottish appearance. There is a peat moor nearby and four of the six stills are direct-heated by coal. Now managed by Nikka which is itself a subsidiary of the Asahi Group. Nikka have recently renovated the former home of Masataka Taketsuru on the site.

10 *yrs*, 45% *abv*

Sweetness – 6	Peatiness – 5	Price – ∗∗

Colour – Amber with pale gold highlights. *Nose* – Medium-bodied and delicately toffeeyed with citrus and delicately peated; water opens out the richness and gives liquorice, marzipan, hazelnut and lemon zest. *Palate* – Medium-dry, quite round and smoothly toffeeyed, a touch of spice and good maltiness. *Finish* – Good length, with the peat rising to the top and a little butterscotch on the tail. *Notes* – D.o.b.

M I Y A G I K Y O   In order to produce different styles from those produced at Hokkaido, Nikka built a new distillery at Sendai, Miyagi in 1969. It was previously named "Sendai", but has recently been renamed "Miyagikyo". It has eight stills, all of which are steam-heated. The distillery is located in a mountain area between the Rivers Nikkawa and Hirose.

MIYAGIKYO, 10 *yrs*, 45% *abv*

Sweetness – 7	Peatiness – 4	Price – **

Colour – Amber with gold highlights. *Nose* – Medium-bodied showing wood; water pulls out some liquorice/fennel and an underlay of toffee. *Palate* – Medium-sweet, clean, spicy, quite full-bodied and round. *Finish* – Long and quite spicy with a sooty peat note. *Notes* – D.o.b.

MIYAGIKYO, 12 *yrs*, 45% *abv*

Sweetness – 3	Peatiness – 6	Price – **

Colour – Mid-amber with gold highlights. *Nose* – Quite full-bodied, and rich with notes of treacle toffee, honey and citrus; water brings out rich fruitcake. *Palate* – Quite big-bodied, medium-dry and delicately peated with an edge of lemon and lime and some honey. *Finish* – Long and softly smoky. *Notes* – D.o.b.

NIKKA PURE MALT BLACK, No age statement, 43% *abv*

Sweetness – 8	Peatiness – 3	Price – *

Colour – Amber with old-gold highlights. *Nose* – Quite big-bodied and rich with a dark chocolate peat note; water brings out oak and vanilla, creamy toffee and a slight herbal note. *Palate* – Medium-sweet and rich with some chocolate, a touch of spice and a youthful note to the peat. *Finish* – Long, rich, quite elegant and smooth. *Notes* – Vatted malt from Nikka.

NIKKA PURE MALT WHITE, No age statement, 43% *abv*

Sweetness – 5	Peatiness – 5	Price – *

Colour – Amber with gold highlights. *Nose* – Medium-bodied, medium-sweet, rich and honeyed with some vanilla; water brings out a quite delicate charred oak note, a touch of burnt orange and ginger and some nectarines. *Palate* – Medium-dry with gently chewy oak tannins, some fruit and spice. *Finish* – Long and quite elegant with dark chocolate and cocoa and clean smoke. *Notes* – Vatted malt from Nikka.

TAKETSURU, 21 *yrs*, 43% *abv*

Sweetness – 6	Peatiness – 3	Price – ***

Colour – Amber with gold highlights. *Nose* – Quite full-bodied and malty with nutty toffee and digestive biscuits; water softens the aroma and brings out a touch of mint and some tablet. *Palate* – Rich, medium-sweet, fresh and toffeeyed with a touch of spice. *Finish* – Long, quite ethereal and perfumed with a fresh peat note on the end. *Notes* – Vatted malt from Nikka.

H A N Y U   Owned by Toa Shuzou, the distillery was founded in April 1946 in a rice field at Saitama with one pot still. Latterly, there were two pot stills and a continuous still as well as the bottling plant within the complex. Water was transported by tanker from Kaminoizumi in Chichibu, where the company was originally established. Now silent and the stills have been removed and put into storage by Ichiro Akuto, who intends to establish another distillery.

CHICHIBU, 8 yrs, 60% abv

Sweetness – 3	Peatiness – 7	Price – *

Colour – Mid-amber with old-gold highlights. *Nose* – Quite dark and nutty, unctuously smooth, medium-bodied and dry with a hint of toffee and honey. *Palate* – Quite big-bodied, dark and nutty, dry with quite solid tannins and a good green peat note. *Finish* – Quite long and tangy with a big belt of smokiness on the tail. *Notes* – D.o.b.

HANYU, 15 yrs, 46% abv

Sweetness – 5	Peatiness – 5	Price – ***

Colour – Deep amber with old-gold highlights. *Nose* – Quite simple, rich, round and warm with nutty vanilla; water brings out an edge of greenness to the peat. *Palate* – Medium-sweet with quite overpoweringly chewy tannins and a dark nuttiness. *Finish* – Long, bitter and nutty. *Notes* – Ichiro's Malt bottling.

ICHIRO'S MALT, 20 yrs, 46% abv

Sweetness – 3	Peatiness – 4	Price – ***

Colour – Deep amber with bronze highlights. *Nose* – Medium-bodied, with beeswax, Sherry rubber, butterscotch and vanilla; water brings out plasticine, white spirit, some orange and apple and a sooty peat note. *Palate* – Medium-dry, quite rich and of good weight, quite intense with cooked apples and a little spice. *Finish* – Long, gently peated and quite full-bodied. *Notes* – Ichiro's Malt bottling.

NINE OF HEARTS, 2000, 46% abv

Sweetness – 7	Peatiness – 2	Price – *

Colour – Mid-amber with gold highlights. *Nose* – Peppery, medium-dry and medium-bodied with a sooty peat character; water brings out toffee, white pepper and a good maltiness. *Palate* – Medium-sweet, of good weight with a banana note, a touch of spice and delicately peated. *Finish* – Long and rich with a touch of fruit and some honey/beeswax. *Notes* – Ichiro's Malt bottling.

QUEEN OF HEARTS, 1990, 54% *abv*

Sweetness – 7	Peatiness – 2	Price – ✱✱✱

Colour – Amber with old-gold highlights. *Nose* – Quite perfumed with vanilla oak and a slight vegetal touch; water brings out honeyed and fruity – oranges – notes and a slightly green delicate peatiness. *Palate* – Medium-sweet and quite rich with good body and toffee flavoured. *Finish* – Long, clean and malty. *Notes* – Ichiro's Malt bottling.

ACE OF SPADES, 1985, 55% *abv*

Sweetness – 4	Peatiness – 2	Price – ✱✱✱✱

Colour – Deep amber with bronze highlights and a ruby hue. *Nose* – Nutty, quite delicate and dark; water brings out a rich fruitcake aroma, a quite delicate, dark peat note and some banana. *Palate* – Medium-bodied, of good weight and medium-dry, nuttily sherried with chewy tannins. *Finish* – Long and rich with a delicate touch of liquorice and tar. *Notes* – Ichiro's Malt bottling.

S H I R A K A W A   Originally owned by the Mercian Company, it was bought by Takara Shuzou, which owns Tomatin in Scotland, in 1947. Currently mothballed, although the bottling plant is working.

27 yrs, 55% *abv*

Sweetness – 6	Peatiness – 4	Price – ✱✱✱✱

Colour – Amber with gold highlights. *Nose* – Full, quite round and medium-sweet, rich, malty and nutty with a hint of toffee. *Palate* – Medium-sweet, quite full-bodied, rich with slightly chewy tannins and a good, quite creamy weight of peat in the background. *Finish* – Long, smooth and pleasantly smoky. *Notes* – D.o.b.

K A R U I Z A W A   Built in 1955 by winemaker Daikoku Budoushu to the west of Karuizawa, Nagano, at the foot of Mt Asama, an active volcano, in an area popular as a summer resort. The distillery has four stills and the warehouses are ivy-clad, which helps keep summer temperatures down. Bottles of *Karuizawa* malt contain 90% malt whisky from Karuizawa distillery and 10% malt whisky from another Mercian-owned distillery in Yamanashi. Now managed by Kirin following the takeover of Mercian by the Kirin Group in December 2006. Two warehouses were replaced by an art museum and visitor centre in 1995.

12 yrs, 40% abv

Sweetness – 3	*Peatiness* – 6	*Price* – ✱

Colour – Amber with old-gold highlights. *Nose* – Medium-bodied, quite rich and medium-dry; water rounds it out and brings out toffee and syrup notes. *Palate* – Medium-dry and gently chewy with vanilla and tablet notes and a dry smokiness. *Finish* – Long, quite smoky and dry. *Notes* – D.o.b.

17 yrs, 43% abv

Sweetness – 3	*Peatiness* – 7	*Price* – ✱✱

Colour – Mid-amber with bronze highlights. *Nose* – Quite big, fruity and rich with a cough-linctus note, some American Cream Soda and leafy orange; water pulls out mahogany and muscovado sugar. *Palate* – Dry and gently chewy with a soft peat note, a little spice and a hint of citrus. *Finish* – Long with softly chewy tannins and a dark, cocoa-flavoured peat note. *Notes* – D.o.b.

F U J I - G O T E M B A   Completed in 1973 in Shizuoka by Kirin-Seagram Ltd, a joint venture between Kirin Brewery Co., Seagram and Chivas Brothers. Now operated by Kirin. Its make is only used for blending. Located in an ancient forest at the foot of Mt Fuji, the buildings also house a grain distillery and a blending and bottling plant.

SINGLE CASK, 12 yrs, 40% abv

Sweetness – 5	*Peatiness* – 3	*Price* – ✱✱✱

Colour – Quite full amber with light bronze highlights. *Nose* – Full-bodied, quite intense and rich with an unctuous oily-oak smoothness and medium-sweet with lime and vanilla notes. *Palate* – Medium-dry, quite full-bodied, rich and gently chocolate-peated. *Finish* – Long and rich with cocoa notes on the tail. *Notes* – D.o.b.

18 yrs, 43% abv

Sweetness – 4	*Peatiness* – 5	*Price* – ✱✱✱

Colour – Mid-amber with old-gold highlights. *Nose* – Rich and quite full with oaky vanilla and a slight medicinal note; water brings out a floral touch, some pine and cedar and a cough-linctus character. *Palate* – Medium-dry with chewy tannins, a medium peat note, some toffee and a slight vegetal touch. *Finish* – Long and quite ethereal with rich vanilla-flavoured toffee. *Notes* – D.o.b.

Australia

Bakery Hill

BALWYN NORTH, VICTORIA [AU] EST. 1999
Website: *www.bakeryhilldistillery.com.au*

Established by David and Lynne Baker. Schooner is the favoured strain of barley at Bakery Hill. All bottlings are single cask bottlings. One still.

Location – In Balwyn North, a suburb 25 km to the north-east of the centre of Melbourne.

Notes – Until 2007, Bakery Hill's wash was produced by the Mountain Goat brewery, a craft microbrewery in Richmond. David's intention is to install his own mashing and brewing operation during 2007.

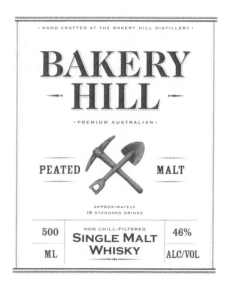

PEATED, *No age statement,* **60% abv**

Sweetness – 4	*Peatiness* – 7	*Price* – ✸✸

Colour – Deep amber with bronze highlights and a pale ruby hue.
Nose – Quite soft, delicate and medium-bodied with notes of red-skinned apples; water brings out baked apples with cloves and a delicate, perfumed peat character. *Palate* – Medium-dry with gently chewy apple skins, very Calvados-like and some citrus. *Finish* – Long with a little touch of spice and smoky with a touch of cocoa.
Notes – D.o.b.

Sullivan's Cove

CAMBRIDGE, TASMANIA [AU] EST. 1994
Website: *www.tasmaniadistillery.com*

Originally established on the banks of the River Derwent at Sullivan's Cove, the site of the first British settlement in Tasmania. The distillery changed hands once or twice between 1994 and 2001 and in November 2003, after a two-year break, the casks, still and equipment were purchased by a small group of enthusiasts and moved to Cambridge on the outskirts of Hobart. Here production was restarted. One still.

Location – In the Hobart suburb of Cambridge.

Notes – The wash is produced at Hobart's Cascade Brewery, Australia's oldest brewery, using Tasmania's Franklin barley, a species created in Tasmania in 1981 and in high demand across Asia and Australia for malting.

Water – Springs on 1,270-metre-high Mt Wellington, which provides the distillery's backdrop.

SULLIVAN'S COVE DOUBLE CASK, No age statement, 40% *abv*

Sweetness – 4	*Peatiness* – 0	*Price* – **

Colour – Straw with pale gold highlights. *Nose* – Quite full and youthful with a chocolate malty note and a rancio character; water brings out chocolate raisins, a touch of citrus and rich, honeyed vanilla. *Palate* – Medium-dry, rich and smooth with a smoky chocolate character. *Finish* – Quite good length with a little touch of spice, some American Cream Soda and ripe peaches. Notes – D.o.b. Hand bottled from a mixture of Port and Bourbon casks.

SULLIVAN'S COVE PORT MATURATION, No age statement, 60% *abv*

Sweetness – 4	*Peatiness* – 0	*Price* – ***

Colour – Deep amber with bronze highlights and a pink hue. *Nose* – Quite delicate, medium-bodied with a hint of raisins and spirity; water brings out hints of Olde English marmalade, neoprene, new Wellington boots and very ripe tangerines. *Palate* – Medium-dry, dark and rich with some citrus fruit. *Finish* – Neoprene follows through with good length and gently chewy. *Notes* – D.o.b. Bottled from ex-Port casks.

Rest of the World
Amrut

BANGALORE, INDIA   [IN]   EST. 1948
Website: *www.amrutdistilleries.com*

Founded by Radhakrishna Jagdale, the company began as a blending and bottling unit. They then moved into distilling rum and brandy for the local market, distilling their first malt whisky in the early 1980s. This was used for the blending of Indian whiskies until 2004, when *Amrut* was launched in Glasgow. Amrut Distilleries Ltd is part of the Jagdale Group. Two stills.

Location – 15 km south of Bangalore, India on the edge of the Bannerghatta National Park.

Notes – They use barley grown in the Punjab and Rajasthan and malted by commercial maltsters in Jaipur and Delhi. At 3000 feet above sea level and in the heat of Karnataka province's tropical climate, the whisky matures quickly, with the sample tasted below being barely over three years old.

Water – An aquifer beside the distillery.

No age statement, 40% *abv*

Sweetness – 6	Peatiness – 2	Price – ✳

Colour – Nose – Medium-bodied, rich and soft with sweet vanilla; water brings out fruit – fresh coconut, apples and peaches with a touch of ginger and a little maltiness. *Palate* – Fresh, medium-sweet, medium-bodied and rich with some honey, red fruit and spice and delicately peated. *Finish* – Of good length, sweet and hazelnutty with a rather bitter tail. *Notes* – D.o.b.

Clear Creek

PORTLAND, OREGON   [US]   [V]   EST. 1985
Website: *www.clearcreekdistillery.com*

Created by Steve McCarthy to use the fruit from his family's orchard to make fruit spirits. Originally with one still, a second was added in 1987, a third in 2005 and the fourth in 2007. Steve and his wife were holidaying in Ireland in the wet summer of 1991 and developed a taste for peated whisky. In 1992, Kurt Widmer began brewing and McCarthy's has doubled production every year since 2004. Four Holstein pot stills.

Location – On N.W. Wilson Street, close to the centre of Portland.

Notes – The wash is produced from peated malt imported from Scotland and mashed and fermented by Widmer Brothers, a local brewery. The whiskey is aged for three years in a mixture of old Sherry wood, old Cognac wood, and new Oregon oak.

CLEAR CREEK DISTILLERY

McCARTHY'S

OREGON SINGLE MALT

POT DISTILLED

WHISKEY

*Distilled from a Fermented Mash
of Peat-Malted Scottish Barley,
Barrel-Aged 3 Years and Bottled by
Clear Creek Distillery*
PORTLAND, OREGON, U.S.A.
ALC. 40% BY VOL. (80 PROOF)
750 ML

McCARTHY'S OREGON, No age statement, 40% *abv*

Sweetness – 6	*Peatiness* – 6	*Price* – ✱✱

Colour – Amber with gold highlights. *Nose* – Medium-bodied and youthful with a slightly green vegetal note; water widens the aroma and brings out apple, an earthily smoky peat note, a hint of rubber and some candle wax. *Palate* – Medium-sweet, fresh and clean with good peat integration, a touch of tarry rope and toffee and ripe citrus. *Finish* – Long, squeaky clean, rich and herby with bergamot and tea on the tail. *Notes* – D.o.b.

Mackmyra

VALBO, SWEDEN [SE] EST. 1999

Founded by eight friends in December 1999 when they created a pilot distillery, producing 3000 litres between then and spring 2002. The full-blown distillery came on stream on 30 October, 2002 following the installation of full-sized distilling equipment into the landmark-declared Mackmyra Bruk buildings, a former power station.

Location – Located just outside Valbo, which is 15 km west of Gävle.

Notes – The product is wholly Swedish, they add juniper twigs to the peat to give their spirit a point of difference and use Swedish barley and Swedish oak casks as well as ex-Bourbon, ex-Sherry and ex-Champagne woods.

Water – A spring in Valbo which rises through a sandstone ridge, "rullstensås" in Swedish, formed during the last ice age.

PRELUDIUM 03, *No age statement*, 52.2% *abv*

Sweetness – 5	*Peatiness* – 4	*Price* – **

Colour – Straw with yellow highlights. *Nose* – Medium-bodied with a little rich maltiness and some caramel; water brings out a youthful perfume. *Palate* – Medium-sweet, fresh, rich and of good body with notes of toffee and apples. *Finish* – Clean, long, quite ethereal and dry. *Notes* – D.o.b.

PRELUDIUM 04, No age statement, 53.3% *abv*

Sweetness – 6	*Peatiness* – 3	*Price* – **

Colour – Straw with pale yellow highlights. *Nose* – Fresh, citrus, of quite good body with a quite soft maltiness; water brings out an earthy and sooty peat note, hints of honey and leafy citrus and a touch of perfume. *Palate* – Medium-sweet, soft and rich with milk chocolate and coconut notes and a little peat. *Finish* – Long, chocolate lingers with a smoky underlay and rich, dessicated coconut on the tail. *Notes* – D.o.b.

Warenghem

LANNION, BRITTANY, FRANCE [FR] EST. 1900
Website: *www.distillerie-warenghem.com*

Established by Leon Warenghem, the distillery produces Fine Bretagne, a Breton Calvados, and other fruit spirits and liqueurs from a continuous still and pot stills. In 1999, they released their first Breton single malt under the Armorik label. It has been aged in cask for "several years" in their cool Breton store.

Location – North of the D767 on the south-east edge of the town of Lannion.

Notes – The distillery also produces a range of beers. The casks are stored in the Breton warehouses vertically, rather than in the traditional Scottish/Irish horizontal style.

Water – A local spring.

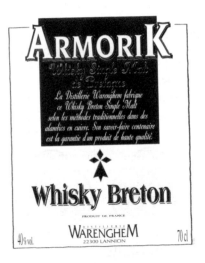

ARMORIK, No age statement, 40% *abv*

Sweetness – 4	*Peatiness* – 4	*Price* – *

Colour – Amber with gold highlights. *Nose* – Medium-bodied, rich and round with a dark vanilla note and some delicate peat; the addition of water makes almost no difference other than to open out the peat character. *Palate* – Quite full, dark and rich with sweet vanilla pods, medium-dry, creamy and smooth with a touch of honey and almond – a liquid Toblerone! *Finish* – Quite long and ethereal with a drying edge to the oak. *Notes* – D.o.b.

Ones to Watch
Daftmill

CUPAR, FIFE   [L]   EST.   2005

Farming brothers Ian and Francis Cuthbert both work on the family farm, where they have grown malting barley for the past 60 years. Like many, their dream was to make whisky. Unlike many, they received their license on St Andrew's Day 2005 and produced their first spirit in December. A true farm distillery, they will produce only from the barley they grow on their own 800-acre farm (around 150 acres of which is under barley, producing around 250 tonnes of Optik per annum). Two stills.

Location – Just off the A91, immediately to the south-west of Bow of Fife.

Notes – The distillery was constructed inside a listed building of indeterminate date, but which certainly dates back to Napoleonic times (records show that it was renovated in 1809), and was costing a considerable sum to keep wind and watertight. Apart from the stills, which were made by Forsyth's of Rothes, all the work was carried out by people living within a five-mile radius of the farm.

NEW MAKE SPIRIT (7 months old)

Sweetness – 4	Peatiness – 0	Price – NA

Colour – Water white. *Nose* – Clean and quite fruity with notes of tobacco and herbs, not hugely mashy with a hint of slightly green coffee. *Palate* – Young, spicy, medium-bodied and medium-sweet with a fresh, green note. *Finish* – Long, rich, showing slight toffee-and-hazelnut ice cream. *Notes* – Sample tasted from an Oloroso butt at 7 months old. Surprisingly forward at this young age.

Glann ar Mor

CREC'H AR FUR, BRITTANY, FRANCE [FR] EST. 2005
Website: *www.glannarmor.com*

Established on a farm which was originally built in 1668, conversion to a distillery was completed early in 2004 and production began in June 2005. Two stills.

Location – To the north-west of the village of Pleubian in the Presqu'île Sauvage (the Wild Peninsula) of northern Brittany's Tregor district.

Notes – Spirit is being filled in either Sauternes barriques (225 litres) or Bourbon barrels.

Water – A bore hole drawing water from a supply in the granite 50 metres below the distillery.

NEW MAKE, 62% abv

Sweetness – 3	Peatiness – 6	Price – *

Colour – Clear with water-white highlights. *Nose* – Young and mashy with a slight cocoa peat character; with water it opens out with more of the same and a hints of chocolate and mint and a more vegetal than fruity character. *Palate* – Quite soft and mashy, smooth and medium-dry with a perfumed peat note. *Finish* – Long, surprisingly appealing and waxy. *Notes* – D.o.b.

Mitchell's Glengyle

CAMPBELTOWN, ARGYLL   [C]   EST. 1872
Website: *www.kilkerran.com/scottish-whisky/index*

Originally established in 1872 by William Mitchell & Co. When Alfred Barnard visited circa 1876, William Mitchell was away from home, so Barnard's information is scant, although he describes it as neat and compact with a fine view. At this time there were two stills, "one containing 3,100 gallons and the other 1,860 gallons". It had an annual output of 90,000 gallons and employed 14 men. After the collapse of Pattison's, Glengyle was sold to West Highland Malt Distilleries Ltd (WHMD) in 1919, the same year that WHMD bought Glen Scotia and the now long-defunct Ardlussa, Glen Nevis, Dalintober and Kinloch distilleries. WHMD was a consortium led by Robertson & Baxter Ltd, but included such pillars of the industry as James Watson & Co. of Dundee, Taylor, Ferguson of Glasgow and Macdonald & Muir of Leith amongst its members. West Highland Malt Distilleries Ltd went into voluntary liquidation in 1924 and Glengyle ceased production in 1925, with its stock being auctioned off on 8 April 1925. The building was bought by J. & A. Mitchell, who also own Springbank, in 2002. A great deal of work was necessary to return the building to its original purpose, but Frank McHardy and James McGowan were able to structure the building so that the process flows in a natural manner. They acquired some equipment at more economical prices than brand new, with stills coming from the Ben Wyvis operation at Invergordon. A stainless steel semi-lauter mash tun and Boatskin Larch washbacks were installed in late 2003. The distillery officially opened on 28 March 2004 and the first spirit flowed from its stills on 9 April 2004.

Location – On Glebe Street, close to the centre of Campbeltown.

Notes – One slight fly in the Mitchells' ointment is that they are not allowed to call the spirit "Glengyle", because that brand name was registered to Glen Catrine Bonded Warehouse Ltd. The spirit which originates from Glengyle distillery is called *Kilkerran*, a name which derived from the Gaelic "Ceann Loch Cille Chiarain", which is the name of the original settlement where Saint Kerran had his religious cell and where Campbeltown now stands.

KILKERRAN, 3 *yrs*, 46% *abv*		
Sweetness – 3	Peatiness – 7	Price – *

Colour – Straw with pale gold highlights. *Nose* – Quite big-bodied with a chunky peat character, a touch of lemon and some muscovado sugar; water brings out green fruit, some spice and a meaty note, together with fresh campfire embers among the sand dunes. *Palate* – Big, quite dark and youthful, quite rich with a pineapple note. *Finish* – Long, quite powerful and youthful. *Notes* – D.o.b.

Kilchoman

ISLE OF ISLAY, ARGYLL   [I]   [V]   EST. 2005
Website: *www.kilchomandistillery.com*

Established at Rockside Farm as a traditional farm distillery. Everything from growing the barley, through malting and distilling, to bottling the product is carried out on the farm. Once their home-grown barley has all been malted and distilled, production ceases until the next harvest. Two stills.

Location – Situated at Rockside Farm, 2 km west of the B8018 and about $1\frac{1}{2}$ km inland from Machir Bay with its spectacular sandy beach on the west coast of Islay.

Notes – Kilchoman is now officially the most westerly distillery in Scotland.

Water – A spring on Cnoc Dubh, the hill above the farm.

NEW MAKE, 63.5% *abv*

Sweetness – 3	Peatiness – 8	Price – *

Colour – Water-white with white highlights. *Nose* – Fresh, clean and slightly peppery; water brings out big, dark, clean peat, quite full-bodied with a mashy cereal character and a herbal note. *Palate* – Medium-dry with notes of peanuts and pistachios, of good body with rich, cocoa-flavoured peat. *Finish* – Long, quite spicy and rich with the peanuts lingering *Notes* – D.o.b.

Vatted Malts

BERRY'S BEST ISLAY, 14 yrs, 43% *abv*

Sweetness – 1	*Peatiness* – 9	*Price* – ✳✳

Colour – Pale amber with honeyed gold highlights. *Nose* – Big-bodied and smoky with a burnt-bone character; with water, the sea influence comes out as well as a fish note. *Palate* – Dry, of good body, quite powerful, well-balanced with seashore characters, a touch of tar and some floral notes. *Finish* – Long, pleasantly pungent, tangy and quite complex. *Notes* – Bottled by Berry Brothers & Rudd.

BLUE HANGER SECOND RELEASE, 25 yrs, 45.6% *abv*

Sweetness – 8	*Peatiness* – 4	*Price* – ✳✳

Colour – Mid-amber with bronze highlights. *Nose* – Medium-bodied and toffeeyed with light peat and a hint of Seville marmalade; water brings out vanilla, fresh lemon and leather. *Palate* – Rich, medium-sweet and smooth with good body and notes of creamy toffee and citrus. *Finish* – Long, clean and appealing with quite delicate peat and juicy orange on the tail. *Notes* – A Berry's Own Selection bottling.

CLAN DENNY, 46% *abv*

Sweetness – 1	*Peatiness* – 9	*Price* – ✳

Colour – Pale straw with pale lemon highlights. *Nose* – Quite big-bodied with a smoky chocolate peat note and burnt heather roots; water brings out cocoa, tobacco, leather and a touch of carbolic with a floral edge. *Palate* – Dry with good richness, some cocoa-flavoured peat, a hint of the sea and wind-blown heather. *Finish* – Long, quite ethereal with a touch of spice and chocolate on the end. *Notes* – A vatted Islay from Hunter Hamilton Co.

GLENALMOND, 1988, 40% *abv*

Sweetness – 4	Peatiness – 7	Price – ✱✱

Colour – Amber with old-gold highlights. *Nose* – Medium-bodied, spicy and slightly green with cardamom and a hint of Christmas-cake richness; water makes it fresher with a menthol note, some beeswax and linoleum. *Palate* – Smooth and medium-dry with quite a solid peat note and a dark edge. *Finish* – Long, quite smoky and ethereal. *Notes* – Bottled by The Vintage Malt Whisky Co.

JOHNNIE WALKER GREEN LABEL, 15 *yrs*, 43% *abv*

Sweetness – 6	Peatiness – 5	Price – ✱

Colour – Amber with gold highlights. *Nose* – Quite big, soft and fragrantly floral; water brings out tangerines, soft, sweet vanilla, toffee, beeswax, some exotic fruits and exotic spices to match. *Palate* – Quite full-bodied, medium-sweet and creamily smooth, delicately sea-breeze peated, some coffee and toffee and stewed apples. *Finish* – Long with a delicate burnt heather roots note and some warm spice. *Notes* – Bottled by Johnnie Walker.

MONKEY SHOULDER, 40% *abv*

Sweetness – 8	Peatiness – 2	Price – ✱

Colour – Mid-amber with gold highlights. *Nose* – Rich and unctuous with a touch of hazelnut and a green freshness; water rounds it out, adding warm toffee and coffee, some delicate peating, tangerine and apple. *Palate* – Sweet, round, smooth and toffeeyed with a wee touch of spice, slightly green, delicate peat and a note of cappuccino. *Finish* – Long, rich, mellow and soft. *Notes* – Bottled by William Grant & Sons Ltd.

POIT DHUBH, 21 *yrs*, 43% *abv*

Sweetness 5	Peatiness – 4	Price – ✱✱✱

Colour – Mid-amber with old-gold highlights. *Nose* – A rich, almost fruity note, medium-sweet, quite restrained and delicate, gently peated with a soft toffee/vanilla note. *Palate* – Medium-dry and of good body with a nutty peatiness, slightly chewy and smooth with a soft vanilla flavour. *Finish* – Long, tangy and complex with a final elegance. *Notes* – An unchill-filtered vatted malt from Praban-na-Linne.

PRIDE OF ORKNEY, 12 *yrs*, 40% *abv*

Sweetness – 2	Peatiness – 5	Price – ✷

Colour – Light to mid-amber with gold highlights. *Nose* – Quite light and rich with dried-fruit characters and hints of honey. *Palate* – Off-dry, smooth, lightly smoky and malty. *Finish* – Clean with a refreshing greenness. *Notes* – Bottled by Gordon & MacPhail.

THE RICH SPICY ONE, No age statement, 40% *abv*

Sweetness – 4	Peatiness – 6	Price – ✷

Colour – Mid-amber with old-gold highlights. *Nose* – Big and warm with notes of liquorice and rubber; water brings out a touch of fruit, some smoky weight, a touch of neoprene, dried apricots, raisins and cloves. *Palate* – Big, round, rich, softly chewy and medium-dry with dried fruit, some apples, ginger and cinnamon. *Finish* – Long, rich and quite ethereal with medium-peat in the background – a wee blockbuster. *Notes* – Bottled by Jon, Mark & Robbo.

THE SIX ISLES, No age statement, 43% *abv*

Sweetness – 2	Peatiness – 8	Price – ✷

Colour – Pale straw with pale lemon highlights. *Nose* – Quite a smoky peat character with quite good body; with water, the smokiness becomes burnt paper with a slight hint of chocolate. *Palate* – Dry and smoky with a gentle charred note, quite soft and rich with good weight. *Finish* – Long, with good richness, and finishing with cocoa and chocolate. *Notes* – Bottled by William Maxwell & Co. Ltd.

SMOKEHEAD, No age statement, 43% *!!!*

Sweetness – 1	Peatiness – 9	Price – ✷

Colour – Amber with pale gold highlights. *Nose* – Quite big-bodied, peaty, smoky and dry with touches of perfume and medicinal notes; water rounds it out and pulls out a rich kiwi fruit character. *Palate* – Big, powerful, smoky and dry with a charred peat character. *Finish* – Long, softly chewy, warm, spicy and clean. *Notes* – Bottled by Ian MacLeod & Co.

TAMBOWIE, 12 *yrs*, 40% *abv*

Sweetness – 5	Peatiness – 4	Price – ✷

Colour – Mid-amber with pale bronze highlights. *Nose* – Quite full-bodied with cereal and dark peat notes; water brings out slightly creamy, medium-sweet, toffee and cocoa notes with a touch of shortbread. *Palate* – Medium-dry, round and smooth with soft vanilla, quite delicately peated and quite full-bodied with flavours of coffee and cocoa. *Finish* – Long, rich and quite spicy with lingering cocoa and chocolate. *Notes* – Bottled by The Vintage Malt Whisky Co.

Independent Bottlings

BLACK CUILLIN, 8 yrs, 40% abv

Sweetness – 4	Peatiness – 8	Price – *

Colour – Pale amber with yellow/green highlights. *Nose* – Big, yet delicate with dark fruit and vegetal leather; water brings out notes of shellfish and oaky beeswax with a touch of floral perfume. *Palate* – Quite big-bodied, rich and medium-dry with softly chewy oaky tannins, a quite big peat smokiness and some charred oak. *Finish* – Long and quite ethereal with a richly smoky touch and a note of cocoa on the tail. *Notes* – Single Hebridean Island malt from the Highlands & Islands Scottish Whisky Co. Ltd.

BLAIRFINDY, 1980, 57.6% abv

Sweetness – 8	Peatiness – 4	Price – ***

Colour – Deep amber with full bronze highlights. *Nose* – Rich, dark, nutty, full-bodied and fruity; water brings out a slightly charred, unctuous oak note and some warm, raisins/dried fruit notes. *Palate* – Big-bodied, medium-sweet, smooth and round with a rich fruitcake flavour, some dark nuttiness and sweet vanilla. *Finish* – Long, smooth and quite ethereal. *Notes* – Blackadder Raw Cask bottling.

THE BURNS MALT, 5 yrs, 40% abv

Sweetness – 4	Peatiness – 4	Price – *

Colour – Pale straw with pale lemon highlights. *Nose* – Medium-bodied with vinous, Riesling-like characters of lime and petrol; with water it almost loses the vinous character and pulls out a youthful maltiness. *Palate* – Medium-bodied, medium-dry with a youthful, green, mashy character and a delicate but dark peat note. *Finish* – Long, with notes of lemon sherbet, almost a sea character and a touch of cocoa. *Notes* – Single Malt from Isle of Arran Distillers.

CLONTARF, No age statement, 40% *abv*

Sweetness – 7	Peatiness – 2	Price – ✳

Colour – Pale straw with pale lemon highlights. *Nose* – Fresh, clean, quite light and delicate; water brings out a nettley perfumed note and maltiness. *Palate* – Medium- sweet, rich, clean and smooth with a distinctive grassy note. *Finish* – Long, clean, quite elegant and slightly vinous. *Notes* – Single Irish malt from Clontarf.

GLEN ANDREW, 10 *yrs*, 40% *abv*

Sweetness – 8	Peatiness – 2	Price – ✳

Colour – Amber with old-gold highlights. *Nose* – Medium-bodied, sweet, citrus (lime)-flavoured and malty with a little floral note; water brings out rich, ripe and juicy tangerines with honey and apple notes. *Palate* – Rich, medium-sweet, toffeeyed and smooth with a touch of citrus and honey. *Finish* – Long, soft and rich with a slight green edge to the peat. *Notes* – Single Highland malt from the Highlands & Islands Scottish Whisky Co. Ltd.

GLENTROMIE, 12 *yrs*, 40% *abv*

Sweetness – 6	Peatiness – 3	Price – ✳

Colour – Mid-amber with gold highlights. *Nose* – Quite light, elegant, medium-sweet and peppery, quite rich with slight tablet and sweet vanilla oak notes. *Palate* – Quite sweet, round, smooth, soft and quite delicately peated. *Finish* – Long, clean, quite ethereal and peppery on the tail. *Notes* – Single Highland malt from Speyside Distillers Ltd.

GLENTROMIE, 17 *yrs*, 40% *abv*

Sweetness – 6	Peatiness – 3	Price – ✱✱

Colour – Mid-amber with old-gold highlights. *Nose* – Quite light, elegant, rich and medium-sweet with notes of toffee/vanilla and Demerara sugar and slightly peppery. *Palate* – Quite sweet with gently chewy tannins, a touch of a charred oak character and quite lightly peated. *Finish* – Long, soft, quite smooth and peppery on the tail. *Notes* – Single Highland malt from Speyside Distillers Ltd.

GLEN TURNER, 12 *yrs*, 40% *abv*

Sweetness – 4	Peatiness – 3	Price – ✱

Colour – Mid-amber with pale old-gold highlights. *Nose* – Of good body with a slight herbal, hedgerow peat character and medium-dry; with water, it is clean, almost wine-like with a green menthol note. *Palate* – Medium-dry, medium-bodied, quite rich with a green freshness and notes of apples and pears. *Finish* – Long, clean and rich with a note of spearmint. *Notes* – Single malt from La Martiniquaise.

HUNTING LODGE HOTEL MALT, 15 *yrs*, 46% *abv*

Sweetness – 4	Peatiness – 6	Price – ✱✱

Colour – Amber with yellow/gold highlights. *Nose* – Medium-bodied, with slight herbal and vegetal notes; water pulls out the maltiness, a slight hedgerow character and liquorice/fennel with a hint of citrus. *Palate* – Medium-dry, smooth and softly chewy with notes of chocolate digestive biscuits and coffee. *Finish* – Long, gently tarry, distinctive and salty. *Notes* – Single Campbeltown malt bottled for the Hunting Lodge Hotel, Bellochantuy.

LOCKE'S, 40% *abv*

Sweetness – 7	Peatiness – 0	Price – ✱

Colour – Amber with pale old-gold highlights. *Nose* – Fresh, clean and slightly honeyed with a slight grassy/hedgerow character and sherbet/lemon notes. *Palate* – Fresh, medium-sweet and clean, quite creamy and soft. *Finish* – Long, very clean and grassy. *Notes* – An Irish single malt whiskey from Cooley's.

MACPHAIL'S MALT, 10 *yrs*, 40% *abv*

Sweetness – 6	Peatiness – 6	Price – ✱

Colour – Mid-amber with old-gold highlights. *Nose* – Quite light, fresh, dark and smoky, medium-dry. *Palate* – Medium-dry with good body, an earthy peatiness and a touch of spiciness. *Finish* – Fresh, quite smoky and long-lasting with a touch of oak. *Notes* – Single malt from Gordon & MacPhail.

Sweetness – 7	Peatiness – 7	Price – ✳

Colour – Amber with yellow-gold highlights. *Nose* – Big, with dark, smoky peat and slightly unctuous sherried rubber; with water the aromas of a highland burn and boiled potatoes come out, the rubber disappears and the peat develops a burnt-stick character. *Palate* – Big, rich and medium-sweet with dark-chocolate peat notes, of good weight, smooth and smoky. *Finish* – Long, smoky and rich with a clean, green touch to the peat. *Notes* – Single Speyside malt from Angus Dundee.

PEAT REEK, 46% *abv*

Sweetness – 2	Peatiness – 10	Price – ✳

Colour – Pale straw with very pale lemon highlights. *Nose* – Big, powerful with dark, charred peat and puffed wheat; water brings out an edge of richness. *Palate* – Big-bodied and dry with chewy tannins and breakfast cereal notes. *Finish* – Long, darkly smoky with a burnt note on the tail. *Notes* – Blackadder bottling.

SMOKING ISLAY, 55% *abv*

Sweetness – 2	Peatiness – 10	Price – ✳✳

Colour – Pale straw with pale lemon highlights. *Nose* – Big-bodied, with burnt heather roots and charred oak; water brings out a touch of richness. *Palate* – Big, powerful, smoky and round with a touch of richness, softly chewy tannins and clean and smooth. *Finish* – Very long, very smoky with just a hint of sweetness and quite complex. *Notes* – Blackadder bottling from cask 2002/01.

OLD MAN OF HOY, No age statement, 43% *abv*

Sweetness – 6	Peatiness – 4	Price – *

Colour – Mid-amber with old-gold highlights. *Nose* – Medium-bodied, malty and medium-sweet with a slight herbaceous character and a rich, honeyed edge. *Palate* – Medium bodied and quite fresh with a slightly rich greenness and a sweet edge. *Finish* – Long, medium-sweet and rich, a touch tangy with a slight nuttiness on the end. *Notes* – A single Orcadian malt.

THE PIBROCH, 12 yrs, 43% *abv*

Sweetness – 5	Peatiness – 8	Price – *

Colour – Amber with gold/green highlights. *Nose* – Quite big, dark peat character, burnt heather roots and slight hint of the sea; with water it has a slightly charred note and hints of fruit and honey. *Palate* – Big, medium-dry, rich, round and smooth with pear fruit and a touch of spice. *Finish* – Long, smoky, softly chewy and elegant. *Notes* – Single Islay malt from the Highlands and Islands Scotch Whisky Co. Ltd.

Specialist Whisky Shops

Although some of the major retail chains and many of the so-called "tax free" shops at airports offer good selections of single malt whiskies at competitive prices, they cannot hope to compare with the whisky specialist for depth of choice and knowledge. If there is a whisky you particularly want, then the specialist will usually try to get it for you. Many offer a mail order service. Here are just a few.

SCOTLAND

The Cadenhead Whisky Shop, 172 Canongate, Edinburgh EH8 8BN
Cairngorm Whisky Centre, Inverdruie, Aviemore, PH22 1QH
Canape Wines, 85 Main Street, Bothwell, Glasgow G71 8RD
Clifton Coffee Shop, Tyndrum, Crianlarich, Perthshire FK20 8RY
Duncan Taylor & Co. Ltd, 4 Upperkirkgate, Huntly, Aberdeenshire AB54 8JU, *www.duncantaylor.co.uk*
Eaglesome Ltd, Reform Square, Campbeltown, Argyll PA28 6JA
John Scott & Miller, 15–19 Bridge Street, Kirkwall, Orkney KW15 1HR, *www.jsmorkney.co.uk*
Loch Fyne Whiskies, Inverary, Argyll PA32 8UD *www.lfw.co.uk*
Luvian's Bottle Shop, 93 Bonnygate, Cupar, Fife KY15 4LG
J A McKay, 4 Traill St, Thurso, KW14 8EJ
Robbie's Drams, 3 Sandgate, Ayr KA7 1BG, *www.whiskiesrus.co.uk*
Robertsons, 46 Atholl Road, Pitlochry, Perthshire PH16 5BX
Royal Mile Whiskies, 379/381 High Street, Edinburgh EH1 1PW
www.royalmilewhiskies.com
Scott Wines Plus, 60 High Street, Lockerbie DG11 2AA, *www.scottwinesplus.co.uk*
Strachan of Aboyne, Balmoral Terrace, Aboyne, Aberdeenshire AB34 5HL
T B Watson Ltd, 11–17 English Street, Dumfries DG1 2BU
Valvona & Crolla, 19 Elm Row, Edinburgh EH7 4AA, *www.valvonacrolla.co.uk*
Villeneuve Wines Ltd, 1 Venlaw Court, Peebles, EH45 8AE
The Whisky Castle, Main Street, Tomintoul AB37 9EX, *www.whiskycastle.com*
The Whisky Shop, Now a national chain with branches in Callander, Glasgow, Edinburgh, Fort William and Oban in Scotland and Gateshead, Lakeside, London, Norwich, Oxford and York in England. *www.whiskyshop.com*
Whisky Spirit, 83 Victoria Street, Newton Stewart DG8 6NL, *www.whiskyspirit.co.uk*

ENGLAND AND WALES

D Byrne & Co., 12 King Street, Clitheroe, Lancs BB7 2EP
Connolly's, Arch 13, 220 Livery Street, Birmingham B3 1EU,
www.connollyswine.co.uk
Constantine Stores Ltd, 30 Fore St, Falmouth, Cornwall TR11 5AB,
www.drinkfinder.co.uk
Cornerwise, 13 Lake Road, Keswick, Cumbria CA12 5BS,
www.cornerwise-keswick.com
The County Stores, 52 North Street, Taunton, Somerset TA1 1ND
Cadenhead's Covent Garden Whisky Shop, 3 Russell St, London, WC2B 5JD,
www.coventgardenwhiskyshop.co.uk

Carringtons, 322 Barlow Moor Road, Chorlton, Manchester M21 8AY
Gauntleys, 4 High Street, Exchange Arcade, Nottingham NG1 2ET,
www.gauntleywine.co.uk
Milroys, 3 Greek St, Soho, London W1A 1ER *www.milroys.co.uk*
The Vintage House, 42 Old Compton St, Soho, London W1V 6LR,
www.vintagehouse.co.uk
The Whisky Exchange, London, *www.thewhiskyexchange.com*
Also now a shop at: Vinopolis, 1 Bank End, London SE1 9BU
The Whisky Shop, 87 Bailgate, Lincoln, *www.lincolnwhiskyshop.co.uk*
The Wright Wine Co., Skipton, *www.wineandwhisky.co.uk*

AUSTRIA
Potstill, Strozzigasse 37, Vienna, *www.potstill.org*

BELGIUM
Drankenshop Broekmans, Molenstraat 19, Zolder, *www.drankenshop.be*
TasTToe, Leuvensesteenweg 22, Kampenhout, *www.tasttoe.com*
Villers, Villerslei 130-132, Schoten

CZECH REPUBLIC
Kratochvílovci, Týnská 15, Praha 1, *www.kratochvilovci.cz*
The Whisky Shop, Dum pánu z Lipé, Nám. Svobody 17, Bruno
www.thewhiskyshop.cz

DENMARK
Juuls Vinhandel, Værnedamsvej 15, 1819 Frederiksberg, Copenhagen,
www.juuls.dk
Kjær Sommerfeldt, Gammel Mønt 4, 1117 Copenhagen, *www.kogs.dk*
Skjold Burne Aarhus, Storetorv 18, 8000 Aarhus C., *www.skjoldburne-aarhus.dk*

FRANCE
Archibald Lauder's, Zone d'Activité de Marticot, Chemin de Marticot, 33610
CESTAS, Paris, *www.archibald-lauders.fr*
La Maison du Whisky, 20 rue d'Anjou, Paris, *www.whisky.fr*

GERMANY
Excalibur, Löwengasse 7, 61348 Bad Homburg, *www.celtic-spirit.de*
Getränke Weiser, Darmstädter Str. 97, 64646 Heppenheim, *www.thewhiskytrader.de*
Weinquelle Lühmann, Lübecker Str. 145, 22067 Hamburg, *www.weinquelle.com*
Malt Whisky Company, Am Fleith 24, 31275 Lehrte,
www.malt-whisky-company.de
Scoma, Am Bullhamm 17, 26441 Jever, *www.scoma.de*
Whisk(e)y Shop Tara, Rindermarkt 16, 80331 München, *www.whiskyversand.de*

LUXEMBOURG
Le Bouchon, 2, rue des Celtes, 6615 Wasserbillig, *www.lebouchon.lu*

JAPAN
Liquors Hasegawa, Yaesu Shopping Mall, 2-1, Yaesu, Chuo-ku, Tokyo,
www.liquors-hasegawa.com

Liquor Villa Aizawa, 570-9, Dairakuji-machi, Hachioji, *www.aizawa-web.com*
Shinanoya Shokuhin, 1-34-13, Daita, Setagaya-ku, Tokyo, *www.shinanoya.co.jp*

THE NETHERLANDS
Hein Post Wijnen & Gedistilleerd, Nieuwe Ebbingestraat 104, 9712, NP Groningen,
www.heinpost.nl
Slijterij Reijnders, Kade 12, Sluis, *www.whiskeyhouse.nl*
Slijterij 't Raadhuis, Raadhuisplein 1a, Maastricht
Gall & Gall van der Boog, Dr H. Colijnlaan 289, Rijswijk
Van Genderen's Wijnen en Gedistilleerd, Voorstraat 31, Spijkenisse
Slijterij Stroomberg, Brink 1, Zwolle
Whiskyslijterij De Koning, Hinthamereinde 41, 's-Hertogenbosch,
www.whiskykoning.nl

POLAND
Scottish House, Modniczka 299, Centrum Handlowe A4 Kraków,
www.scottishhouse.pl

RUSSIA
Whisky World, 9, Tverskoy Boulevard, Moscow, *www.whiskyworld.ru*

TAIWAN
Whisky & Wine, Ta An District, No. 185, Sec. 3, Ta An Rd, Taipei,
www.w-shop.com.tw

USA
Arrow Wine & Spirits, Dayton, OH
Bayway World of Liquor, Elizabeth, NJ
Binny's Beverage Depot, 300 North Clarke, Lakeview, IL, *www.binnys.com*
Cork 'n Bottle, Covington, KY, *www.corknbottle.com*
D&M Wines & Liquors, San Francisco, *www.dandm.com*
Dundee Dell, Omaha, NE, *www.dundeedell.com*
K&L Wine Merchants, San Francisco, CA, *www.klwines.com*
Federal Wine & Spirits, 29 State St, Boston MA, *www.federalwine.com*
Park Avenue Liquors, New York City, NY, *www.parkaveliquors.com*
Pearsons Wine of Atlanta, 3072 Early St NW, Atlanta GA, *www.pearsonswine.com*
Red Dog Wine & Spirits, 1031 Riverside Drive, Franklin, TN,
www.reddogwineandspirits.com
Sam's Wine & Spirits, Chicago, IL, *www.samswine.com*
The Party Source, 95 Riviera Drive, Bellevue KY, *www.thepartysource.com*
The Red Wagon Wine Shoppe, 2940 S. Rochester Road, MI,
www.redwagonshoppe.com
The Whisky Shop, 360 Sutter St, San Francisco, CA, *www.whiskyshopusa.com*
The Wine Merchant, 20 South Hanley, Clayton MO, *www.winemerchantltd.com*
Town Wine & Spirits, Rumsford, RI, *www.townwineri.com*
Wine & Liquor Depot, Van Nuys, CA (L.A. area), *www.wineandliquordepot.com*

Acknowledgements

*O**ur grateful thanks are due to a great many people for their assistance
in completing this book:*

Jo Lennon of Agency Brazil, Alastair Sinclair of Amrut, Aaron Hillman of Angus
Dundee, David Baker of Bakery Hill, Colin Ross of Ben Nevis, Billy and Alastair Walker
of BenRiach, Doug McIvor of Berry Brothers & Rudd, Raymond Armstrong of
Bladnoch, Lynne McEwan of Bruichladdich, Katherine Crisp of Burn Stewart, Peter
Schmid of Campari, Dominic McKay of Chivas, Steve McCarthy of Clear Creek, John
Glaser of Compass Box, Ian Cuthbert of Daftmill, Suzy Russell of John Dewar & Sons
Ltd, Frances Dupuy of Dewar Rattray, Anne Baekkelund of Diageo, Michael Cockram
of Fortune Brands, Jean Donnay of Glann ar Mor, Andy Davidson of Glencairn Crystal,
Robert Ransom of Glenfarclas, Morna McLelland of Glenmorangie, Ian Chapman of
Gordon & MacPhail, Sara Browne of Willam Grant, Jason Craig of Highland Park,
Gareth Stanley and Karen Walker of Inver House, Euan Mitchell and Jaclyn Kelly of
Isle of Arran, Anthony Wills of Kilchoman, Fred Laing, Stewart Laing of Douglas
Laing, Ian Weir of Ian MacLeod, Sheila Kennedy of Macallan, Lars Lindberger of
Mackmyra, John Milroy, Alison Getty of Morrison Bowmore, Des McCagherty of
Signatory, Jim Gordon of Speyside, Kate Wright of Springbank, Mike Kuo and Richard
Liao of Sun Favorite, Taiwan, Patrick Maguire of Tasmania Distillery, Euan Shand
of Duncan Taylor, Stephen Bremner of Tomatin, Andrew Crook of Vintage Malt
Whisky Co., Mike Drury of the Whisky Castle, Tomintoul, Cara Laing from Whyte
& Mackay and Junichi Fukutani, Takeshi Mogi and Anna Russell.

Our sincere apologies to anyone who has been omitted from the above list. You
know who you are – we thank you.

TASTING SAMPLES FOR FUTURE CONSIDERATION . . .

John Lamond is constantly reviewing new whiskies and writing new tasting
notes. If you have a whisky that has not been included in this book, or a
new bottling you would like John to review, please send a tasting sample
to John Lamond, 22 Delph Wynd, Tullibody, Clackmannanshire, FK10
2TW, Scotland. All submissions will be considered, however, because of
space considerations, we regret we will be unable to include all of the
whiskies John receives.

THE MALT WHISKY FILE IS NOW ALSO ONLINE . . .

We hope that you have enjoyed our book. We are constantly adding to
the tasting notes and whisky information in this book and all of the latest
notes, information and much, much more can now be found online at
our website: *www.maltfile.com*

If you have information about whiskies, distilleries, whisky shops, history
and anecdotes you would like to share with us please email Robin:
robin@maltfile.com